BASEBALL'S BEST

BASEBALL'S
BEST

The All-Time Major League Baseball Team

BY

TOM MEANY AND TOMMY HOLMES

FRANKLIN WATTS, INC.
575 Lexington Avenue, New York 22

ACKNOWLEDGMENTS

To Grosset & Dunlap, Inc. for permission to use material on Bob Feller, Lefty Grove, Carl Hubbell, Ted
Williams, Willie Mays and Stan Musial from BASEBALL'S GREATEST
PLAYERS by Tom Meany. Copyright
1953 by Grosset & Dunlap, Inc.

CONTENTS

v

BASEBALL'S BEST

1

CASEY STENGEL
The Old Perfesser

THE SELECTION of a manager for an all-time all-star base-ball team presented the editors of this book with no problem whatever.

It took about thirty seconds on a stopwatch to agree on Casey Stengel.

To be sure, there is no thought here that the appointment of Mr. Stengel will provide universal satisfaction any more than the selection of twenty-five baseball players out of the past and present to form a dream team equipped with the high-est imaginable skills.

There are still those who call it heresy to intimate that the greatest baseball leader of all time was any other than John J. McGraw of the New York Giants. A possibly quieter but equally insistent bloc of old-timers would vote for Connie Mack, who became the ancient mariner of the Philadelphia Athletics.

There have been many other good baseball managers. They come and go. Sometimes they come and go again. And again. You can feel reasonably certain that men like Bucky Harris and Charley Dressen managed well. They didn't get so many chances because club owners like to throw money away. Joe McCarthy, Bill McKechnie, and Wilbert Robinson are among those who reached the baseball Hall of Fame on their reputa-tions as more or less peerless leaders.

I

As a matter of fact, you'll find dissenters on Stengel and many of them. Back in the past, he managed the Dodgers in Brooklyn for three years and the Braves in Boston for six seasons, and his teams finished in the second division nine times.

Ultimately he took over the Yankees and his Yankee teams won ten pennants in twelve years. Scoffers will say that anybody could have won with those clubs, but Casey didn't miss often. It may be worth noting, as an oddity, that the Yankee team to win the most games under Stengel was the aggregation of 1954. They won 103 games and lost the pennant to the Cleveland Indians by eight games.

A year after the Yankee front office retired Stengel because of his age, he unretired himself and cast his fortunes with the New York Mets. Presumably nobody blames the old boy for what happened then. The task he assumed would have baffled all the baseball brains that ever existed plus those of Dr. Robert Oppenheimer.

The argument that Casey could only win with the Yankees isn't entirely sound anyway. In his long life, Stengel also managed triple-A teams in Toledo, Milwaukee, Oakland, and Kansas City; and his teams won pennants in all except the last named.

Summed up, it is fair to assume that Stengel is a good manager when he has the material and only human when he hasn't, and you may say the same about every successful baseball leader who ever flashed a sign.

But the reason why Stengel is selected to manage this team is that he is unique. Of all the baseball men who ever lived, he stands out as the only one who personally knew and, as player or manager, had competitive association with every one of the 25 athletes who are to make up this mythical squad.

Casey hit against old Pete Alexander, Walter Johnson, and Christy Mathewson and played on teams against Honus Wagner, Rogers Hornsby, Pie Traynor, Ty Cobb, and Babe Ruth.

2

With the Giants, he was a teammate of Frankie Frisch. He hit against Dazzy Vance and later managed Vance in Brooklyn. He managed Yogi Berra, Joe DiMaggio, and Johnny Mize with the Yankees.

He managed against Stan Musial and Carl Hubbell in the National League and against Bob Feller, Hoyt Wilhelm, and Ted Williams in the American League. He managed against Jackie Robinson and Roy Campanella in the heat of World Series competition. He found out all he had to know about Lou Gehrig, Lefty Grove, and Bill Dickey, managing against them in Florida exhibition games.

And, in the National League, he is still managing against Willie Mays and Warren Spahn.

Perhaps Casey's acquaintance with a few of these was a bit sketchy, but he knew them all right. For instance, he saw Walter Johnson early. This was just about the time Stengel had reached the majors and Johnson already had been famed as the outstanding flamethrower in the American League.

Johnson lived in Coffeyville, Kansas, not far from Stengel's native Kansas City. A post-season exhibition game was arranged for Coffeyville roughly between National and American Leaguers.

"Johnson beat us, 1 to 0," recalls Stengel, "and struck out about 18 of us. The thing I best remember about the game was a line in the Kansas City *Star* next day. It went, 'the National Leaguers lost because of Dutch Stengel's inability to hit with men on base.'

"It seems he struck me out twice with a runner on second."

One spring Stengel trained with the Dodgers in Augusta, Georgia, home of Ty Cobb, the famed Detroit Tiger who happened to be a holdout.

"Imagine this happening today," Casey will tell you. "Darned if Cobb didn't arrange an exhibition game with us and it packed the park. The gate was split down the middle—half to the Brooklyn club and half to Cobb.

3

"Of course, we Brooklyn players didn't get an extra red cent although our club made about $3,000. Cobb made that much personally, less maybe a couple of hundred he had to pay the farm boys who made up the rest of his club.

"I saw enough of Cobb to know what made him a great ball-player and learned enough about him that afternoon to know how he became a millionaire long before he died."

As a member of the 1916 champion Dodgers, Stengel sat on the bench the day Ruth beat Brooklyn, 2 to 1, in 14 innings. Actually, he had taken note of Babe more than two years before when he hadn't even heard Ruth's name.

In the spring of 1914, the Dodgers, coming north, stopped in Baltimore for an exhibition game.

"There was this big left-handed kid with black hair hanging down over his eyes pitching against us," recalled Stengel, "and doing pretty good, too. I was playing center field and the first time he came to bat I played for him just about where you'd play for any pitcher.

"He hit one over my head and Wilbert Robinson didn't care very much for that and bawled me out. How was I to know that a sugar-bush pitcher could hit one that far and besides I thought it was probably an accident.

"The next time the kid came to bat I walked out and stood with my shoulder blades pressed against the fence. My idea was to show Robbie up. The only guy I showed up was myself. He hit one over my head again—this time out of the park."

With his amazing powers of recall, Stengel undoubtedly can recite succinct early impressions of each one of the other 22 ball players on the squad.

Since Casey has been selected as a manager, not a player, his playing career shall receive the once-over-lightly treatment here.

Charles Dillon Stengel was born July 30, 1890 and, after a false start toward left-handed dentistry, took to baseball as a profession. In his third season in the minor leagues, he was dis-

4

covered by Larry Sutton, a Brooklyn scout. His contract, purchased from Montgomery, Alabama, of the Southern Association, cost $300.

He lasted in the National League for more than a dozen years. The Dodgers traded him to the Pittsburgh Pirates in 1918. One of the players to go to Brooklyn in the deal was Burleigh Grimes, who was was to succeed Stengel as Dodger manager eighteen years later.

Casey enlisted in the Navy before the 1918 season was over, was traded to the Phillies in 1919, and went from there to John McGraw's Giants in 1921. After the 1923 campaign, he was traded to the Braves and finished his major league playing career in 1925.

Stengel batted and threw left-handed. He was a good left-handed hitter, especially against right-handed pitchers and McGraw platooned him in New York with a right-handed hitter named Bill Cunningham. Casey also was a better than average base runner, threw well and played either center field or right field with skill.

Stengel's lifetime batting average in the National League was a respectable .284. His World Series batting average was a splendid .393—11 hits for 28 times at bat. In his last World Series he hit two home runs, one an inside-the-park wallop at Yankee Stadium that beat Sam Jones, 1 to 0.

A story goes with that home run.

As Stengel, himself, would put it, he was quite a while past the third reader and his weather-beaten features were well wrinkled even then. Still he wasn't as old as some of the next day's news stories made him appear to be as he staggered madly around the bases, his pace complicated by a painfully bruised heel. There were references to his long white beard, the wheel chair that awaited him, etc.

In far-off California, the parents of Edna Lawson, the charming lady who was Casey's fiancee, read of the exploits of their prospective son-in-law at the breakfast table. They had never met Stengel.

"My goodness," said Mrs. Lawson, unaccustomed to sports page flights of fancy, "what kind of a man is our Edna marrying, anyway?"

"I hope he lives long enough for us to find out," was the gloomy rejoinder of Mr. Lawson.

That was in October of 1923. Edna and Casey Stengel have lived happily ever since and Casey still is a vibrant figure in the game of baseball.

EDITOR'S NOTE——The 25-player squad herein handed over to Professor Stengel is his to employ as he sees fit.

It is the general idea that he might like to use a lineup with Dickey behind the plate, Gehrig, Hornsby, Wagner, and Traynor as infielders, and Ruth, Cobb, and DiMaggio in the outfield, then select as opening day pitcher Alexander, Johnson, or Mathewson.

But if Casey wishes to change that alignment he is at liberty to do so. The batting order naturally is his responsibility. He may select his own coaches and a general manager, if he thinks he needs one. If for any reason, he becomes dissatisfied with his squad, let him make some trades.

CHARLES DILLON STENGEL

Born, July 30, 1890, Kansas City, Missouri.
Height 5'10". Weight 175. Batted and threw left-handed.

Year	Club	League	Pos.	G	AB	R	H	2B	3B	HR	RBI	BA
1912	Brooklyn	Nat.	OF	17	57	9	18	1	0	1	12	.316
1913	Brooklyn	Nat.	OF	124	438	60	119	16	8	7	44	.272
1914	Brooklyn	Nat.	OF	126	412	55	130	13	10	4	56	.316
1915	Brooklyn	Nat.	OF	132	459	52	109	20	12	3	43	.237
1916	Brooklyn	Nat.	OF	127	462	66	129	27	8	8	53	.279
1917	Brooklyn [1]	Nat.	OF	150	549	69	141	23	12	6	69	.257

[1] Traded with Second Baseman George Cutshaw to Pittsburgh for Infielder Chuck Ward and Pitchers Burleigh Grimes and Al Mamaux, January 9, 1918.

6

CHARLES DILLON STENGEL (*Continued*)

Year	Club	League	Pos.	G	AB	R	H	2B	3B	HR	RBI	BA
1918	Pittsburgh	Nat.	OF	39	122	18	30	4	1	1	13	.246
1919	Pittsburgh [2]	Nat.	OF	89	321	38	94	10	10	4	40	.293
1920	Philadelphia	Nat.	OF	129	445	53	130	25	6	9	50	.292
1921	Philadelphia-											
	New York [3]	Nat.	OF	42	81	11	23	4	1	0	6	.284
1922	New York	Nat.	OF	84	250	48	92	8	10	7	48	.368
1923	New York [4]	Nat.	OF	75	218	39	74	11	5	5	43	.339
1924	Boston	Nat.	OF	131	461	57	129	20	6	5	39	.280
1925	Boston	Nat.	OF	12	13	0	1	0	0	0	2	.077
	Major League Totals			**1277**	**4288**	**575**	**1219**	**182**	**89**	**60**	**518**	**.284**

[2] Traded to Philadelphia for Outfielder George Whitted, August, 1919, but failed to report due to salary dispute.

[3] Traded with Second Baseman Johnny Rawlings to New York for Third Baseman Goldie Rapp, Outfielder Lee King, and First Baseman Lance Richbourg, July 1, 1921.

[4] Traded with Shortstop Dave Bancroft and Outfielder Bill Cunningham to Boston for Outfielder Billy Southworth and Pitcher Joe Oeschger, November, 1923.

WORLD SERIES RECORD

Year	Club	League	Pos.	G	AB	R	H	2B	3B	HR	RBI	BA
1916	Brooklyn	Nat.	OF	4	11	2	4	0	0	0	0	.364
1922	New York	Nat.	OF	2	5	0	2	0	0	0	0	.400
1923	New York	Nat.	OF	6	12	3	5	0	0	2	4	.417
	World Series Totals			**12**	**20**	**5**	**11**	**0**	**0**	**2**	**4**	**.393**

MANAGERIAL RECORD

Year	Club	League	Position	Won	Lost
1934	Brooklyn	Nat.	Sixth	71	81
1935	Brooklyn	Nat.	Fifth	70	83
1936	Brooklyn	Nat.	Seventh	67	87
1938	Boston	Nat.	Fifth	77	75
1939	Boston	Nat.	Seventh	63	88
1940	Boston	Nat.	Seventh	65	87
1941	Boston	Nat.	Seventh	62	92
1942	Boston	Nat.	Seventh	59	89
1943	Boston	Nat.	Sixth	68	85
1949	New York	Amer.	First	97	57
1950	New York	Amer.	First	98	56
1951	New York	Amer.	First	98	56
1952	New York	Amer.	First	95	59
1953	New York	Amer.	First	99	52
1954	New York	Amer.	Second	103	51
1955	New York	Amer.	First	96	58
1956	New York	Amer.	First	97	57
1957	New York	Amer.	First	98	56

MANAGERIAL RECORD (*Continued*)

Year	Club	League	Position	Won	Lost
1958	New York	Amer.	First	92	62
1959	New York	Amer.	Third	79	75
1960	New York	Amer.	First	97	57
1962	New York	Nat.	Tenth	40	120
1963	New York	Nat.	Tenth	51	111

* key

Pos. = position
G = games
AB = at bat
R = runs
H = hits
2B = two-base hits or doubles
3B = three-base hits or triples
HR = home run
RBI = runs batted in
BA = batting average

GROVER CLEVELAND ALEXANDER
Alex the Great

His NAME was Grover Cleveland Alexander, but no one can be found who ever called him by either one of his given names. For many years, he was simply called Alex or sometimes Alex the Great. Toward the end of a pitching career that covered two decades in the National League, he was called "Old Pete."

Whatever they called him seemed all right with Alexander. He never complained, never alibied. He was never known to criticize a teammate or call an opposing ballplayer lucky. He accepted his great successes modestly and the many vicissitudes of his life in silence. He was easy to like and hard to know. Probably no contemporary knew him thoroughly although many thought they did.

His life began on a farm near St. Paul, Nebraska, on February 26, 1887. It ended November 4, 1950, in a shabby furnished room in St. Paul (population: about 2,000).

In between those dates, he roamed far and wide. The full story of his curiously erratic life would read like a mixture of Burt L. Standish, creator of Frank Merriwell, and Eugene O'Neill, the American master of dramatic tragedy.

What cannot be obscured is that Alexander was a tremendous pitcher . . . one of the greatest . . . perhaps the greatest.

He was a freckled farmer of 24 when he first reached the majors with the Phillies in 1911. At six-feet-one, he weighed 185 pounds and those were just about his specifications when he bowed out 373 National League victories later. Weight was never one of his many problems. Neither were his strong legs and good right arm.

His constitution was rugged and his strength was deceptive. His appearance on the ball field was unimpressive. Somehow, Alex always managed to look as if he had put on his uniform in a pitch-black cellar and his cap never seemed to fit. The motif of carelessness carried to his pitching style. He used a short, three-quarter delivery that suggested a boy skipping flat stones across the surface of a pond.

His outwardly casual approach to pitching makes it easy to believe that Red Dooin, the veteran catcher who managed the Phillies, wanted to release Alex before the end of spring training. But Pat Moran, another old catcher with the club, thought he saw something and persuaded Dooin to give the young right-hander a chance in a final Philadelphia exhibition game against the Athletics, then champions of the world.

Alexander pitched five hitless, shutout innings. That sold Dooin, who made Alex a rotation starter. He lost his first National League decision, 5 to 4, to Boston and then went on to compile the greatest record achieved by a first-year major league pitcher in this century. He won 28 games, lost 13.

One of his late season victories was notable. Boston's Cy Young, then 44, had won 511 big-league games. He tried for No. 512 on September 26, and Alexander beat him 1 to 0, in 12 innings. Old Cy never pitched again, but nobody in the Boston pressbox seemed to have had the wisdom and the foresight to have written something like: "The King is dead; long live the King!"

Before reaching the Phillies, Alexander had two years in the minors. His schooling was brief and his hard, early life on the farm built a physical frame that stood up under cruel and unusual punishment in later years. Behind a pair of mules, he guided a plow through furrows which, laid end-to-end, would have stretched miles and miles and miles. And when he could he played town ball.

At 19, he got a job as a telephone lineman. He still played town ball and eventually was fired because one of his sandlot games went into extra innings and made him late for work. By this time (1909), his reputation as a pitcher was a bit more than local and he was signed at $50 a month to a contract with Galesburg of the Illinois-Missouri League. He had won 15 and lost 8 when an injury almost brought his career to an abrupt end.

Running from first to second, Alex was skulled by a wild throw as a strong-armed shortstop tried for a double play. He was unconscious for 56 hours. When he came to, he was cross-eyed and suffered from acute double vision. No doctor could assure the disconsolate young man that the condition ever would clear up.

Possibly while still unconscious, Alexander's contract was sold to Indianapolis of the American Association. He reported apprehensively and was assigned to pitch batting practice as his first chore. He tried to oblige although he could plainly see two batters at home plate. The first fast ball he threw broke a rib of one of these and, unfortunately, the one he hit was Charley Carr, manager of the team.

He was sent back to the Nebraska farm before he could cripple anybody else. Then, so the investment shouldn't be a total loss, Indianapolis sold him during the winter to Syracuse of the New York State League.

Meanwhile, Alexander was home filled with worry that approached despair. "For months," he said in one of his rare observations about his early life, "I saw two of everything whenever my eyes were open. And then one morning I woke up and everything was back in focus again. It was like a miracle."

So he went to Syracuse where he won 29 games and lost 14. A scout named Patsy O'Rourke recommended him to Horace

Fogel, who then operated the Phillies. Fogel wasn't sufficiently impressed to buy Alexander outright, but when no other club did either, the Phillies contrived to draft him for $750.

Alexander's first contract with the Phillies called for $250 a month, which, roughly translated, means that he was paid at a rate of a little more than $50 for each of his 28 victories. Of course, as economists like to point out, there was no federal income tax in 1911.

The unique feature of Alexander's early career was his practically instantaneous rise to the top once he arrived in the major leagues. In his first seven seasons, he won 190 games, an average of 27 victories a year. No one ever claimed to have taught Alex anything about pitching, yet he arrived on the scene with an unsurpassed knowledge of that skill.

On the subject of the early Alexander, there was no greater authority than the late Bill Killefer, a fine catcher who joined the Phillies late in 1911 to become Alexander's battery mate in Philadelphia and Chicago for the next ten years.

"No one else was like him," said Killefer. "He had the skills and the pitching instinct to take charge of a good hitter, even one he saw for the first time. He was a master improviser on split-second notice."

Killefer said he couldn't quarrel with the frequently expressed opinion that Alexander was the best of all curve ball pitchers. "Yet," said old Bill, "that estimate did not quite do him justice because his best pitch actually was his fast ball."

Alexander was different from all the others, according to Killefer. The instinct of pitchers who can throw hard is to switch to a curve after a batter had been set up by speed pitching. Alex worked in reverse. He started off with curves and, if that didn't do the job, had his great fast ball in reserve.

"Any good hitter will tell you," said Killefer, "that he must be ready to hit a fast ball and, if the pitch turns out to be a curve, he'll have time to readjust.

"But if a batter looks for the curve, a fast ball leaves him for dead. Alexander's secret, if you want to call it that, was to throw so many curves that the hitter never was ready for the fast ball when he threw it.

"He wasn't as fast as Walter Johnson and I don't think anyone else ever was. But he was as fast as Christy Mathewson, for example, although he didn't throw his fast ball nearly as often. Nor did Alex have what you might call a great change of pace although he did throw curves at different speeds, which amounted to the same thing."

Killefer recalled one of the first games in which he ever handled Alexander. They had two strikes on Larry Doyle of the Giants, a good left-handed hitter.

"I gave the curve ball sign," said the old catcher, "figuring that Alex would tease Doyle with a breaking pitch off the plate. He blazed a fast ball and Larry's swing was half a second late.

"I walked out to the box to straighten out our signs. Alex grinned and said he hadn't missed the signal. 'But gee, Bill,' he said, 'as I wound up I saw Doyle lean for a curve and I thought I'd startle him a little.'

" 'You startled me to,' said the catcher, 'but that's all right.' "

After that, according to Killefer, they still used signs, but signs that were subject to change without notice.

Obviously, such great success wouldn't have been possible without Alexander's great control.

Over a stretch of three seasons, Alexander won 94 games for the Phillies—31 in 1915, 33 in 1916, and 30 in 1917. In those three years, he worked 1,153 innings and gave up only 170 bases on balls—an average of less than three walks for every two complete games.

At the close of the 1917 season, William F. Baker, owner of the Phillies who rarely overlooked an opportunity to realize a profit, sold Alexander and Killefer to the Chicago Cubs for assorted players and $60,000, a huge chunk of cash in those days. Baker sensed that Alex, a bachelor, surely would be drafted for the armed forces, which is exactly what happened.

World War I changed many things, many people and the game of baseball. Alex was never the same after he returned although he came back a good pitcher, occasionally a great one, and the moments of the 1926 World Series for which he is so vividly remembered still were far in the future.

He never won 30 games again although he did have a good run at that figure in 1920 when he won 27 for the Cubs. He was a 20-game winner in two subsequent seasons, the last time in 1927 when he was 40 years old.

He finished with 373 victories, tying Mathewson's National League record. He lost 208 games, which gave him a career winning percentage of .642. He pitched 90 shutouts, a National League record surpassed only by Johnson's American League total of 113. His 2,199 strikeouts compared to 955 bases on balls testify to his control.

It was in 1918 that the aforementioned Burt L. Standish would have given up on the Alexander story and the also aforementioned Eugene O'Neill would have picked up the pieces.

Alex was drafted on schedule and just before his outfit was shipped overseas he married. His wife, Aimee, was and, if still alive, is a wonderful person.

He served as a sergeant of artillery with the 89th Infantry Division in France. He returned deafened in one ear as the result of battlefield cannonading, a fact hidden from everyone except Aimee for quite a while. And still later, Mrs. Alexander discovered that in France Alex had suffered his first epileptic seizure.

In 1926, Joe McCarthy managed the Cubs for the first time and there were those who thought that greater understanding on McCarthy's part might have helped Alexander. That is only a remote possibility. Remember that Killefer had managed the Cubs the year before and Killefer had been Alexander's pal.

14

Now it seems inevitable. Alex and McCarthy did not get along. On June 22, the Cubs asked waivers on Alexander. The St. Louis Cardinals claimed him. Rogers Hornsby, the young manager of the Cardinals, was a lifelong teetotaler but one of his coaches was Bill Killefer. "Grab him," begged Killefer, "let me handle him and he'll help us."

That was the year the Cardinals won the pennant for the first time in their history. Alex won some games for them but no one could fairly say that he was the big wheel of the pitching staff although he may have meant the difference between success and failure. But he and no one else took charge of the World Series against the powerful Yankees.

The Yankees won the first game. Alex pitched the second and beat Urban Shocker, 6 to 2. At the end of five games, the Yankees led, three victories to two. Alex pitched the sixth game and beat Bob Shawkey, 10 to 2, on a Saturday in New York.

In the last and final game they needed him in the seventh inning when Jess Haines, leading by 3 to 2, broke a blister on his pitching hand. Haines got wild and the bases were filled with two out. Hornsby sent the message to the bullpen and met Alexander at second base.

"You see how it is, Pete," said Hornsby as he handed Alexander the ball. Alexander nodded and said, "I guess we gotta get Lazzeri out."

It took four pitches—all curves. Tony Lazzeri, one of the toughest of clutch hitters, laid off the first two, one called a strike, the second a ball. He tied into the third—a little too fast—but pulled a line drive into the left field bleachers 20 feet foul. The fourth was perfect—low and away—and Tony swung and missed.

Alex retired the Yankees in order in the eighth. With two out in the ninth, he walked Babe Ruth but not intentionally. "I had him struck out," he insisted, "but the umpire didn't give me the corner on the three-and-two pitch." It didn't matter. The game and the Series ended when Ruth was thrown out trying to steal.

The grateful Cardinals gave Alexander a $17,000 contract for 1927 and that is the highest salary he ever received. He reciprocated by winning 21 games. He was a 16-game winner in 1928 when the Cardinals won the pennant again but this time he was just another spear-carrier as the Yankees won a World Series in four straight games.

In 1929, Alexander's ninth victory was the 373rd of his career and the old boy, thinking he had set a National League record, took off on a rip-roaring celebration. By the time he sobered he had been suspended. That winter, he was traded back to the Phillies in a minor deal. His 20th major league season in the city in which he started resulted in no victories and three defeats, the only losing year he ever had.

There is a story that the night Alexander received his unconditional release from the Phillies, he said to an old friend, "I'm leaving this town just as I first came here—with nothing."

Ironically, Alexander didn't even have the National League record for most victories he thought he had. Some busybody, checking the old files, discovered that a game unaccountably charged as a defeat for Mathewson in 1902 actually had been a victory for Mathewson. So the final tally was 373 victories for each of these great right-handers. Alexander was elected to the Baseball Hall of Fame in 1938.

GROVER CLEVELAND ALEXANDER

Born, February 26, 1887, St. Paul, Nebraska.
Died, November 4, 1950, St. Paul, Nebraska.
Height 6'1". Weight 185. Threw and batted right-handed.

Year	Club	League	G	IP	W	L	Pct.	H	SO	BB	ERA
1911	Philadelphia	Nat.	48	367	28	13	.683	285	227	129	..
1912	Philadelphia	Nat.	46	310	19	17	.528	289	195	105	2.81
1913	Philadelphia	Nat.	47	306	22	8	.733	288	159	75	2.82

GROVER CLEVELAND ALEXANDER (*Continued*)

Year	Club	League	G	IP	W	L	Pct.	H	SO	BB	ERA
1914	Philadelphia	Nat.	46	355	27	15	.643	327	214	76	2.39
1915	Philadelphia	Nat.	49	376	31	10	.756	253	241	64	1.22
1916	Philadelphia	Nat.	48	389	33	12	.733	323	167	50	1.55
1917	Philadelphia [1]	Nat.	45	388	30	13	.698	326	200	56	1.83
1918	Chicago	Nat.	3	26	2	1	.667	19	15	3	1.78
1919	Chicago	Nat.	30	235	16	11	.593	180	121	38	1.72
1920	Chicago	Nat.	46	363	27	14	.659	335	173	69	1.91
1921	Chicago	Nat.	31	252	15	13	.536	286	77	33	3.39
1922	Chicago	Nat.	33	246	16	13	.552	283	48	34	3.62
1923	Chicago	Nat.	39	305	22	12	.647	308	72	30	3.19
1924	Chicago	Nat.	21	169	12	5	.706	183	33	25	3.03
1925	Chicago	Nat.	32	236	15	11	.577	270	63	29	3.39
1926	Chicago [2]-										
	St. Louis	Nat.	30	200	12	10	.545	191	47	31	3.06
1927	St. Louis	Nat.	37	268	21	10	.677	261	48	38	2.52
1928	St. Louis	Nat.	34	244	16	9	.640	262	59	37	3.36
1929	St. Louis [3]	Nat.	22	132	9	8	.529	149	33	23	3.89
1930	Philadelphia	Nat.	9	22	0	3	.000	40	6	6	9.00
	Major League Totals		**696**	**5189**	**373**	**208**	**.642**	**4868**	**2198**	**951**	**2.56**

[1] Traded with Catcher Bill Killefer to Chicago for Pitcher Mike Prendergast, Catcher Pickles Dilhoefer and $60,000, November 11, 1917.

[2] Waived to St. Louis, June 22, 1926.

[3] Traded with Catcher Harry McCurdy to Philadelphia for Outfielder Homer Peel and Pitcher Bob McGraw, December 11, 1929.

WORLD SERIES RECORD

Year	Club	League	G	IP	W	L	Pct.	H	SO	BB	ERA
1915	Philadelphia	Nat.	2	17⅔	1	1	.500	14	10	4	1.58
1926	St. Louis	Nat.	3	20⅓	2	0	1.000	12	17	4	0.89
1928	St. Louis	Nat.	2	5	0	1	.000	10	2	4	19.80
	World Series Totals		**7**	**43**	**3**	**2**	**.600**	**36**	**29**	**12**	**3.35**

* key

G = games
IP = innings pitched
W = won
L = lost
Pct. = percentage of games won
H = hits given up
SO = strikeouts
BB = bases on balls or walks
ERA = earned-run average

3

WALTER JOHNSON
The Big Train

As TIME goes by the number of baseball fans to actually have watched the Big Train roll diminishes constantly. Yet the legend is still so alive that the yardstick of speed pitching is the fast ball of Walter Johnson after a full half-century.

"Almost as fast as Johnson was" remains high praise for any pitcher. "As fast as Johnson" is an accolade bestowed on a very few—Dazzy Vance and Bob Grove, Dizzy Dean and Bob Feller, and a strange and unsuccessful Brooklyn right-hander named Van Lingle Mungo.

Was Johnson actually the fastest pitcher who ever lived? We'll never really know. But if you settle for the theory that Johnson threw the best fast ball ever seen in the major leagues you cannot be far off the mark.

Speed is a relative thing and Johnson's great natural talent was enhanced by a trick of delivery that has defied identical duplication. A modern watching Don Drysdale of the Dodgers can get some idea of Johnson's motion. But Drysdale's sidearm delivery is long and sweeping. Johnson's was somewhat shorter.

Great hitters said that Johnson's pitch was halfway to the plate before their eyes could pick up the flight of the ball and, by that time, it was usually too late.

After all these years, the best word picture of the young Johnson still is that drawn by Ring Lardner in a short story called "Horseshoes."

These are the words of a fictional rookie named Grimes, trying to make the grade with the Philadelphia Athletics:

"They can't never tell me he throws them balls with his arm. He's got a gun concealed about his person and he shoots 'em up there. I was leadin' off in Murphy's place and the game was a little delayed in startin' because I'd watched the big guy warm up and wasn't in no hurry to get to that plate. Before I left the bench Connie says:

" 'Don't try to take no healthy swing. Just meet 'em and you'll get along better.'

"So I tried to meet the first one he throwed; but when I stuck out my bat, Henry was throwin' the pill back to Johnson. Then I thought: Maybe if I start swingin' now at the second one I'll hit the third one. So I let the second one come over and the umps guessed it was another strike, though I'll bet a thousand dollars he couldn't see it no more'n I could.

"While Johnson was still windin' up to pitch again I started to swing—and the big cuss crosses me with a slow one. I lunged at it twice and missed it both times and the force of my wallop threw me clean back to the bench. The Ath-a-letics was all laughin' at me and I laughed too, because I was glad that much of it was over.

"McInnes gets a base hit off him in the second innin' and I ast him how he done it.

" 'He's a friend of mine,' says Jack, 'and he lets up when he pitches to me.'

"I made up my mind right there that if I was goin' to be in the league next year I'd go out and visit Johnson this winter and get acquainted.

"I wished before the day was over I was hittin' in the catcher's place, because the fellers down near the tail end of the batting order only had to face him three times. He fanned me on three pitched balls again in the third and when I came up in the sixth he scared me to death by pretty near beanin' me with the first one.

" 'Be careful!' says Henry. 'He's gettin' pretty wild and he's liable to knock you away from your uniform.'

" 'Don't he ever curve one?' I ast.

" 'Sure!' says Henry. 'Do you want to see his curve?'

"So he give me three hooks in succession and I missed 'em all; but I felt more comf'table than when I was duckin' his fast ball. In the ninth he hit my bat with a curve and the ball went on the ground to McBride. He booted it, but throwed me out easy—because I was so surprised at not havin' whiffed that I forgot to run!"

That was Johnson. It took a brave hitter to dig in at the plate when he was pitching. Walter's control was generally excellent but, occasionally, a fast ball did get away from him and, when that happened, Johnson was likely to be upset for a couple of innings. His own fear of seriously injuring a player with an accidental bean ball amounted to a phobia.

One time someone remarked in Casey Stengel's presence that it was a good thing Johnson wasn't mean.

"It was a good thing for the hitters," agreed the inimitable Stengel, "and a good thing for Johnson too. If he had been mean with that fast ball he woulda hadda been destroyed."

In his autobiography, Ty Cobb revealed that Johnson's fear was the basis of some psychological warfare that helped the great Cobb hit Johnson with some success. Cobb started by crowding the plate which, he knew, made Walter nervous. Trying to pitch outside, Johnson frequently fell behind in the count. Then Cobb would fall back into normal hitting position hopeful that Johnson would let up on his fast ball to make sure of a strike.

"It worked sometimes," said Cobb. "But Johnson's fast ball, even with something taken off it, wasn't easy to hit."

Walter Perry Johnson was born at Humboldt, Kansas, on

November 6, 1887, and almost 20 years passed before the city of Washington ever heard of him. Then on June 29, 1907, readers of the Washington *Star* read the following dispatch under a New York dateline:

"Manager Joe Cantillon has added a great baseball phenom to his pitching staff. The young man's name is Walter Johnson. This premier pitcher of the Idaho State League was signed by Cliff Blankenship. Cantillon received word from Blankenship today telling of the capture! Johnson pitched 75 innings in the Idaho State League without allowing a run and had a wonderful strikeout record of 166 in 11 games, or more than 15 strikeouts per game. Blankenship is very enthusiastic, but fails to state whether the great phenom is right or left-handed."

Blankenship was a Washington catcher recovering from an injury. Somebody thought it might be a good idea if he helped earn his salary by doing some scouting. Just before getting Johnson, he uncovered Clyde Milan in the minor leagues.

Milan was a crack Washington outfielder for 15 years and Johnson was a Washington pitcher for 21 seasons, so one assumes that Blankenship conducted a pretty successful operation.

When Pongo Joe Cantillon finally got to see the young marvel, his discoveries in order of importance were: (1) Johnson was right-handed; (2) he already stood six feet, one inch, but hadn't yet filled out to 200 pounds; (3) he really did have a wonderful arm.

He was a handsome youth, strikingly blond, and developed into a stalwart man. He also was diffident and unused to city ways and his success was not immediate.

In 1907, he won five games and lost nine. In 1908, he won 14 and lost the same number. In 1909, he won 13 games, but lost 25, yet was adding experience and gaining confidence. After all, the Idaho State League, from which he sprung, was little more than a semi-pro league which did not even keep official records.

Then in 1910, Johnson was off in a cloud of dust. He won 25 games and this was the first of ten straight seasons in which he won 20 or more. Twice he won more than 30.

His peak season was 1913 when he won 36 games and lost only seven. One-third of his victories that season were shutouts. He pitched 346 innings and gave up only 38 bases on balls, while striking out 243. His earned run average was 1.14.

When Johnson finished up at the end of the 1927 campaign, he had 416 victories, a record total for one league.

Sure Cy Young won 511, but Young's total was spread through both the National and American Leagues.

Johnson lost 280 games, which also is a record for one league, but bear in mind that the Senators finished in the second division in ten of his 21 seasons. How many heartbreakers he lost no one knows. He was beaten, 1 to 0, 20 times which is probably another record although nobody knows how to check that figure.

He led his league in strikeouts 12 times, another record. His lifetime strikeout total was 3,497. That not only is a major league record, but tops by more than 600 the mark set in both leagues by Young, his closest rival. It is almost 1,000 higher than the National League record held by Christy Mathewson.

And he did almost all of it with a fast ball. In spite of Lardner, hitters who faced Johnson say that Walter's curve was little more than a wrinkle, effective because it, too, was unusually fast like a modern slider. And again, in spite of Lardner, the old timers say he just played around with a change-up and never developed one which he could control consistently.

He never was with a really good team until 1924 when he was crowding 37 and his once devastating speed pitch had dwindled to the point where it merely was a good fast ball. That year, under Bucky Harris, then called the "boy manager," the Senators won their first pennant.

Now, at long last, Johnson was in a World Series. Naturally, he started in the first game and although he struck out 12 of

John McGraw's Giants, he was beaten by the left-handed Art Nehf, 4 to 3, in 12 innings. He pitched and lost the fifth game to Jack Bentley, also left-handed, 6 to 2.

But this series went the limit and when the Senators rallied to tie the seventh game in the the eighth inning, Harris sent Johnson in to relieve. He pitched four shutout innings, fanning five, and received his reward in the last of the 12th when a ground ball hit by Earl McNeely hopped weirdly over the head of third baseman Freddy Lindstrom to drive in the winning run.

For once, the breaks were with Johnson and there wasn't a nonpartisan fan in the country who didn't feel happy for the gallant veteran.

In 1925, the Senators again won the pennant and Johnson's World Series experiences were in exact reverse. This time he beat the Pittsburgh Pirates in the first game and the fourth, yielding only one run in the two games.

But again it went seven games and Johnson started the finale. This was a wild one, which started in a drizzle and continued in a downpour. At nine innings, the score was tied at 7 to 7. Johnson lost in the 12th when Kiki Cuyler hit a ground-rule double with the bases filled.

Among those who criticized Harris for keeping Johnson in the game was Ban Johnson, the president of the American League who had a notoriously low boiling point. The telegram Ban Johnson sent read: "You have sacrificed a World's Championship which the American League should have won to maudlin sentiment."

Bucky's reply was dignified and to the point.

"I am satisfied," said the young manager, "that we lost with our best."

When the rubber finally stretched out of his arm, Johnson tried managing at Washington and in Cleveland without much success. They said, probably with truth, he was too nice a guy.

He had a farm in Maryland, not too far from the capital, and he retired there after the death of his wife in 1930. He tried politics and achieved some local success but was beaten by a narrow margin when he ran for Congress on the Republican ticket.

That was another 1 to 0 defeat but Johnson did not seem to mind too much and lived in reasonable content until his final illness. When he died of a brain tumor on December 10, 1946, with his five children at his bedside, President Truman made a formal announcement of White House grief and Clark Griffith, who operated the Senators for so many years, wept openly.

There are not too many personal anecdotes about Johnson. His life off-field was private and quiet. He never was known to swear and he actually said "goodness gracious" to emphasize a point.

Johnson had various nicknames. Throughout his career, he answered to "Barney" in the dugout and in the clubhouse. This was adapted from Barney Oldfield, the pioneer automobile racing driver who had been America's earliest recognized king of speed.

"The Big Train" was pinned on Johnson late in his career. Before that, he had been for many years known as "the Big Swede" because of his rawboned strength and Nordic complexion.

The validity of that nickname was so generally accepted that an old friend was astonished one night to hear Johnson say that there was no Scandinavian strain whatever in his ancestry, that his forebears had been English, Holland Dutch, and Scotch-Irish.

Johnson seemed surprised when his friend asked him why he hadn't bothered to correct the impression that he was a Swede.

"Why," he answered, "the Swedes are nice people and I wouldn't want to hurt their feelings by intimating that I didn't wish to be known as one."

That was Walter Johnson.

WALTER PERRY JOHNSON

Born, November 6, 1887, Humboldt, Kansas.
Died, December 10, 1946, Washington, D.C.
Height 6'1". Weight 200. Threw and batted right-handed.

Year	Club	League	G	IP	W	L	Pct.	H	SO	BB	ERA
1907	Washington	Amer.	14	111	5	9	.357	100	70	16	...
1908	Washington	Amer.	36	257	14	14	.500	196	160	52	...
1909	Washington	Amer.	40	297	13	25	.342	247	164	84	...
1910	Washington	Amer.	45	374	25	17	.595	262	313	76	...
1911	Washington	Amer.	40	322	25	13	.658	292	207	70	...
1912	Washington	Amer.	50	368	32	12	.727	259	303	76	...
1913	Washington	Amer.	48	346	36	7	.837	232	243	38	1.14
1914	Washington	Amer.	51	372	28	18	.609	287	225	74	1.72
1915	Washington	Amer.	47	337	27	13	.675	258	203	56	1.55
1916	Washington	Amer.	48	371	25	20	.556	290	228	82	1.89
1917	Washington	Amer.	47	328	23	16	.590	259	188	67	2.28
1918	Washington	Amer.	39	325	23	13	.639	241	162	70	1.27
1919	Washington	Amer.	39	290	20	14	.588	235	147	51	1.49
1920	Washington	Amer.	21	144	8	10	.444	135	78	27	3.13
1921	Washington	Amer.	35	264	17	14	.548	265	143	92	3.51
1922	Washington	Amer.	41	280	15	16	.484	283	105	99	2.99
1923	Washington	Amer.	42	261	17	12	.586	263	130	69	3.48
1924	Washington	Amer.	38	278	23	7	.767	233	158	77	2.72
1925	Washington	Amer.	30	229	20	7	.741	211	108	78	3.07
1926	Washington	Amer.	33	262	15	16	.484	259	125	73	3.61
1927	Washington	Amer.	18	108	5	6	.455	113	48	26	5.08
Major League Totals			**802**	**5924**	**416**	**279**	**.599**	**4920**	**3508**	**1353**	...

WORLD SERIES RECORD

Year	Club	League	G	IP	W	L	Pct.	H	SO	BB	ERA
1924	Washington	Amer.	3	24	1	2	.333	30	20	11	3.38
1925	Washington	Amer.	3	26	2	1	.667	26	15	4	2.08
World Series Totals			**6**	**50**	**3**	**3**	**.500**	**56**	**35**	**15**	**2.70**

* key
G = games
IP = innings pitched
W = won
L = lost
Pct. = percentage of games won
H = hits given up
SO = strikeouts
BB = bases on balls or walks
ERA = earned-run average

25

4

CHRISTY MATHEWSON

Big Six

AND THEN there was Matty, earliest of the three right-handed Titans to grace the pitching mound in the first quarter of this twentieth century although the last to be considered here.

Christy Mathewson . . . Grover Alexander . . . Walter Johnson. Who was really top man of this illustrious trio? With all in their graves, it seems fruitless to revive an argument never resolved when all were alive and pitching.

The evidence points to conclusions which may be accepted as reasonably certain.

Mathewson was fast—as fast as Alexander, but not as fast as Johnson.

Matty had a good curve—not as good as Alexander's perhaps, but far better than Johnson's.

Matty had a third pitch—one that didn't even have a name when he first introduced it to the major leagues. It was George Davis (Matty's first manager with the Giants), who christened the revolutionary "reverse curve" a *fadeaway*. Some 25 years later they started to call the same pitch a *screwball*.

Johnson had good control. Alexander had great control. Mathewson, according to Johnny Evers (fiery second baseman of the Chicago Cubs), "could pitch into a tin cup." This qualifies as rare praise. In those days, the rivalry of the Giants and Cubs attained the frenetic bitterness of a holy war.

Mathewson's control figures are incredible. In his 17 seasons in the National League, he pitched 4,779 innings and walked only 831 men—an average of a trifle more than 1.5 bases on balls per nine inning game.

In 1908, he pitched 391 innings and walked only 42—an average just slightly above one base on balls a game.

In 1913, he pitched 306 innings and walked 21—one base on balls each 15 innings. He was almost as good in 1914, his last winning season, when he worked 312 innings and walked 23. He once pitched 68 consecutive innings without walking anybody.

Matty had one advantage over the other two—he pitched for more good ball clubs. The Giants of his time won five pennants and almost always were in the race. Consequently, his career percentage of .665 on 373 victories and 188 defeats tops the .642 of Alexander and the .599 of Johnson.

Mathewson's victory total and Alexander's are identical. They share the National League record. Obviously the reason why he did not top Alexander's mark and approach Johnson's American League record of 416 is that he wasn't as durable as either of the others. In retrospect, it seems likely that the wearing effects of throwing the fadeaway or screwball caused him to be washed up at 35.

To a degree that far transcended his ability, Mathewson made contributions to the game that probably surpassed those of any other individual.

Through force of character and personality, Mathewson altered turn-of-the-century conceptions about men who played the game. Through him, the public learned that a professional ballplayer need be neither a hayseed nor a tough-talking, tobacco-chewing, whiskey-guzzling refugee from the poolrooms of the teeming cities.

He was one of the earliest college graduates to play in the big leagues and the first of the college graduates to become a great star. He moved with a calm serenity but with a certain air of command. Baseball was a great part of his life, but not all of it, for here was a man of unusual intelligence who kept himself well-informed throughout his tragically short life.

He happened to be fascinated by games and was good at almost everything he tried. In the days when motoring was adventuresome sport, he was probably the first ballplayer to own an automobile and certainly the first to be fined for speeding (37 miles per hour).

He loved all kinds of card games. He played excellent chess. He earned such renown playing checkers that he was frequently called upon for exhibitions in which he faced 20 opponents simultaneously. He was among the first ballplayers to try golf and the first ballplayer to play it well. He consistently shot in the mid-70's when few professionals did with the hickory-shafted clubs and gutta-percha balls of that time.

Usually in the fall, he turned hunter and was a crack shot in the fields.

He forced his religious leanings upon no one, yet he made it plain that he did not care to pitch on Sundays and he never did. (This, incidentally, posed less of a problem than it would today. In Matty's time, there was no Sunday baseball in New York, Massachusetts, and Pennsylvania, and five of the eight National League cities were located in those states.)

He was presented as a model for American youth, which embarrassed him, and so did the well-intended effort to portray him as a plaster saint, which he wasn't.

He smoked—pipes, sometimes cigars, occasionally cigarettes. He was a temperate man but didn't mind if he did indulge in a snort once in a while. His poise was rarely ruffled but, when he did become angry, he could express himself in terms which his pastor might not have approved.

Christopher Mathewson was born August 12, 1880, and was raised on a farm outside Factoryville, Pennsylvania. It was a reasonably prosperous farm and his parents had no trouble fitting him out for a good start in life.

Christy was only 13 years old—but so large for his age that his boyhood nickname was "Husk"—when he pitched town ball against grown men who wore moustaches and even beards. Although he liked the game, the thought of playing it professionally doesn't appear to have come until much later.

He attended Keystone Academy and then Bucknell, where he attained his principal fame as a football player, but also was president of his class, a member of the glee club and of two literary societies.

He majored in forestry and seemingly had every intention of making this his career, but . . .

In those carefree days, it was quite customary for accomplished college athletes to pick up loose money in the summer months in semiprofessional baseball.

The summer of 1899 found young Mathewson pitching for Taunton, Massachusetts, in a league composed of New England mill towns. He won five, lost two, and discovered the fadeaway which, he admitted, he did not invent.

It seems that another pitcher named Williams, first name unknown, showed Matty the trick. Williams only threw it as a freak pitch on the sidelines and couldn't control it well enough to employ it in a game. Christy made it a useful addition to his repertoire.

That fall, it was back to Bucknell and football. Matty was a fast, hard-hitting fullback and a dropkicker of exceptional skill. The morning before a game with the University of Pennsylvania, Matty was approached in a Philadelphia hotel lobby by a character named Phenom Ed Smith, who was going to operate Norfolk in the Virginia League the following year.

Smith offered Mathewson $80 a month to pitch in Norfolk and Christy said he'd think it over. Bucknell upset Penn that afternoon and Mathewson kicked field goals of 42 and 45 yards. The exuberant Smith raised the ante to $90 a month.

Christy was too good for the Virginia League. He won 21 games and lost 2, then late in the season of 1900, was sold to the Giants "conditionally."

He pitched in five games for New York that year, won none and lost three, was returned to Norfolk, presumably a failure. Then the Giants got him back by ways that are dark and tricks that are vain.

The Cincinnati Reds drafted Mathewson for the ridiculous price of $100, then traded him to the Giants before the 1901 season began for Amos Rusie, who had been a celebrated fast ball pitcher in the early '90's but who hadn't won a game since 1898.

The Norfolk club bitterly complained that Andrew Freedman, owner of the Giants, had conspired to gyp Norfolk of the "conditional" price of $1,500 agreed upon for Mathewson. Circumstantial evidence supports the claim.

The long and intimate association of Matty and John J. McGraw, the colorful and vibrant manager of the Giants, is responsible for the widely held notion that McGraw had discovered and developed the great pitcher.

Actually, Matty worked for three managers in New York before McGraw took over toward the end of the 1902 season and one of these—Horace Fogel—was charged with trying to convert him into a first baseman. And, as a pitcher, Christy needed little help from anybody.

He won 20 games while losing 17 for George Davis in 1901. In 1902, when the Giants finished in the cellar, his record slipped to 14 victories and 17 defeats. Then, in 1903 with McGraw in charge, the Giants were on the rise and Mathewson rose with them.

In each of the next 12 years, Matty won more than 20 games. In four of these seasons he won more than 30. His peak years were 1903 (30–13); 1904 (33–12); 1905 (31–9); and 1908 (37–11).

Although his lifetime total of 2,505 strikeouts is a National League record, Matty was not primarily a strikeout specialist. He preferred giving his opposition a piece of the ball to hit, never forgetting there were eight other men on his team.

Joe Tinker, another old Chicago Cub and one who had a reputation for hitting Matty well, summed it up this way. "He didn't fool with you. A lot of pitchers had to throw six, seven or eight times to get rid of one hitter. Matty wanted to get you out with one pitch if he could. He averaged fewer pitches a game than any good pitcher who ever lived."

Matty's first famed battery mate was Frank Bowerman, later his hunting companion on many an autumn trip. Afterwards came Roger Bresnahan, one of the greatest of catchers, and still later, "Chief" Meyers, a redoubtable Indian. All three agreed he was a delightfully easy pitcher to handle.

Because he won so often, it is inevitable perhaps that Matty's best remembered games are a handful of heartbreaking defeats.

One was the final game of the 1908 pennant race, the re-play of the disallowed Giant victory in which Fred Merkle failed to touch second base. This was his 56th game of the season and for once Matty was tired. He lost to the Cubs, 4 to 2, but that might not have happened if Cy Seymour had obeyed instructions and had played back toward the fence on Matty's signal.

Actually, Seymour did move back but then crept in as Matty turned to pitch and Tinker hit a triple over the center fielder's head to drive in two runs.

Matty pitched in a World Series for the first time in 1905 when the Giants beat the Athletics in four out of five. Mathewson pitched three games and three shutouts. He held Connie Mack's fine team to 14 hits in 27 innings, struck out 18 and walked one.

But after that blazing start, Mathewson was unlucky in

31

World Series competition, winding up with five victories and five defeats.

The worst was in 1912 when Matty pitched three fine games against the Boston Red Sox, failed to win any of them and lost two, including the decisive game.

Merkle's single in the top of the tenth inning off Boston's Smoky Joe Wood had given the Giants a 2 to 1 lead. Matty had to retire three men for game, set, and match.

Clyde Engle, a pinch hitter for Wood, led off the Boston half with an easy fly to center. Fred Snodgrass muffed the ball. Harry Hooper hit a similar fly which Snodgrass held for out one, but then Steve Yerkes walked to put two on with the redoubtable Tris Speaker coming up.

Fooled on a pitch, Speaker lifted a soft foul fly. Either Meyers, catching, or Merkle, playing first, should have caught the ball. Both started for it, then both stopped.

Then Speaker singled to right, scoring Engle with the tying run and moving Yerkes around to third.

Matty then gave Duffy Lewis an intentional walk to fill the bases, but there was only one out and the Giants couldn't get well. Larry Gardner hit a long fly to Josh Devore for what should have been the fourth out of the inning and Yerkes easily scored on the sacrifice fly.

An interesting footnote was the mass meeting staged by Boston fans at Faneuil Hall to celebrate the championship that night. After congratulating the Red Sox, Boston Mayor Fitzgerald—the "Honey Fitz" whose grandson later sat in the White House—called for three cheers for the real hero of the World Series—Mathewson. And the beams in the ceiling of the historic shrine literally shook as the Boston fans obliged.

The mighty McGraw's relationship with Mathewson had always been unusual, to say the least. After Christy was married in 1903 to Jane Stoughton, who, as a Bucknell co-ed, had been

32

his campus sweetheart, the McGraws and the Mathewsons shared a large apartment in Manhattan. The arrangement was for the McGraws to take care of the rent and the Mathewsons to provide the table.

The idea of a manager living with his star pitcher staggers imagination and yet it worked for many years. Perhaps the reason why other players weren't as resentful as they might have been was an idea that Matty's calm good judgment often saved them from the sharpest edge of McGraw's irascible temper. Long after both were widowed Jane Mathewson and Blanche McGraw remained devoted friends until Mrs. McGraw's death.

In 1915, Christy still was a magnificent figure of a man—six feet, one and a half inches, 195 pounds, and graceful in every movement on the ball field.

But something had happened to his fast ball. It still looked good, but it had straightened out. Good hitters waited for the pitch—and then waylaid it. The word went out that "Big Six"— a nickname pinned on Mathewson after a famed New York City fire engine—no longer could work up a full head of steam.

Matty won eight games in 1915 and lost 14. In 1916, he floundered even worse and, in July, McGraw traded him to the Cincinnati Reds where he took over as manager until the end of 1917 when he went to war.

There is little doubt that McGraw was priming Matty to be his successor as manager of the Giants. When Matty returned from France he was immediately engaged as a coach of the New York club. In the meantime, he had been fingered by fate as a delayed casualty of 1918.

He had been a captain in the chemical warfare division of the army and when something went wrong in a poison gas test conducted in France, Matty inhaled a deep breath of the lethal stuff. By the summer of 1921, he was in Saranac with tuberculosis in both lungs. He beat the original diagnosis, which had given him only six months to live, then perhaps foolishly returned to baseball as part owner and president of the Boston Braves. That was in 1923 and within two years he was back in Saranac.

The end came on October 7, 1925. That was an afternoon a World Series started with Walter Johnson pitching the first game for Washington against the Pittsburgh Pirates.

This was the time of crystal radio sets and this was one of the first World Series ever broadcast. Early in the afternoon, Matty is said to have asked how the game was going. He was told that Johnson had allowed only two hits and was well ahead of the Pirates.

"Fine," murmured Mathewson, who barely knew Johnson but who had a tremendous professional admiration for the great Senator. He never knew that Walter maintained his lead and won the game, for, by that time, Matty was dead.

He was only 45.

CHRISTOPHER MATHEWSON

Born, August 12, 1880, Factoryville, Pennsylvania.
Died, October 7, 1925, Saranac Lake, New York.
Height 6'1½". Weight 195. Threw and batted right-handed.

Year	Club	League	G	IP	W	L	Pct.	H	SO	BB	ERA
1900	New York	Nat.	5	30	0	3	.000	29	15	14	...
1901	New York	Nat.	40	336	20	17	.541	281	215	92	...
1902	New York	Nat.	34	276	14	17	.452	241	162	74	...
1903	New York	Nat.	45	367	30	13	.698	321	267	100	...
1904	New York	Nat.	48	368	33	12	.733	306	212	78	...
1905	New York	Nat.	43	339	31	9	.775	252	206	64	...
1906	New York	Nat.	38	267	22	12	.647	262	128	77	...
1907	New York	Nat.	41	316	24	12	.667	250	178	53	...
1908	New York	Nat.	56	391	37	11	.771	278	259	42	...
1909	New York	Nat.	37	275	25	6	.806	192	149	36	..
1910	New York	Nat.	38	319	27	9	.750	291	190	57	...
1911	New York	Nat.	45	307	26	13	.667	303	141	38	...
1912	New York	Nat.	43	310	23	12	.657	311	134	34	2.12
1913	New York	Nat.	40	306	25	11	.694	291	93	21	2.06
1914	New York	Nat.	41	312	24	13	.648	314	80	23	3.00

34

CHRISTOPHER MATTHEWSON (*Continued*)

Year	Club	League	G	IP	W	L	Pct.	H	SO	BB	ERA
1915	New York	Nat.	27	186	8	14	.364	199	57	20	3.58
1916	New York [1]-										
	Cincinnati	Nat.	13	74	4	4	.500	74	19	8	3.04
	Major League Totals		**634**	**4779**	**373**	**188**	**.665**	**4195**	**2505**	**831**	...

[1] Traded with Outfielder Eddie Roush to Cincinnati for Infielder Charles (Buck) Herzog and Outfielder Wade Killefer, July 20, 1916.

WORLD SERIES RECORD

Year	Club	League	G	IP	W	L	Pct.	H	SO	BB	ERA
1905	New York	Nat.	3	27	3	0	1.000	14	18	1	0.00
1911	New York	Nat.	3	27	1	2	.333	25	13	2	2.33
1912	New York	Nat.	3	28⅔	0	2	.000	23	10	5	1.57
1913	New York	Nat.	2	19	1	1	.500	14	7	2	0.47
	World Series Totals		**11**	**101⅓**	**5**	**5**	**.500**	**76**	**48**	**10**	**1.15**

* key

G = games
IP = innings pitched
W = won
L = lost
Pct. = percentage of games won
H = hits given up
SO = strikeouts
BB = bases on balls or walks
ERA = earned-run average

5

ROBERT WILLIAM ANDREW FELLER

The Fireballer

CONVERSATION AMONG the writers traveling with the Giants was brisk and stimulating that Easter Sunday morning in 1937 as they moved from Jackson, Mississippi, to Vicksburg for an exhibition game with the Cleveland Indians. They were going to get a look at Bob Feller, the schoolboy who broke in so sensationally with the Indians late in the preceding season. The kid had fanned eight Cardinals in three innings in a July exhibition game, struck out fifteen of the St. Louis Browns in his first major league start, but so far none of the writers with the Giants had seen him.

The ball park at Vicksburg was built with an eye to convenience. Home plate was within fifty feet of the first row of the grandstand and the press box was in the first row. There were three writers accompanying the Indians and ten with the Giants. The press box was built to accommodate about a half-dozen and the overflow press sat on a bench on the playing field. When Feller cut loose with his first warm-up pitch, somebody tipped the bench and everybody keeled over. It was a gag, of course, but one which had its foundations in truth, for Robert William Andrew Feller, of Van Meter, Iowa, was the original blow-'em-down kid in those days.

It didn't take the New York writers more than a few pitches to realize that their Cleveland brethren weren't kidding when they said young Feller was out of this world. He had a fast ball

36

as explosive as any they had ever seen—Dazzy Vance, Walter Johnson, Lefty Grove or Van Lingle Mungo. And the boy was only eighteen years old!

Feller pitched the first three innings, held the Giants without a hit, fanned six, four of them in succession. For once, a sports writer could employ the adjective "sensational" and be well within the bounds of accuracy. Bob walked only one man, facing a total of ten in the three innings he worked.

Bill Klem, the veteran National League umpire who worked behind the plate that afternoon in Vicksburg, was loud in his praise of Feller after the game. "The boy has a chance to be the greatest of them all," said Bill. The Giants, for the most part, agreed with Klem. Manager Bill Terry cautiously added the phrase "if he has control" to his encomia of Feller. Mel Ott admired his curve ball and Carl Hubbell said he thought Bob was "about as fast as anybody I've ever seen."

There was one dissenter—Dick Bartell, the Giant shortstop. Battling against Feller in the first inning, Dick popped out. While taking fielding practice between innings a ball took a bad hop and hit Dick in the face, so he was excused from further duty. Maybe it was the fact that his acquaintance with Feller was thus curtailed which warped Dick's judgment but the shortstop was unimpressed.

"We've got several guys in our league who can throw just as hard," stoutly maintained Richard. "I know he isn't as fast as Mungo."

Feller continued to strike out the Giants, seemingly leveling at Bartell. He fanned Dick something like thirteen times in eighteen turns at bat. As the late Bill Slocum wrote, "Bartell went all the way to Fort Smith before he got so much as a loud foul against Feller."

No ballplayer in modern times broke in as sensationally as Feller. He was an unknown who burst into national prominence with his exhibition performance against the Cardinals.

Harry Grayson, sports editor of the Newspaper Enterprise Association, which then had its home office in Cleveland, was the first to bring word East of Feller's fireball. Harry burst in on a group of New York writers in Pittsburgh's Schenley Hotel one night and began to sing the praises of Feller, whom he had seen in the night exhibition against the Cards.

"You never saw anything like this kid!" sputtered Grayson excitedly. "He practically steps toward third base when he throws, and the ball just explodes.

"I was sitting on the bench with Frisch the other night when he brought the Cards to Cleveland. Feller started warming up and Frank said 'Who in the hell is that fireballer?' I told him he was a kid Cy Slapnicka had picked up and that he was selling peanuts. 'Peanuts,' Frisch screams. 'That kid's the fastest pitcher I ever saw.' Then he turns to Stu Martin and says, 'Stu, how'd you like to play second base tonight?' He turned aside to me and winked, saying, 'They're not gonna get the old Flash out there against that kid.'"

The first batter to face Feller, Bruce Ogrodowski, the St. Louis catcher, bunted and was out and then Bob faced Leo Durocher, who became the first major leaguer he ever fanned. He got Leo twice during his three-inning stint and also Les Munns, the Card pitcher. The woods are probably full of pitchers who struck out Durocher and Munns twice, but Bob also managed to bag four other Cardinals, Pepper Martin, Charley Gelbert, Rip Collins, and Art Garibaldi.

Feller went on from that night exhibition game against the Cardinals to face the Browns in an American League game and fanned fifteen of them, an impressive total and one which hasn't been topped by many pitchers. This was in late August, 1936, and Rapid Robert's achievement was a sensation, but not for long, because he tangled with the Athletics only three weeks later and fanned seventeen! This tied the National League

38

strikeout record, which had been set by the great Dizzy Dean only three years earlier, and it was the first time an American League pitcher, any American League pitcher—Johnson, Grove, Waddell or the rest—ever had scored so many strikeout victims.

Young Bob had nothing but speed in those closing weeks in 1936, speed and what little he was able to remember of the advice Steve O'Neill gave him. Stout Steve, who was Feller's first manager, even cooperated to the point of catching the fire-baller in the exhibition game against the Cardinals, so as to give him additional confidence. And Steve, then fat and forty, took no inconsiderable risk in getting behind the plate to handle the explosive fast ball of the kid.

Feller broke in with the greatest of all natural gifts for a pitcher—the ability to fire a baseball as though it were jet-propelled. Uncle Wilbert Robinson, who managed the Dodgers for so many years, was adjudged a great handler and developer of pitchers, whatever opinions may have been held on his strategic maneuverings. It was Uncle Robbie who claimed that a pitcher could develop anything he needed, control, a curve, fielding skill, anything except a fast ball.

"Only God can give a man a fast ball," said Robbie.

Although Feller had only one attribute, he had the most important. He was to develop the others as time went on, to develop them painstakingly, through perseverance and practice. Bob was fortunate that his first manager was O'Neill, for there was something of Uncle Robbie in the brawny Irishman from the anthracite country of Pennsylvania. Like Robbie, Steve had been a catcher, and like Robbie, Steve appreciated good pitching. He saw from the beginning that Feller had a chance to become one of the greatest.

Bob, at the outset, didn't have much of a curve and tipped off when he was going to throw it. A change of pace was merely a bit of baseball nomenclature to him, and on the subject of

39

holding base runners to their bases, he knew rather less than a Hindu. Players stole second—and even home—while Feller was holding the ball in his hand. He was the biggest green pea baseball had ever seen—and he was to become one of its greatest pitchers.

It is a moot question whether Feller's lack of control in the early days was a curse or a blessing. To be sure, the bases on balls he issued got him into many a jam, but the fact that nobody, not even Bobby, ever was quite sure where any given pitch was going, certainly padded his strikeout records. Nobody took any toeholds when Feller's forked lightning began striking around home plate.

To quote Uncle Robbie once again, the roundest of all the old Orioles had a phrase for this lack of control in a fast ball pitcher, a phrase which was so much the *mot juste* that he used it over and over when he spoke of Dazzy Vance. Robbie called this trait, "pleasingly wild," which meant that while the pitcher's wildness wasn't enough to get him into serious trouble, it was sufficient to keep the batters footloose and fancy-free at the plate.

Feller's fireball hardly had burst upon the baseball horizon when Bobby found himself a cause célèbre for entirely different reasons. Lee Keyser, who owned the Des Moines franchise in the Western League and who, it irrelevantly must be noted, was the first man to play organized baseball under lights, filed a protest with Commissioner Kenesaw Mountain Landis, that Cy Slapnicka had illegally signed Feller to a Cleveland contract.

At the time it caused a dandy rhubard, for Feller completed his first season with five victories in eight decisions and the amazing number of 76 strikeouts in 62 innings, which gave him an average of better than 11 per regulation game! If the Commissioner were to declare him a free agent, Feller could have commanded at least $100,000 on the open market.

The circumstances under which Feller became Cleveland's property were not uncommon for that period, even though contrary to baseball law. Bob had been pitching sandlot ball in Iowa when Slapnicka signed him to a contract to pitch for Fargo-Moorehead (North Dakota) in the Northern League. Bob, who came up with a sore arm in the winter, probably as the result of playing basketball at Van Meter High, never reported to Fargo-Moorehead. Instead, he was brought to Cleveland and worked out at League Park when the Indians were on the road and pitched for the Cleveland Rosenblums, under the watchful eye of Slapnicka. Cy was ready to transfer Feller's contract to another Cleveland farm, New Orleans in the Southern League, when Bobby burst like a bombshell on the Cardinals.

After that, Slapnicka decided the boy had to stay with the Indians. Keyser's beef to Landis opened a fine kettle of fish, but by December of 1936, the Judge ruled that Bobby was to remain the property of Cleveland, although he ordered the Indians to pay Keyser and the Des Moines Club $7,500 as damages. The Judge went further than that—he rescinded the rule which forbade major league clubs to deal with sandlot players, since he realized that many of them were doing so anyway.

It wasn't to be as easy as Cy hoped, despite Feller's sensational work in the barnstorming games against the Giants in the spring of 1937, when he fanned 37 in 27 innings and climaxed the tour by drawing 31,486 into the Polo Grounds when he faced Carl Hubbell in the finale.

Feller pitched against the Browns in Cleveland's second home game of the season, April 24. On his first pitch of the ball game, Bobby tried to break off a curve against Bill Knickerbocker and almost broke off his arm instead. Before the inning was over, Feller had walked four, given up two hits and had been scored

41

on four times. He contemplated walking off the mound but instead tried to get by with his fast ball alone.

Bob lasted until the sixth, when he tried another curve, with the same searing pain in his right elbow. He told Manager O'Neill he was through, explaining that he had injured his arm in the first inning and had believed he pitched out the soreness until he tried another curve.

It is doubtful if any pitcher in baseball got more publicity than Feller did by *not* pitching. His arm refused to respond to treatment and he wasn't able to pitch again until July 4, an absence of more than two months from the firing line. All sorts of treatments were tried but nothing proved effective until a bone and muscle manipulator a few blocks from the ball park, one A.L. Austin, restored Bobby to normalcy by deciding that Feller's ulna bone was out of his socket and snapping it back into place. He told Bobby to get 24 hours' rest and then go out and pitch.

The kid with the plowboy's walk did just that. He didn't pitch well but he got back into the swing of things. He concluded the season with a record of nine wins and seven defeats, after losing his first four decisions. Feller was on the way back.

Feller's dead arm was a tremendous strain on a youth of eighteen. First of all, he was beset with the morbid fear that his pitching career was over before it started. Secondly, his every visit to a doctor, osteopath, or chiropractor was subjected to pitiless publicity. Even when he went home to Van Meter to receive his high school diploma, his sore arm was the principal subject of conversation.

In addition to his dad, Feller had two men to lean upon, the tireless Slapnicka and the patient and generous Steve O'Neill. Although a slovenly season by the Indians had placed Stout Steve's job in jeopardy, he stuck by Bobby and paid as much attention to the kid as if Feller already were the established star he was destined to be, instead of a boy who had won precisely five major league games and who wasn't able to throw a ball at all, let alone throw it hard.

It was in 1938, under a new manager, the dynamic Oscar Vitt, that Feller really started to move. Feller played under four Cleveland managers before he came under the guidance of Al Lopez in 1951—O'Neill, Vitt, Roger Peckinpaugh, and Lou Boudreau—and he gave them all the same loyal service. The chances are Bobby was closer to O'Neill than any of them, for the paternal Irishman stayed with him during the rough spots of his arm trouble in 1937.

Beginning in 1938, Rapid Robert fanned the amazing number of 1,007 American League hitters in four years, while pitching 1,238 innings and winning 93 games. Then he entered the Navy, not to return to the uniform of the Indians again for almost four full seasons, four seasons when he assuredly would have been at the peak of his career and in a position to challenge all of the all-time strikeout records. He almost certainly would have moved into the select circle of pitchers who have won 300 games.

There was a curious pattern through all of Feller's pitching, an overall greatness, tinged with frustration. Throughout his career, Bobby was consistently balked on the threshold of his finest achievements. The sore arm he developed in 1937 was a forerunner of things to be. His entrance into the Navy at the height of his career was symbolic.

Nowhere was the Feller jinx more noticeable than in the World Series of 1948, which Bobby finally reached a dozen years after he first burst upon the baseball scene. The fireballer didn't have a particularly good season—good for him, that is—as the Indians won their first pennant in 28 years through the virtue of Lou Boudreau's hitting in the first play-off game in American League history, which broke the tie with the Red Sox.

43

Bobby won nineteen games that year, the first full season since 1938 in which he failed to reach twenty. His winning percentage, .559, was the poorest he had ever had up until that time. Although he led the American League in strikeouts for the seventh time, his total, 164, was the lowest he had had for a full season in ten years. And he gave up more base hits than any other pitcher in the league.

Nevertheless, Feller was magnificent in the opening game against the Braves in Boston. He gave up only two hits, yet bowed to Johnny Sain by a score of 1 to 0. It was the first 1–0 World Series decision since Casey Stengel had beaten the Yankees with a home run when he was playing with the Giants, a quarter of a century before. And it was the first 1–0 Series opener since Babe Ruth had pitched the Red Sox to a victory over Hippo Jim Vaughn and the Cubs thirty years earlier.

Marvin Rickert—who played the outfield for the Braves through special dispensation after Jeff Heath sustained a fractured leg in the last week of the season—made the first hit in the fifth, and the second and last hit, a single by Tommy Holmes, beat Feller in the eighth, one of the most controversial innings in World Series history.

Bill Salkeld, Boston catcher, opened the eighth by drawing Feller's second pass of the game. Phil Masi went in to run for Bill and was sacrificed to second by Mike McCormick. Manager Boudreau ordered an intentional pass for Eddie Stanky, with the obvious aim of setting up a double play situation for Sain.

Boudreau also was setting up something else, the famed pick-off play of the Tribe which had proved effective quite frequently during the regular American League season. While pitching to Sain, Bobby suddenly whirled and threw to Boudreau covering second. It seemed from the stands that Masi was definitely picked off, that Lou had the ball on him before he could dive back into second base. National League umpire Bill

Stewart, who, after all, was closer to the play than anybody else, ruled that Masi's headlong slide had beaten Boudreau's tag, that Lou had put the ball on Phil's upper arm after the runner's hand had reached the bag.

When the excitement subsided, Sain flied for the second out, but Holmes, a left-handed batter, singled home Masi from second with the only run of the ball game, and Feller was beaten, although far from disgraced, in his first World Series appearance.

Cleveland took the next three straight, Bob Lemon winning 4 to 1 in Boston, while Gene Bearden won the first game in Cleveland by 2 to 0. For the Saturday game in Cleveland, Boudreau pulled Steve Gromek as a surprise starter and Steve came through with a 2–1 triumph. In four games, the hapless Braves had scored exactly three runs and Feller seemed a cinch to wind up the Series when he made his second start on Sunday before the largest World Series crowd at that time—86,288.

Feller simply didn't have it that day, although Boudreau, with an eye on history's pages, persevered with him far longer than he would with an ordinary pitcher. Bobby was being well belted, but Nelson Potter, the desperation pitching selection of Manager Bill Southworth, wasn't exactly a puzzle and Lou kept hoping that Feller would get a grip on himself.

Bob Elliott tagged Feller for a three-run homer over the right field screen in the first inning and then hit a homer into the left field stands in the third. Boudreau's tenacity with Feller seemed justified when a three-run home run by Jim Hegan put the Tribe in front by 5 to 4 in the fifth.

Feller couldn't hold the lead, however, and gave up his third home run in the sixth, this by Bill Salkeld. Then in the seventh, the game came apart at the seams and Lou finally had to lift Bobby. Boston eventually won the game by a score of 11 to 5.

In many respects, Feller enjoyed in 1946 the greatest season of any modern pitcher, even though he wasn't a thirty-game winner as Lefty Grove and Dizzy Dean had been. Bob won 26 games, pitched 371 innings and broke Rube Waddell's old strikeout mark by five, bagging 348 victims in the course of this laborious season.

More than that, Feller finally made the Yankees, his chief tormentors since he had entered baseball, holler "Uncle!" On the last day of April that season, Bob threw the second no-hitter of his career against the Bombers in Yankee Stadium, winning 1 to 0 on a home run by his catcher, Frankie Hayes, against Floyd Bevens in the ninth. Bevens, who in his brief career with the Yankees was to prove baseball's unluckiest pitcher, later was to lose a no-hit World Series game in Brooklyn when Cookie Lavagetto hit a pinch-double with two out in the ninth.

Although Feller walked five and George Stirnweiss opened the ninth by reaching first on Les Fleming's palpable error, Bobby's no-hitter never really was in danger after Boudreau had come in behind the pitcher's box to make an acrobatic play on a grounder by the speedy Stirnweiss for the second out in the first inning. Boudreau also made a spry play later on a ball hit by Phil Rizzuto but it wasn't as spectacular as the one on George.

The last play of the game was a throat-choker, as Ray Mack stumbled fielding Charley Keller's ordinary grounder but scrambled to his feet in time to throw him out at first and preserve Rapid Robert's no-hitter. In all, Feller fanned a dozen Yankees getting Nick Etten, the first baseman, three times, and Bevens the same number. He fanned Stirnweiss twice and Rizzuto, Keller, Joe Gordon, and Bill Dickey once. He missed only Tommy Henrich, who walked twice, and Joe DiMaggio, who went four-for-oh.

DiMaggio in particular and the Yanks in general always had been a nemesis to Feller. In Bob's first start in New York,

46

in 1936, he lasted exactly one inning, giving up three hits, three walks, and contributing a balk to general debacle as the Yanks scored five times. The following year, when Bobby was making his comeback after his sore arm, he had the Yanks in a 1–1 tie before 59,000 in a Sunday afternoon game in the Municipal Stadium, and DiMaggio broke the tie and Feller's heart with a grand-slam home run high into the left-center stands. Bob had thrown two fast balls by the Clipper and tried to fool him with a curve.

DiMaggio beat Feller with home runs more than once, as did Lou Gehrig. In one game, in 1938, Joe batted in seven runs against Feller, quite possibly the all-time high for a single batter in one game against the fireballer.

Feller's 1946 achievements are all the more remarkable when it is remembered that he was in service from two days after Pearl Harbor until a week after V–J Day. Bob served 44 months and had eight battle stars. He appeared in nine games in what was left of 1945 and then really went to work the following season.

Bob, who pitched a no-hitter against the White Sox to open the 1940 season, considers his Yankee no-hitter his masterpiece. One of his greatest games, however, was the final game of the 1938 season, when he struck out eighteen Tigers, including Hank Greenberg, who hit 58 home runs that year to threaten Ruth's record.

Feller fanned Chet Laabs five times in the course of the game. He had ten strikeouts out of a possible dozen in the first four innings, five more in the next three and needed only three strikeouts in the last two innings to break the record he held jointly with Dizzy Dean. He finally made it by fanning Laabs for the fifth time for the final out in the ninth.

Bob's game is still spoken of reverently, yet only those who saw the game can remember the name of his opponent. It was

Harry Eisenstat, a left-handed kid from Brooklyn who threw mostly soft stuff. If there aren't many who can remember the name of Eisenstat, there are even fewer who remember that he beat Feller that day, 4 to 0!

Written off after a 16–11 season in 1950, Bobby came back in 1951 to get into the twenty-win column again for the sixth time in his career. His pitching put the Indians into the heat of the American League's pennant race and he topped it all with a no-hit game against Detroit on July 1. It was the third no-hitter of his career and gave Feller the distinction of being the only pitcher to ring up three no-hitters in the era of the lively ball. The lively ball held no terrors for Bob as long as there was life in his own fast one and in his curve.

It was Bob's curve which became pretty much his stock in trade as time wore on. He improved on his 9–13 season of 1952 with a 10–7 record the next year, although he fanned only 60, his all-time low for a full season.

With a pitching staff boasting Bob Lemon, Early Wynn, and Mike Garcia, Cleveland drove to a pennant in 1954, breaking the five-year hold the Yankees had held over the American League. Although Rapid Robert was in the second wave, so to speak, he had a remarkable 13–3 record and scored some spot victories at a time when they helped the Indians the most.

In the debacle of the World Series, in which the Giants won four straight, Feller was merely a spectator. Manager Al Lopez had pre-series plans of starting Feller in the fourth game, after Lemon, Wynn, and Garcia, but the Giants had knocked off all three and Lopez decided to come back with Lemon, who had lost the opener 5 to 3 on Dusty Rhodes' three-run homer in the tenth. The Giants beat Lemon and that was that.

There were many who believed that a rested Feller would have been a better bet against the National Leaguers than Lemon with only two days between starts. Feller was not among the critics of Lopez.

48

"Al is the boss," said Bob.

Apparently the kid fireballer knows how to grow old gracefully.

ROBERT WILLIAM ANDREW FELLER

Born, November 3, 1918, Van Meter, Iowa.
Height 6'. Weight 185. Threw and batted right-handed.

Year	Club	League	G	IP	W	L	Pct.	H	SO	BB	ERA
1936	Cleveland	Amer.	14	62	5	3	.625	52	76	47	3.34
1937	Cleveland	Amer.	26	149	9	7	.563	116	150	106	3.38
1938	Cleveland	Amer.	39	278	17	11	.607	225	240	208	4.08
1939	Cleveland	Amer.	39	297	24	9	.727	227	246	142	2.85
1940	Cleveland	Amer.	43	320	27	11	.711	245	261	118	2.62
1941	Cleveland	Amer.	44	343	25	13	.658	284	260	194	3.15
1942–1943–1944	(In Military	Service)									
1945	Cleveland	Amer.	9	72	5	3	.625	50	59	35	2.50
1946	Cleveland	Amer.	48	371	26	15	.634	277	348	153	2.18
1947	Cleveland	Amer.	42	299	20	11	.645	230	196	127	2.68
1948	Cleveland	Amer.	44	280	19	15	.559	255	164	116	3.57
1949	Cleveland	Amer.	36	211	15	14	.517	198	108	84	3.75
1950	Cleveland	Amer.	35	247	16	11	.593	230	119	103	3.43
1951	Cleveland	Amer.	33	250	22	8	.733	239	111	95	3.49
1952	Cleveland	Amer.	30	192	9	13	.409	219	81	83	4.73
1953	Cleveland	Amer.	25	176	10	7	.588	163	60	60	3.58
1954	Cleveland	Amer.	19	140	13	3	.813	127	59	39	3.09
1955	Cleveland	Amer.	25	83	4	4	.500	71	25	29	3.47
1956	Cleveland	Amer.	19	58	0	4	.000	63	18	23	4.97
	Major League Totals		570	3828	266	162	.621	3271	2581	1762	3.25

WORLD SERIES RECORD

Year	Club	League	G	IP	W	L	Pct.	H	SO	BB	ERA
1948	Cleveland	Amer.	2	14⅓	0	2	.000	10	7	5	5.02

* key

G   = games
IP   = innings pitched
W   = won
L   = lost
Pct. = percentage of games won
H   = hits given up
SO   = strikeouts
BB   = bases on balls or walks
ERA = earned-run average

6

ROBERT MOSES GROVE
Old Man Mose

UNLESS YOU happened to be a National Leaguer, the very first of the All-Star baseball games, played at Chicago's Comiskey Park in 1933, was an outstanding success. It had been devised by Arch Ward, sports editor of the Chicago *Tribune* as an added fillip to *A Century of Progress*, the pageant which was sprawled along the lake front doing a howling business.

There were 49,200 fans in the stands, the stars of both leagues had been on the field, John McGraw had come out of retirement to face his old foe, Connie Mack, and Babe Ruth and Frankie Frisch had hit home runs. Babe's homer, which came with a man on, had given the Americans a 4–2 lead which looked comfortable enough as the ninth inning rolled around.

With two out McGraw sent Tony Cuccinello of the Dodgers up to pinch-hit for Carl Hubbell. Tony, a chunky Italian infielder, looked like a mascot as he stood up there to face the altitudinous Lefty Grove. Grove breezed three fast balls by Tony and the first All-Star game was history.

Cuccinello was still somewhat dazed that night as the Dodgers entrained to open their Western trip in St. Louis. It wasn't the strikeout which bothered Tony, nor the fact that the Nationals were defeated. Tony was an old pro and he could take strikeouts and defeats in stride but he still was awed by the lightning fast ball of Grove.

"Aspirin tablets," he muttered that evening, "just like aspirin tablets those balls were. I've hit against Dazzy Vance and Van Mungo, and I thought they were pretty swift, but I never saw anything like that Grove."

Such was the speed of Grove in those days that National Leaguers were invariably astounded when they got their first glimpse of the star left-hander of the Philadelphia Athletics. The speed of Grove was famous throughout both leagues but it had to be seen to be appreciated.

Cuccinello wasn't the first big leaguer to be amazed when he saw Grove from the proximity of the batter's box for the first time, nor was he the last. The Cubs had a rude shock in the World Series of 1929 when they saw Lefty for the first time.

In the opening game of that Series at Wrigley Field, Mack had pulled Howard Ehmke out of a hat and Ehmke proceeded to make Series history by fanning thirteen Cubs. The next day Connie came up with George Earnshaw, who was relieved by Grove in the fifth. The Big Moose had fanned seven when he needed help from Grove and Lefty struck out another six Cubs to bring the total to thirteen for the second day in a row. And Grove pitched only 4⅓ innings in getting six strikeout victims out of a possible thirteen. In the fourth game, after the Athletics had had a ten-run inning against the Cubs at Shibe Park, Grove came in to pitch the last two innings and fanned four of a possible six, giving him a Series record of ten strikeouts in 6⅓ innings.

Grove could throw a ball by a batter as few pitchers ever could. It wasn't only National Leaguers seeing him for the first time who were put into a coma by his speed. It happened to American Leaguers who had seen him time and again and who were simply overpowered, not surprised.

Against the Yankees one day, when the Athletics held a 1–0 lead in the last half of the ninth, Mark Koenig led off with a triple against Grove. With Ruth, Gehrig, and Bob Meusel coming up, the customers in Yankee Stadium settled back to await a tie ball game.

Grove simply reared back and flung his fast ball right by the Yankee Murderers' Row, fanning the Babe, Lou, and Meusel on nine pitched balls, one of which Meusel came close enough to foul off.

Grove was particularly proud of achieving his 300th victory, as well he should be since he was the first since Grover Cleveland Alexander's day to reach that number and will be the last for many years to come. When Cy Young's 511 victories cropped up, in conversation or even the marks of Walter Johnson, Christy Mathewson or Alexander, Lefty was quick to enter a demurer.

"I might have won 500 games if I pitched forty years ago," he would snort. "Consider all the things those guys had going for 'em that I didn't. First of all they had the dead ball. Guys used to lead the league with a half-dozen home runs. Second, a ball was hardly ever thrown out of play. You could pitch with a discolored ball or a scuffed one. The dirty baseball was hard to follow and the scuffed one 'sailed,' which made it harder to hit. Third, they had the privilege of throwing trick deliveries like the shine ball, the emory ball, and the spitter."

Another point, too, was that in Grove's day—and all 300 of his victories were scored in the era of the lively ball—Babe Ruth had set the style. The choke-hitter had almost disappeared and all the batters were swinging from their heels in an effort to clear the fences. While this was in some ways an asset to a pitcher, since he could get the ball past the hitter who was swinging freely, it also meant trouble if the pitch were the least bit off, if it went anywhere in the zone where the batter had a chance to get the "fat" part of his bat on the ball.

Grove's complaints against comparisons with the pitchers of the pre-Ruthian era may seem conceited but he has a sound argument. To begin with, Lefty is the only pitcher who won 300 games all in the era of the lively ball. Young, Matty, and Eddie Plank reached the 300-mark pitching exclusively with the dead ball, while Alexander had a decade with the dead ball and Johnson enjoyed it for thirteen seasons.

Not only is Grove the only jackrabbit pitcher to reach 300 victories but he has an even more important distinction and one generally overlooked. The lean left-hander won 300 games while losing 141, which gives him the highest won and lost percentage of any pitcher elected to the Hall of Fame at Cooperstown, .680. The closest Hall of Famer to Bob in winning percentage is Babe Ruth with .676, but Ruth was voted into Cooperstown on the strength of his home-run hitting, not his pitching.

Grove had a deep appreciation of what it meant to win 300 games and he hung on until he made it. In 1939, Lefty won fifteen games while losing four for the Red Sox and led the American League pitchers in earned runs with an average of 2.54. Those fifteen triumphs boosted his lifetime total to 286 but it took him two more seasons to get to 300, two seasons in which his overall won-and-lost record was 14–13 and in which his earned-run mark was four per nine-inning game and higher.

Robert Moses Grove was born in Lonaconing, Maryland, on March 6, 1900. He was born in circumstances which it would be euphemistic to call "modest." His dad and most of the menfolk in his family worked in the coal mines and Grove, quitting school after his elementary grades, went to work in a silk mill for a half dollar a day, finally working his way, after a couple of years, up to seven bucks a week.

Bob wanted no part of the coal mines and eventually, when he was eighteen, he was working in a glass factory at $5.25 a day. He played ball with other boys in the neighborhood, crude, cow-pasture ball, but finally, in 1919, landed with an organized

53

amateur team at Midland, near his hometown. Here he was a first baseman simply because no one could handle his blazing fast ball.

Eventually the Midland team obtained a catcher who could hold Grove's speed and his pitching began receiving attention. He was offered a job pitching for Martinsburg, West Virginia, in the Blue Ridge League at $125 a month and he leaped at the chance to get away from the drudgery of manual labor.

Grove was a lean, lanky kid of twenty when he joined Martinsburg and, although he didn't know it at the time, he already was on his way to glory and gold. He was in Martinsburg only a few months when the Baltimore Orioles paid $3,500 for his contract and upped his salary $50 a month. The Orioles at that time, managed by the famous Jack Dunn, the discoverer of Ruth, were one of the greatest minor league teams in history.

Dunn had great stars with the Orioles, players who might have been in the majors long before they actually made it had it not been Dunn's whim to keep them in Baltimore where they continued to tear the International League apart, year after year. It was with the Orioles that Grove ran across players like George Earnshaw, Jack Bentley, Max Bishop, Joe Boley, Rube Parnham, and Dick Porter.

Baltimore won seven International League pennants in a row, breaking the record for minor league teams set in the Texas League by Jake Atz's Fort Worth team. Grove joined the team when it was in the process of winning its third pennant in that string, and winning it by taking the last 25 games of the season in a row. Lefty stayed with the Orioles while they won the last five of these pennants.

Dunn had sold Ernie Shore, a pitcher, Ben Egan, a catcher, and Ruth to the Red Sox in 1914 for a grand total of $8,500, with the Babe's price tag reported to be $2,900. Less than six years later, Harry Frazee, the Red Sox owner, found himself caught in a financial squeeze and sold Ruth to the Yankees for

$100,000. It was a monumental price for those times and Dunnie, when he arranged to sell Grove, wanted to set a new record for baseball ivory. Connie Mack obliged by tacking $600 extra onto the check. It was the top figure at the time but, of course, has since been exceeded.

With the Athletics, Grove not only rejoined some of his Oriole teammates but he was to find himself with a team which shortly was to dominate the American League as Baltimore had dominated the International. Mack had broken up a pennant-winning team after the 1914 season and now was laboriously piecing together another one. He eventually was to have a three-time pennant winner, a club which ended the Yankees' position as baseball's Number One team.

Grove, who never had a losing year at Baltimore (he was 12–2 in his first season there), found the American League a little rough at the start. Accustomed to firing the ball past the hitters in the International League, Lefty found that didn't work in the majors. For one thing, big leaguers were more inclined to wait a pitcher out and not chase after bad balls.

At Baltimore, Grove never had to pay much attention to his control. It was nothing for him to fill the bases on walks and then strike out the side. It didn't pan out that way with the A's. In 1925, his first year on the big wheel, Lefty won ten games and lost twelve. He led the American League in bases on balls with 131, the only time he ever won that booby prize but he also led it in strikeouts with 116.

There were several significant items in Grove's first year with the Athletics, not the least of which was the fact that Lefty learned that he would have to alter his pitching tactics. That 1925 season was the only one in Grove's entire career, major or minor, in which he finished with a percentage of lower than .500 and it was the only time he ever walked more men than he fanned. It also was the first of seven straight seasons in which he was to lead the league in strikeouts.

The temperament Grove brought to the majors with him was as remarkable as his fast ball. Dealing with temperamental ballplayers was nothing new to Mack, who had handled Rube Waddell and Ossie Schreckengost, fun-loving Rover Boys if ever there were, and Joe Jackson, who threatened to pine away with lonesomeness for the Carolinas. Grove was a different problem. He wasn't a dissipater and he wasn't lonesome. Lefty was merely ornery.

Grove wanted to win but couldn't see that it was his fault when he didn't. In four and a half years with Baltimore, Lefty had won 108 games while losing only 36. When things started to go wrong with him in the American League, when his control was off or when the hitters were tying into his high hard one, Grove took it as a personal insult. He couldn't wait to get the ball back from the catcher so he could fire it at the batters again.

It was Cy Perkins, a catcher out of Gloucester, Massachusetts, who taught Grove patience. Cy served a long time under Connie. He had come to Mack when the 1914 A's were broken up and dispersed over the American League market and he labored with Connie during the long, lonesome stretch when the Athletics spent seven consecutive seasons in the cellar.

The cure, of itself, was a simple one but teaching it to Grove was far from simple. Perkins finally made Lefty step off the rubber as he took the throw from the catcher and remain off the rubber while he took the ball in his left hand and plunked it into his gloved right hand three times. You've seen pitchers fiddle around thus on the mound. With most it is merely a reflex action, with Grove it acted as a checkrein. After he had plopped the ball into his mitt three times, then Grove stepped on the mound, leaned forward and took the sign from the catcher.

Having learned to space himself between pitches, Grove taught himself to pace his pitching. No longer did he fire every ball as hard as he could. He saved his fireball for the clutches and found he was able to finish with something in reserve, that he wasn't running out of gas in the closing innings.

With the help from Perkins and the self-study imposed upon him by necessity, Grove had adjusted himself so that he was a winning pitcher in his third year with the Athletics. After his 10–12 season as a freshman, Lefty split 26 decisions right down the middle in 1926, cut his bases on balls down to 101, the last time in the majors he walked more than 100, and managed to lead the American League in earned runs with a mark of 2.51.

Grove won twenty games for Mack in 1927 and for the next six seasons he never failed to win that many. In those seven years before he was sold to the Red Sox, Lefty won a total of 172 games for the A's, an average of nearly 25 per season. This stretch is unparalleled in the era of the lively ball.

Not only was Grove winning twenty or better for Connie, but he was leading the league in strikeouts and in earned runs. The earned-run tabulation was introduced into baseball in 1912 and Grove is the only pitcher who for three straight seasons led the league in both earned runs and won-and-lost percentage. Grove also is the holder of the major league record for the most number of seasons leading the league in earned-run percentage, nine, and the most number of years in leading the league in won-and-lost percentage, five.

Grove had two remarkable seasons in 1930 and 1931, the most amazing pair any modern pitcher has enjoyed. He was 28–5 in 1930, which was sensational enough, but the following year he turned in a 31–4 record. This was the highest winning percentage (.886) ever attained by a pitcher in this century who had twenty decisions. Percentagewise the mark is topped by Freddie Fitzsimmons' 16–2 record with Brooklyn in 1940 and Johnny Allen's 15–1 mark with Cleveland in 1937, but neither stands comparison with Grove's record. Indeed, Lefty's 31 victories in that one year equaled the combined victory total of Fitzsimmons and Allen in their record-breaking seasons.

If Grove had his greatest season in 1931—and only one pitcher, Dizzy Dean in 1934, has won as many as thirty games since—it also was the year which led to his most memorable display of temper. At one stretch Grove had a sixteen-game winning streak going and he seemed a cinch to break the American League record which Joe Wood of the Red Sox and Walter Johnson of the Senators had established in 1912.

When Grove set his cap for his seventeenth in a row he had the great power of the Athletics going for him against the lowly St. Louis Browns. The A's were to win 107 games that year and beat the Yankees for the pennant by a comfortable 13½-game margin. Bill Killefer's Browns were to lose 91 games. It didn't seem possible that a better spot could be picked for Grove to write a new page into American League history than Sportsman's Park in St. Louis on that August afternoon in 1931.

Grove's opponent was Dick Coffman, a right-hander with good spirit but nothing like the physical equipment of the Athletic ace. Yet when the smoke had cleared, Dick was the winner by a 1–0 score, the lone run of the game coming when Jim Moore, playing left field for the A's, misjudged a fly ball.

The visitors' dressing room at Sportsman's Park that evening was a shambles. Grove attempted to take it apart, locker by locker. It was the greatest of his towering rages and Lefty's towering rages reached practically into the stratosphere. He was not only mad at everybody present, he was even mad at Al Simmons, who was many miles away in Milwaukee receiving medical treatment.

"If Simmons had been here and in left field, he would have stuck that ball in his back pocket," roared Grove. "What the hell did he have to go to Milwaukee for?"

Despite his ingrown disposition, Grove could adjust himself to conditions—when he was forced to. He proved this by his third year with the Athletics and he was to prove it again with the Red Sox, after Mack had sold him to Tom Yawkey for more than he had paid Jack Dunn for him.

Grove was sold to the Sox after the 1933 season and somewhere along the line during the training session at Sarasota, Florida, the next spring he injured his arm. How or where is a mystery. There were hints that Mack had palmed off damaged goods on Yawkey but the general belief is that Lefty's injury came during training with Boston.

It was a new experience for Grove to find his pitches belted out of the lot. He had an 8–8 record but it was a truly horrible season. He struck out fewer than fifty hitters and the opposition averaged better than seven runs a game against the once invincible left-hander.

If Grove had been hard to get along with before, the Boston writers found him practically impossible. They had been prepared to welcome a great pitcher and instead found themselves with a great grouch. He talked of quitting and going back to his native Lonaconing. Bucky Harris, then in his first and only year of managing the Sox, persevered with him and by the end of the year old man Mose grumpily allowed as how his arm might be getting a mite better.

It was now that Lefty made the great changeover, that he added pitching artistry to his physical assets. Near the end of the 1934 season under Harris, Grove discovered that there were fewer twinges in his arm when he threw a curve than when he threw a fast ball. He began to develop his curve ball and finally had a good one.

Grove always had a curve ball and it was more than just a wrinkle but since he was winning with his fast ball he neglected it. Now he became a pitcher instead of a thrower. Moe Berg, who was with Grove at Boston, makes a nice distinction of Lefty's changeover. "It wasn't that Grove developed a curve ball after he hurt his arm," explained Moe, "but that he im-

59

proved the good curve he already had to the point where it was almost a great curve."

Later Grove added a fork ball to his equipment, a pitch which Bullet Joe Bush had used to implement his own fast ball. It is a pitch which doesn't rotate much, shudders like a knuckler as it nears the plate and usually lures the batter into swinging too soon. The term "fork ball" stems from the fact that the fingers gripping the ball are spread wide instead of held close together as when pitching a curve or fast one.

Thus when the petulant southpaw went back to Lonaconing 22 years after he set out from there to become a pitcher, he had a complete assortment of pitching equipment. He also had 300 victories and he won them with everything from a blazing fireball to a slow curve. Time, and Grove, had marched on.

ROBERT MOSES GROVE

Born, March 6, 1900, Lonaconing, Maryland.
Height 6'3". Weight 204. Threw and batted left-handed.

Year	Club	League	G	IP	W	L	Pct.	H	SO	BB	ERA
1925	Philadelphia	Amer.	45	197	10	12	.455	207	116	131	4.75
1926	Philadelphia	Amer.	45	258	13	13	.500	227	194	101	2.51
1927	Philadelphia	Amer.	51	262	20	12	.625	251	174	79	3.19
1928	Philadelphia	Amer.	39	262	24	8	.750	228	183	64	2.58
1929	Philadelphia	Amer.	42	275	20	6	.769	278	170	81	2.81
1930	Philadelphia	Amer.	50	291	28	5	.848	273	209	60	2.54
1931	Philadelphia	Amer.	41	289	31	4	.886	249	175	62	2.06
1932	Philadelphia	Amer.	44	292	25	10	.714	269	188	79	2.84
1933	Philadelphia [1]	Amer.	45	275	24	8	.750	280	114	83	3.21
1934	Boston	Amer.	22	109	8	8	.500	149	43	32	6.52
1935	Boston	Amer.	35	273	20	12	.625	269	121	65	2.70
1936	Boston	Amer.	35	253	17	12	.586	237	130	65	2.81
1937	Boston	Amer.	32	262	17	9	.654	269	153	83	3.02
1938	Boston	Amer.	24	164	14	4	.778	169	99	52	3.07
1939	Boston	Amer.	23	191	15	4	.789	180	81	58	2.54
1940	Boston	Amer.	22	153	7	6	.538	159	62	50	4.00
1941	Boston	Amer.	21	134	7	7	.500	155	54	42	4.37
Major League Totals			**616**	**3940**	**300**	**140**	**.682**	**3849**	**2266**	**1187**	**3.06**

[1] Traded with Pitcher George (Rube) Walberg and Second Baseman Max Bishop to Boston for Infielder Harold (Rabbit) Warstler, Pitcher Bob Kline and $125,000, December 12, 1933.

WORLD SERIES RECORD

Year	Club	League	G	IP	W	L	Pct.	H	SO	BB	ERA
1929	Philadelphia	Amer.	2	6⅓	0	0	.000	3	10	1	0.00
1930	Philadelphia	Amer.	3	19	2	1	.667	15	10	3	1.42
1931	Philadelphia	Amer.	3	26	2	1	.667	28	16	2	2.42
World Series Totals			**8**	**51⅓**	**4**	**2**	**.667**	**46**	**36**	**6**	**1.75**

* key
G   = games
IP   = innings pitched
W   = won
L   = lost
Pct. = percentage of games won
H   = hits given up
SO   = strikeouts
BB   = bases on balls or walks
ERA = earned-run average

7

CARL OWEN HUBBELL
The Meal Ticket

ONE WARM, humid afternoon in Houston, Texas, Edward Kinsella (a Giant scout) decided he would be much more comfortable at the ball park.

By any standards, "Sinister Dick" saw a rattling, good ball game. A chunky southpaw was pitching for the Houston Buffs—one Bill Hallahan who was to go on to fame with the Cardinals. Hallahan was opposed by another left-hander working for Beaumont, a tall, cadaverous-appearing chap who pitched with great deliberation and consummate skill.

Back at the Rice Hotel, Kinsella wasted no time calling McGraw in New York. "Mac," reported Dick, "I think I saw another Art Nehf today. Fellow pitching for Beaumont. He worked against Hallahan and beat him one to zero in eleven innings."

"Send him along immediately," ordered McGraw, and thus it was that Carl Owen Hubbell reported to the Giants at the old Auditorium Hotel in Chicago a couple of days later. It was to be a long and profitable association for all concerned.

McGraw knew that Kinsella must have been pretty high on Hubbell to compare him with Nehf. What nobody knew at the time was that Dick had understated the case. Hubbell turned out to be another Matty, a left-handed Christy Mathewson.

The comparison between Hubbell and Matty is not out of line. Both were pitching heroes of an entire generation of fans and each used an unorthodox delivery to augment his usual pitching equipment. In Matty's case it was called the "fadeaway"; in Hub's it was known as the "screwball."

Matty's fadeaway broke *in* on right-handed batters, whereas the normal right-hander's curve broke *out* and away from right-handers and in on left-handed hitters. Hubbell's screwball broke *in* on left-handed batters and *out* on right-handers. To generalize, Mathewson's fadeaway behaved like a southpaw's curve ball, Hubbell's screwball like the curve ball of a right-hander. If this sounds somewhat confusing, remember that thousands of National League batters were confused by these two pitches.

In throwing a curve, a pitcher lets the ball come off the tip of his index finger as he breaks his wrist. In throwing a screwball (or a fadeaway), the wrist is broken in toward the body as the ball is released, instead of away from the body. Through the years, Hub threw so many screwballs that the palm of his left hand faces outward when he holds his arms at his sides, whereas in any normal person the palms face inward.

Hubbell was indeed a physical rarity, a left-hander with control. Traditionally, southpaws are wild, and it sometimes takes them years to acquire control. Hub had control almost from the day he started pitching. Only once in professional baseball did the number of bases on balls he issued in a season exceed the number of strikeouts he recorded. And that was in 1925, with Oklahoma City in the Western League when Carl walked 108 while fanning 102. In his sixteen years with the Giants, Hub averaged fewer than two bases on balls per nine-inning game.

The second All-Star game was played at the Polo Grounds in 1934, with Bill Terry as manager of the National Leaguers. Terry had won the pennant and the World Series the year before and he had done so by not overlooking any bets. He was

63

a master of detail and he gathered his All-Stars around him in the clubhouse that they might share his pearls of wisdom. Hubbell, who had won 23 games the season before and two more in the World Series, was to be the starting pitcher for the Nationals.

It was a formidable array of hitters the Americans had grouped together and Hub listened respectfully to Terry's suggestions. He tried to keep his first pitch away from Charley Gehringer and it was belted into center for a clean single. Wally Berger fumbled the ball and Charley raced to second. The game was exactly one pitch old and the Americans already had a man in scoring position.

Still pitching cautiously, Hubbell walked Heinie Manush. With men on first and second and none out, the next three hitters were Babe Ruth, Lou Gehrig, and Jimmy Foxx. If ever a pitcher was on a spot, Mr. Hubbell was the man.

Catching for the National Leaguers was the ebullient Gabby Hartnett of the Cubs. He halted the game, removed his mask and walked toward the pitcher's box with that ponderous stride that always reminded onlookers of a cop who had halted traffic at a busy intersection to hand out a ticket.

"Look, Hub," admonished Gabby, "never mind all that junk about being careful and pitching this way or that way. Just throw that 'thing.' It'll get 'em out. It always gets me out!"

"That thing," of course, was Hubbell's screwball. Hub fired three of them at Ruth and the Babe was out of there. Three more took care of Gehrig, and the fact that Manush and Gehringer worked a double steal while Lou fanned bothered no one.

Having fanned Ruth and Gehrig, Hubbell proceeded to close out the inning by striking out Foxx. Jimmy proved a bit more troublesome than Babe or Lou, however. He managed to hit a foul. Then, in the second inning, Hubbell, still throwing "that thing," struck out Al Simmons and Joe Cronin. It was a demonstration of pitching never equaled before or since. Five straight strikeouts is unusual but the conditions under which Hubbell achieved this feat were even more unusual, for he was facing the flower and power of the American League.

Bill Dickey broke the spell with a single after two were out in the second inning, but Lefty Gomez obligingly became Hub's sixth strikeout victim. It is still a sore point with Lefty that while everybody talks of Hubbell fanning Ruth, Gehrig, Foxx, Simmons, and Cronin in succession, nobody ever mentions that Gomez, too, was one of Hubbell's strikeout victims.

So remarkable was Hubbell's pitching in this All-Star game that it usually obscures his other great deeds on the mound. In the World Series the fall before, Carl had pitched twenty innings against the Senators without allowing an earned run. He opened the Series and fanned the first three men to face him, Buddy Myer, Goose Goslin, and Heinie Manush. He won that game 4 to 2 and won the fourth game 2 to 1 in eleven innings.

Hubbell won 253 games as a Giant and had five consecutive seasons in which he won better than twenty games each year. From 1933 through 1937, the Meal Ticket won 115 games, an excellent total by modern standards. Those were Hub's glory years, and they were the glory years of the Giants, too. They won three pennants in those five seasons but weren't actual pennant contenders again until 1951.

Two marks the maestro of the screwball left behind him are well known—his 46⅓ scoreless-inning streak in 1933 and the sixteen consecutive games he won in 1936, a string which was still intact when the season ended. Unlike his collection of scoreless innings, this was not a National League record. Another Giant left-hander, Rube Marquard, won nineteen straight in 1912, but nobody since Rube has done any better than sixteen. With this string, Hubbell moved into pretty select pitching company—Smokey Joe Wood, Walter Johnson, Lefty Grove, and Schoolboy Rowe, all of whom ran their streaks to sixteen.

The most oft-repeated story about Hubbell is that a Detroit manager—some say Ty Cobb, some say George Moriarty—told him that he never would get anywhere throwing the screwball. Actually, it was George McBride, former Washington infielder and a Tiger coach, who told Hub at the Augusta training camp in 1927 that the screwball was calculated to injure his arm.

"I never threw a screwball while I was Detroit property," declared Hubbell, "after McBride had given me that warning. I pitched for the Tigers with Toronto and with Beaumont but without the screwball."

Carl felt that he was being overlooked by the Tigers, but not because of McBride's admonition about the screwball. In two springs with the Tigers, Hub pitched exactly one inning of one exhibition game—and with the "B" squad against the University of Texas at Austin.

Having discarded the screwball while pitching for the Detroit farm clubs, Hubbell did not employ it when he first came to the Giants. He still remembers distinctly the first screwball he threw in the National League.

"We were playing the Cardinals and I was in a jam with men on base and Chick Hafey at bat," explained Carl. "I consider Hafey one of the best right-handed hitters who ever lived and when the count got to three and one on him, I was plenty worried. Shanty Hogan was catching and he signaled for a fast ball. I threw Chick a screwball and it fooled him. Shanty gave me the fast-ball sign again and I threw another screwball and struck Hafey out."

Hogan encouraged Hubbell in throwing the screwball, and McGraw, who called practically every pitch from the bench, made no objections. Nor, surprisingly enough, any comment. The screwball was, in effect, a secret weapon. Hubbell threw it,

66

Hogan caught it, the batters missed it and nobody ever mentioned it until some years later.

"McBride wasn't kidding about the screwball being a menace to my arm," said Hubbell. "I had arm trouble as early as 1934, although I went on to have a couple of my best years after that. After I pitched a game in 1934, my left elbow would swell up at night and still be swollen and stiff the next afternoon. After I warmed up a little, the stiffness would leave and the swelling would go down.

"I had some X rays taken and they showed I had chips in my elbow, but they were loose and floating around. Later, when I really had arm trouble, the chips were firmly imbedded and my elbow would 'lock' when I tried to throw the ball."

Hubbell's arm trouble in 1934 resulted in a somewhat mediocre season in 1935, mediocre for Hub, that is, yet it forced him to develop his curve ball, which he threw almost exclusively to left-handed batters. By 1936, Hub was able to throw the screwball again and this, added to his improved curve, made him one of the most effective pitchers in National League history while he was pitching the Giants to pennants in 1936 and 1937. In those two years, the Meal Ticket turned in records of 26–6 and 22–8.

Gaunt, lean-visaged, almost Lincolnesque in his angular awkwardness, Hubbell is the soul of modesty. Asked what he considered had been his greatest pitching performance, he didn't leap into the breach and name his sensational five strikeouts in the All-Star game of 1934. He mulled over the question for some time before answering.

"It's like this," he finally said. "I got my biggest pitching thrill out of winning ball games which meant something to the ball club, games when we were fighting for the pennant and they were games we just had to win. That meant something, regardless of the score or the number of strikeouts I got. Those were the games I took pride in winning."

Asked what was the best ball game he ever pitched, Hubbell passed up his 1929 no-hit, no-run game against Pittsburgh and settled for a one-hitter he pitched against Brooklyn at Ebbets Field on Decoration Day, 1940.

"The way I look at it," explained the Meal Ticket, "the best game any pitcher could pitch would be a game in which he got every batter who faced him out—a perfect game.

"This day in Brooklyn, I was gettting the Dodgers out one-two-three. I had sixteen in a row when Johnny Hudson came up with one out in the sixth. I had him two strikes and one ball and I tried to waste a pitch, to get in low and outside. Johnny hit it back through the box, a looping line drive just over my head. Our second baseman dove at the ball but he didn't have a chance for it.

"It wasn't too well hit but it was the only hit Brooklyn got. The next batter hit into a double play, and in the last three innings I got the Dodgers out in order, so I faced only 27 men in the whole ball game. It would have been a perfect game except for Hudson but I guess that's what makes perfect games so rare."

Hubbell engaged in some terrific duels with Dizzy Dean when that great man was at the height of his spectacular but short career with the Cardinals. These were "money" games, with both clubs shooting for the pennant, and it is a matter of fact that Hub beat Dean more often that Diz beat him. One of the Meal Ticket's great games against St. Louis was at the Polo Grounds on July 2, 1933, when he beat the Red Birds 1 to 0 in eighteen innings without giving up a base on balls.

It wasn't only against the Cardinals that Hubbell was effective. He had a decided bulge on every club in the league save Brooklyn. This is rather unusual, since in the days when Hub was the Meal Ticket, the Brooks were usually kicking around in the second division. Outside of 1930, when there was a four-cornered fight for the pennant among the Giants, Cards, Cubs, and Dodgers, Brooklyn rarely was in contention during Hubbell's good seasons.

One of Hubbell's most amazing defeats was administered by the Dodgers before packed Sunday stands at Ebbets Field in 1930. The southpaw was beaten in ten innings by the veteran Dazzy Vance, 1 to 0, which was far from a disgrace, but the manner in which Hub lost was most unusual. After going through nine scoreless rounds, the Dodgers filled the bases against Carl in the tenth, with Jake Flowers at bat. Flowers, who later became a capable baseball executive, was a steady infielder but not regarded as a dangerous batter. Hubbell made four pitches to Flowers and every one was wide of the plate! The winning, and only run, was thus forced across on a base on balls by the master control pitcher of his time. Hub can't recall another occasion when he forced a run across the plate.

The trouble McBride had predicted for Hubbell so many years before finally caught up with him in 1938. He still was a winning pitcher but no longer the workhorse who had led the Giants to pennants three times in five years. His left elbow was operated on and the bone chips were removed, but when he tried to pitch in 1939, it was obvious that he wasn't the Hubbell of old.

There was one flash left in the Meal Ticket and he came through for his old roommate, Mel Ott, who was elevated to the Giant managership in 1942. In July of that year, the Giants lost 4 one-run games in succession. In the fourth of these Harry Feldman had the Cardinals beaten 1 to 0 with two out and nobody on base in the last half of the ninth, and the Cards came up with two runs to win before Ott could get anybody ready to warm up.

Ott sat alone in his room in the dark in the Hotel Chase in St. Louis that night, moodily staring across into Forest Park. He had left a note in Hubbell's box that the pitcher was to come to his room that night before going to bed—"no matter what time you come in." This was a touch of dry humor, since Hub was an exemplary athlete during his entire career.

Long before the midnight curfew, there was a rap on Ottie's door and Hubbell presented himself.

"Sit down, Hub," said Mel. "There's something I've got to say to you." Ott then went on to say that the club was in danger of falling apart because of the succession of one-run defeats. Something had to be done to snap the Giants out of it. And the only thing Mel could think of in this crisis was what McGraw and Terry before him had thought of in similar crises—call on the Meal Ticket.

Hubbell went out the next day against Howie Pollet, then one of the most promising young left-handers in the National League. Hub, with only a trace of his former stuff but with plenty of cunning, proceeded to give Pollet a pitching lesson. The Meal Ticket won, 1 to 0, and went on from there to win six straight, the Giants finishing a surprising third, their only first-division finish between 1938 and 1950, when Leo Durocher brought them home third.

By 1943, it was obvious that the Meal Ticket had been punched full. At the winter baseball meetings in the Hotel New Yorker that December, President Horace C. Stoneham of the Giants summoned the press to his room and announced that Hubbell was being placed in charge of the Giant farm system.

Everybody agreed that it was a nice, sentimental gesture but one cynic remarked what must have been in the minds of several, "What the hell does Hubbell know about the minors? He hasn't been in a minor league in fifteen years!"

Hubbell turned the same thorough concentration on the farm problem that he had turned to his pitching. During the war years, of course, there was little he could do, other than keep the franchises alive, but by 1951, when the Giants finally won the pennant, the fruits of Hub's patient labors became apparent to all. King Carl was still the Meal Ticket.

CARL OWEN HUBBELL

Born, June 22, 1903, Carthage, Missouri.
Height 6'1". Weight 175. Threw left and batted right-handed.

Year	Club	League	G	IP	W	L	Pct.	H	SO	BB	ERA
1928	New York	Nat.	20	124	10	6	.625	117	37	21	2.83
1929	New York	Nat.	39	268	18	11	.621	273	106	67	3.69
1930	New York	Nat.	37	242	17	12	.586	263	117	58	3.87
1931	New York	Nat.	36	248	14	12	.538	211	155	67	2.65
1932	New York	Nat.	40	284	18	11	.621	260	137	40	2.50
1933	New York	Nat.	45	309	23	12	.657	256	156	47	1.66
1934	New York	Nat.	49	313	21	12	.636	286	118	37	2.30
1935	New York	Nat.	42	303	23	12	.657	314	150	49	3.27
1936	New York	Nat.	42	304	26	6	.813	265	123	57	2.31
1937	New York	Nat.	39	262	22	8	.733	261	159	55	3.19
1938	New York	Nat.	24	179	13	10	.565	171	104	33	3.07
1939	New York	Nat.	29	154	11	9	.550	150	62	24	2.75
1940	New York	Nat.	31	214	11	12	.478	220	86	59	3.66
1941	New York	Nat.	26	164	11	9	.550	169	75	53	3.57
1942	New York	Nat.	24	157	11	8	.579	158	61	34	3.96
1943	New York	Nat.	12	66	4	4	.500	87	31	24	4.91
Major League Totals			**535**	**3591**	**253**	**154**	**.622**	**3461**	**1677**	**725**	**2.98**

WORLD SERIES RECORD

Year	Club	League	G	IP	W	L	Pct.	H	SO	BB	ERA
1933	New York	Nat.	2	20	2	0	1.000	13	15	6	0.00
1936	New York	Nat.	2	16	1	1	.500	15	10	2	2.25
1937	New York	Nat.	2	14⅓	1	1	.500	12	7	4	3.77
World Series Totals			**6**	**50⅓**	**4**	**2**	**.667**	**40**	**32**	**12**	**1.79**

* key
G = games
IP = innings pitched
W = won
L = lost
Pct. = percentage of games won
H = hits given up
SO = strikeouts
BB = bases on balls or walks
ERA = earned-run average

8

WARREN SPAHN

Mr. Consistency

WORLD WAR II influenced the careers of a great many ballplayers, some of them stars.

It took three productive baseball years away from Joe DiMaggio and Bob Feller and four such seasons away from Ted Williams, who served two separate hitches as a Marine Corps pilot. Stan Musial lost a year.

The lifetime batting averages of Williams and DiMaggio undoubtedly would have been higher without the war. Unquestionably, Feller would have wound up a 300-game winner. Musial's many lifetime batting records would have been even more impressive than they are.

And then there is the little matter of what the great unpleasantness of twenty years ago did to Warren Spahn.

The remarkable left-hander of the Milwaukee Braves was 20 years old when Pearl Harbor was hit. He pitched in 1942 at Hartford in the Eastern League, winning 17 games. Before the season was over, he was brought up to Boston and worked four games in the National League without a decision.

And the 1946 season was well under way before Spahn pitched again.

These are the things that might have been.

By this time, Warren Spahn might easily have set a new National League record for victories. The present mark is held jointly by Mathewson and Alexander.

Conceivably, Spahn today might be within reach of Walter Johnson's 413 victories. Warren possibly could have won more games in the majors than anyone who did his pitching exclusively in the twentieth century.

This slender, smooth-operating slinger wound up the 1963 campaign with 350 victories. No left-hander, living or dead, ever won that many. The only right-handers to top him are the aforementioned big three—Matty, Alex, and the Big Train.

Of course, there was Cy Young with his 510 victories, but Young properly belongs to another age. His career roughly covered the last decade of the nineteenth century and the first decade of the twentieth.

Young won 284 games before 1901, when the American League was formed. Up until that time, three or four pitchers were considered ample to meet the requirements of a team in the major leagues.

It seems here that the public in general and even a number of baseball men have reacted slowly to Warren Spahn, who embarked upon his twentieth National League campaign with a lifetime earned run average below 3.00.

Among a lot of other things, Spahn had pitched two no-hit shutouts, led the National League in strikeouts four times and finished better than .500 in 17 out of 18 National League seasons. He had been a 20-game winner 13 years, tying a major league record set by Mathewson.

The trouble appears to be that many of Spahn's greatest achievements have occurred at moments when everybody seemed to be looking in another direction.

The 1963 season can be cited as a classic example.

Spahn then was 42. At 42, Matty, Johnson, and Alexander were completely through and even Young was running down like an unwound clock.

Spahn won 23 games and lost only seven and hardly anyone noticed it because this was the year that Koufax went crazy with a 25–5 won-lost record, a new National League strikeout record of 306 and a new World Series record of 15 strikeouts against the Yankees. Sandy naturally collected every award in sight.

This sort of thing to a lesser degree had happened to Spahn before. For instance, Spahn has led the National League in victories three times—in 1949, 1950, and 1957. But in five other seasons, he has been tied for leadership—in 1953 by Robin Roberts, in 1958 by Bob Friend, in 1959 by Lou Burdette and Sam Jones, in 1960 by Ernie Broglio, and in 1961 by Joey Jay.

This line of research uncovers something else. Johnson led the American League in victories six times. Alexander led the National League in victories five times. Feller led the American League five times and tied once.

Only Spahn has gone through eight seasons in which no pitcher in his league topped his victory total.

The story of the skillful Mr. Spahn, of course, is the tale of one ball club and two cities.

It began in Buffalo, New York, April 23, 1921, when Spahnie was born to Mrs. Spahn and a husband, named Edward. Edward had been a semi-pro third baseman and apparently a devout Republican because the heir was named Warren Edward Spahn, the first name coming from Warren G. Harding, then President of the United States.

Time passed and young Warren, a fine student and a keen athlete, was graduated from high school. A scholarship awaited him at Cornell, but then came a bid to hook up with the farm club of the Boston Braves at Bradford, Pennsylvania, of the PONY League at $80 a month.

This was the tail end of the depression years and Warren was one of six children. So he took the baseball bid and, at the tender age of 19, won five games and lost four at Bradford. The next season, he was winning 19 and losing six at Evansville

74

and leading the Three-Eye League in victories. In 1942, he won 17 and lost 12 at Hartford before the Braves brought him up.

Then, of course, came the war. He served with the Army's Corps of Engineers, first as a private and then as staff sergeant. On the field at the battle of the Bulge he was commissioned a second lieutenant. A jagged scar on the back of his neck is the result of a shrapnel wound. He received the Purple Heart and the Silver Star.

Like most soldiers, Spahn talks little about his wartime experience, but there was one incident that unquestionably made a deep impression upon him. As the First Army reached the Rhine, the only bridge that hadn't been destroyed was the one at Remagen. After a beachhead had been established on the other side, Spahn's unit was one of those assigned to lay down a steel tread so that tanks and other heavy equipment could cross into Germany.

Spahn's group was to relieve the men working at the task at a certain hour. They arrived a few minutes early and Spahn walked out on the bridge to discuss the repairs with other officers. Just as he returned to shore to line up his own platoon, there was a tremendous crash behind him. The bridge had collapsed and the men working on it were lost.

"A thing like that," said Spahn long afterwards, "can make a man a fatalist."

Chances are too that his campaign experience in Europe left this young man a calm and resourceful performer, unafraid of anything that might happen to him on the ball field.

Casey Stengel had managed the Braves when Spahn departed and Billy Southworth was there when he returned after the 1946 season was well underway. He won eight and lost five that year and, in 1947, had the first of his 20-victory seasons, winning 21 and losing 10.

75

In 1948, the Braves won the pennant and the importance of Spahn and Johnny Sain, his right-handed partner on South-worth's staff, caused the bards of the Boston pressbox to compose a jingle that went like this:

"It's Spahn and Sain,
Two days of rain,
Then Spahn and Sain again."

Oddly enough, Warren, although he pitched well, did not have a remarkable record in 1948. He won 15 and lost 12. Until 1964, he won more than 15 in every season except one after Boston's pennant year.

He split even in two World Series decisions against the Cleveland Indians that fall, losing the second game to Jim Lemon, but winning the fifth from Bob Feller.

Spahn was a 20-game winner for four straight seasons starting in 1949 and, with a partner, prepared to open a diner on Commonwealth Avenue, close to Braves Field. Just as it was about to open, Lou Perini got permission to move his baseball franchise from Boston to Milwaukee.

Warren accepted the switch in cities philosophically as he accepts almost everything else. It is unlikely that he lost money on his Boston diner venture, anyway, and Milwaukee, for a few years, was to become an exciting summer home.

In the great American cheeselands, Spahn was to become the left-handed half of another one-two pitching punch, this time with the right-handed Lou Burdette. Under Fred Haney, the Braves just missed in 1956, then won pennants in each of the two following years.

The Braves beat the Yankees in the 1957 World Series and again Spahn split two World Series decisions. In 1958, the Yankees beat the Braves although Spahn won two out of three and pitched a shutout in the fourth game to give Milwaukee a 3–1 lead.

76

Meanwhile in 1956 Spahn had started another string of 20-victory seasons that lasted six years.

He has never had a working nickname except perhaps Spahnie. Because he was by no means short-changed when fate passed out noses, an attempt was made to call him "Hooks." But that never really caught on. He ought to be called Mr. Consistency.

He is just six feet tall and a well-built 175 pounds, and his size and shape hasn't changed since he came back from the war. Only his hairline has receded. His graceful left-handed delivery remains the same.

In the beginning, he was definitely a fast ball pitcher. He kicked a hole in the sky with his right foot as he started a big windup and relied mainly on the high, hard one. But he had a good curve too and he could throw it at varying speeds.

As the years have passed, he depends less on the strength of his arm than on finesse. He throws fast balls at varying speeds as well as curves, slips in a screwball once in a while and developed a slider comparatively late in life. So subtle have the changes been from year to year that no one can point to any one season and say this is the time Spahn stopped throwing and started pitching.

Sain, his old sidekick in Boston, remains one of his greatest admirers.

"Every game Spahn pitches," said Johnny while coach of the Yankees, "is an object lesson to every young pitcher in the game. There is a purpose behind every move he makes and behind every pitch he throws.

"He is an object lesson too in the way he lives and the way he regards his job. He has never been complacent and still isn't. He is still trying to learn.

"He helps himself in so many ways. He has developed a great move with runners on base and so its almost impossible to steal on him. His good control helps keep him out of trouble. He has practiced hard for years to become one of the best fielding pitchers. He's a fair hitter too—has hit more home runs than any pitcher in history.

"Fielding and hitting," said Sain, "get little attention from many young pitchers. Spahn's own personal efforts in those departments can make the difference of five or six victories a year."

Application is one answer to Spahn's success and certainly a perfect pitching temperament is another.

Through all of his career, he has been described as a wonderful team man, the kind of a fellow they like to have around. He doesn't grouse if his mates have trouble getting runs, is uncritical of fielding lapses behind him. He never dwells on the bad breaks, rarely disputes an umpire's call.

All concentration on the days he works, he is lighthearted and chatty on the bench between starts. This, he explains, is how he eases his tensions.

He can be happy because his club properly appreciates him. For the 1964 season, the Braves gave him an $85,000 contract. That's the highest ever paid a pitcher although Bob Feller is reputed to have received $135,000 from the Indians in 1946 on $35,000 base pay and a fantastic bonus arrangement.

How much longer Spahn can keep going, of course, is uncertain. When he reaches the end of the road as a pitcher, there still will be a fascinating life ahead for him.

He's now a prosperous ranchman with 1,500 acres and some oil interests in Oklahoma. He happened to settle in the Southwest because, in army boot training, he met Lorene Southard of Tulsa. They were married the year Warren returned from Europe and really got started in the majors.

It has been—and still is—quite a career and one that could scarcely have been imagined by a poor boy of 19 who left home in Buffalo and took the highway to Bradford, Pennsylvania, instead of Ithaca, New York, and Cornell University.

WARREN EDWARD SPAHN

Born, April 23, 1921, Buffalo, New York.
Height 6'. Weight 175. Throws and bats left-handed.

Year	Club	League	G	IP	W	L	Pct.	H	SO	BB	ERA
1942	Boston	Nat.	4	16	0	0	.000	25	7	11	5.63
1943–1944–1945	(In Military Service)										
1946	Boston	Nat.	24	126	8	5	.615	107	67	36	2.93
1947	Boston	Nat.	40	290	21	10	.677	245	123	84	2.33
1948	Boston	Nat.	36	257	15	12	.556	237	114	77	3.71
1949	Boston	Nat.	38	302	21	14	.600	283	151	86	3.07
1950	Boston	Nat.	41	293	21	17	.553	248	191	111	3.16
1951	Boston	Nat.	39	311	22	14	.611	278	164	109	2.98
1952	Boston	Nat.	40	290	14	19	.424	263	183	73	2.98
1953	Milwaukee	Nat.	35	266	23	7	.767	211	148	70	2.10
1954	Milwaukee	Nat.	39	283	21	12	.636	262	136	86	3.15
1955	Milwaukee	Nat.	39	246	17	14	.548	249	110	65	3.26
1956	Milwaukee	Nat.	39	281	20	11	.645	249	128	52	2.79
1957	Milwaukee	Nat.	39	271	21	11	.656	241	111	78	2.69
1958	Milwaukee	Nat.	38	290	22	11	.667	257	150	76	3.07
1959	Milwaukee	Nat.	40	292	21	15	.583	282	143	70	2.96
1960	Milwaukee	Nat.	40	268	21	10	.677	254	154	74	3.49
1961	Milwaukee	Nat.	38	263	21	13	.618	236	115	64	3.01
1962	Milwaukee	Nat.	34	269	18	14	.563	248	118	55	3.04
1963	Milwaukee	Nat.	33	260	23	7	.767	241	102	49	2.60
Major League Totals			**680**	**4874**	**350**	**216**	**.618**	**4416**	**2415**	**1326**	**2.97**

WORLD SERIES RECORD

Year	Club	League	G	IP	W	L	Pct.	H	SO	BB	ERA
1948	Boston	Nat.	3	12	1	1	.500	10	12	3	3.00
1957	Milwaukee	Nat.	2	15⅓	1	1	.500	18	2	2	4.70
1958	Milwaukee	Nat.	3	28⅔	2	1	.667	19	18	8	1.88
World Series Totals			**8**	**56**	**4**	**3**	**.571**	**47**	**32**	**13**	**2.89**

* key
G   = games
IP   = innings pitched
W   = won
L   = lost
Pct. = percentage of games won
H   = hits given up
SO   = strikeouts
BB   = bases on balls or walks
ERA = earned-run average

9

DAZZY VANCE
The Overaged Cyclone

WHEN DAZZY VANCE was elected to the baseball Hall of Fame in 1955, he took it upon himself to set one record straight.

"I actually was born on March 4, 1891," confessed the one-time fireball flinger of the old Dodgers, "and all the while I pitched the books had me two years younger than that."

"Why change it now?"

"Well," said the grizzled old pitcher, "I figure that, at this long range, my advanced age gives me a unique distinction. I'll bet no other pitcher ever lived who reached 30 before he won a game in the majors and then won as many as 100 games.

"I was 31 before I won a game in the majors and wound up with 197 victories."

"As long as you're confessing your right age," needled an old friend, "why don't you tell them your right name?"

"Ah now," protested Mr. Vance, "you're not going to bring that up again."

Here is a flashback to one of those Pullman poker games of long ago. Daz had successfully drawn to a flush and the man, last-carded with two pair, called, read the bad news, then threw his hand away.

"The great Arthur C. Vance," snorted the loser. "By the way, Daz, what does the C stand for?"

"It stands for Charles, you inquisitive so-and-so," retorted Vance.

There was a pause for a few seconds as Vance squinted side-wise at the other fellow.

"I'll bet you're disappointed," Dazzy finally said. "You probably thought it was something high-falutin' like Clarence."

"No, I just thought the C just might stand for Canfield," said the other.

At least twenty years passed and Ollie Holmes, a Brooklyn bowling alley proprietor and Vance's long-time friend, came back with a tale to tell after a fishing vacation at Dazzy's camp on the Florida Gulf Coast.

It seems that Dazzy's brother was along and kept saying things like "Will you pass the bait, Clarence?" or "Give me a chew of tobacco, Clarence?"

Finally, Holmes asked, "What's this Clarence bit, anyway?"

"Didn't you know that's Dazzy's name?" asked the other Vance, innocently.

"It is not," screamed Dazzy. But that night, back in Vance's home, the brother found the Vance family bible and presented the evidence.

"Not only does the C stand for Clarence," revealed detective Holmes, triumphantly, "but that's his first name. He is Clarence Arthur Vance."

But the plaque in the baseball museum at Cooperstown reads "Arthur Charles Vance."

"Let it go," begged Dazzy. "I never was the Clarence-type."

He wasn't either—this tall, broad-shouldered, sandy-haired and pleasantly homely fellow was one of the most colorful and successful of pitchers in that period of the Roaring Twenties when Mathewson was through, Alexander and Johnson were fading, and such as Lefty Grove, Carl Hubbell, and Dizzy Dean had not really arrived.

He was a right-hander with a big delivery. He reared way back at the start of a pitch and kicked his left foot high in the air. He threw overhand and hard and his fast ball was alive.

He was so famed for his speed that generally overlooked was the fact that he threw one of the greatest of curve balls.

"Maybe I shouldn't be talking about hitting," said the aforementioned Hubbell, "but, at the time I faced Dazzy for the first time I hadn't heard anything except raves about his speed. So when I came up to bat I resolved not to look as bad as the eight hitters ahead of me by trying a bunt. On the first pitch, I bunted at what I thought was a high, fast ball and it turned out to be a curve that hit me on the foot."

Starting in 1922, Vance led the National League in strikeouts for seven straight years. He won 15 straight games for the Dodgers in 1924, led the league with an earned-run average of 2.16, won 28 games and lost only six. He gained the Most Valuable Player award and this was the year Rogers Hornsby batted .424.

In 1925, the Dodgers finished only half a game out of the cellar but Vance won 22 and lost nine, pitching a no-hitter against the Phillies.

In 1928, the Dodgers finished sixth—about their norm—but Vance won 22, losing ten and had a league-leading earned-run average of 2.09. In 1931, his 2.61 earned-run average led the league again.

Vance's overall totals are not as impressive as some of his colleagues in the Hall of Fame because it took Dazzy so long to get both feet in the major leagues. Nor can anyone say just how much more impressive the Vance record would be if it were not Dazzy's fate to spend the productive years of his life with Wilbert Robinson's Dodgers, nicknamed "the Daffiness boys" by Westbrook Pegler. Vance's hard-luck defeats would fill a chapter.

But he could pitch. One story of ancient Ebbets Field involves the great Hornsby. One afternoon the Rajah and Daz were fanning away and Hornsby remarked that never had he struck out as many as three times in a single game.

"I'm working tomorrow," said Vance, "and I'll see if I can help you set a new record."

Sure enough, Vance fanned Hornsby three times and, leaving the ball park, the Rajah was razzed by one of those Brooklyn earaches.

"To think I paid my money to see you hit," jeered the customer.

"If I were a Brooklyn fan," answered Hornsby, softly, "I'd pay my money to see Vance pitch."

A farm boy, born in Adair County, Iowa, Vance started out with Red Cloud of the Nebraska State League in 1912. The next season he pitched for Superior of the same league. In neither of these two years did he have a winning record, yet the Pittsburgh Pirates acquired him for a trial.

He pitched at Hastings, Nebraska, and St. Joseph, Missouri, in 1914 and, in 1915, the Pirates let him pitch one game in the National League. He gave up three hits and five walks in three innings and lost the game. Then it was back to St. Joseph and the Yankees bought him late in the season. He had three decisions and three losses in the American League.

Then it was Columbus, Toledo, Memphis, and Rochester and nowhere did Vance do well. Much of the time he suffered from a lame arm. The Yanks brought him back in the war year of 1918, then let him go after he gave up nine hits in two innings. He was a loser at Sacramento in 1919 and in the 1920 season which he divided between Memphis and New Orleans.

At New Orleans in 1921, he won 21 games while losing 11 and the Dodgers purchased him that winter. The circumstances of the deal present one of those vignettes which makes the history of those early Dodgers so delightful. A boo-boo made Dazzy available to the Brooklyn club, which didn't really want him.

In spite of his record with the Pelicans, Vance was not the top pitcher on the New Orleans club. That was another right-hander named Tom Phillips, who had registered no less than 30 victories. The Cleveland Indians had a working agreement with New Orleans giving them the right to pick one pitcher. Naturally, they selected Phillips.

Meanwhile, Larry Sutton, who was practically the entire Dodger scouting staff, was beating the bushes under strict orders from Brooklyn owner Charles H. Ebbets to find a catcher. Sutton chose Hank DeBerry of New Orleans.

Now the New Orleans owner started thinking. Vance had been up and down and around and might never have another good season. The owner wrapped Vance and DeBerry into one package and put a $10,000 price tag on it.

Ebbets screamed. "If we wanted Vance," he yelled, "we could have drafted him."

Sutton finally concluded that the deal might not be too bad.

"DeBerry is the kind of a receiver you want," he told Ebbets, "and maybe Vance is worth a gamble. He wasn't as wild as he used to be last year." And so—

Phillips developed a lame arm and never won a game for Cleveland. Vance started on the trail for Cooperstown. And DeBerry, who had a sense of humor, personally wrote a magazine story in which he referred to himself as "The Tail of the Comet."

When Vance walked into the Dodger clubhouse at their spring training camp at Jacksonville in 1922, Wilbert Robinson was impressed to see about half the members of his squad greet Dazzy like a long-lost brother.

The exhibition games started and Vance knew more people on the other club's bench than Robbie did.

"How come?" the colorful old Oriole wanted to know.

"I've been around," answered Vance, airily. "I'll bet 100 bucks that I can walk into any clubhouse in the country—major or minor league—and know at least three men."

"I guess you could," conceded Robbie.

84

But there were other reasons Robbie liked Vance. Robbie liked his pitchers big. Dazzy stood an inch over six feet and weighed an elastic 200 pounds. Which is to say that Dazzy frequently weighed as high as 215, but he worked hard when he pitched and could frequently melt off as many as a dozen pounds in nine innings on a hot afternoon.

Robbie also suspected that all young pitchers were flighty and nobody could mistake the red-faced Vance for a barefoot boy even though he was actually 31 instead of 29, as recorded. Robbie liked pitchers who could throw hard and that Dazzy could do.

In fact, the veteran skipper liked Vance well enough to let Dazzy call his own shots.

"I need four days of rest between each start," Vance told Robbie. "Give me that rest and I'll do a good job. I've learned from experience that I'm not effective if I work more often than that."

Robbie went along with the idea and the results speak for themselves. Vance won 18 in each of his first two seasons, had his big year in 1924 and led the league in strikeouts in his first seven seasons. He even was the strikeout king in 1926 when he finished with a 9–10 record and did not win a game until the middle of June. That spring, Dazzy was afflicted with the greatest collection of boils since Job.

Ironically although perhaps understandably, two of Vance's best remembered games at Ebbets Field were defeats. In each case, the situation setup made them important.

In 1924, a 15-game winning streak extending well into September made the Dodgers unexpected challengers for a pennant eventually won by the Giants. The turning point came in a game against the Chicago Cubs; Vance fanned 15, gave up only four hits. But he lost, 5 to 4 in ten innings, because three of the four Chicago hits were homers—two by George Grantham and one by Gabby Hartnett.

Six years later, the Cardinals and the Dodgers were virtually tied for first place when the St. Louis team reached Brooklyn to start a three-game series. Vance pitched the first game against Bill Hallahan, again in ten innings but this time by 1 to 0.

This was a wild game. The Cards had a chance to score in the sixth when Vance took his big windup with Sparky Adams on third base. That alert little guy actually stole home, then had to go back because Daz had the presence of mind to hit Chick Hafey in the ribs with the pitch, creating a dead ball situation.

Dazzy got out of that jam all right but in the top of the tenth Andy High, an old pal of Vance's, delivered a pinch double and Taylor Douthit singled to drive High home. And the game was lost in the last of the tenth when the Dodgers, who had missed many chances to score, missed another as Al Lopez grounded into a double play with the bases filled.

In the cold balance of probability, it is unlikely that the Dodgers could have won either pennant even if Vance had reversed the result of these two games. The Dodgers of Dazzy's time just weren't good enough.

After their late bid in 1930, the Dodgers were nothing for two years and age crept up on Vance although Dazzy won 11 games in 1931 and 12 the following year. That winter he was traded to the Cardinals and became a relief pitcher, winning 6 and losing 2 in 1933.

That winter, he was sold to the Reds but the Cardinals reclaimed him at the waiver price in June of 1934. That fall, he made his first and only World Series appearance. He pitched only one and one-third innings of relief, but struck out three of the Detroit Tigers.

In April of 1935, the Cards gave Vance his unconditional release. Casey Stengel had just become manager of the Dodgers and prevailed upon the crazy mixed-up front office in Brooklyn to take the old boy on. For Stengel, Vance did limited relief duty, winning three and losing two in his final season. Then he called it a career—at 44.

86

As players—especially Dodgers—went in those days, Vance was a highly paid performer. After his great year in 1924, he wangled a three-year contract for a total of $50,000 from Squire Ebbets, an achievement that called for a loud and noisy holdout. After that contract expired, Dazzy got $20,000 a year for a couple of seasons. In 1930, he became the first pitcher in baseball history to collect a $25,000 salary.

Like many other players of that era, Vance suffered in the financial crash of 1929 and in the depression of the '30's. But he was far luckier than most because of his sunny philosophy of life.

This was essentially a humorous, fun-loving man, a gifted raconteur who made and held his friends. He loved sports of all kinds and the outdoors. He was an expert marksman with both a pistol or a rifle and a knowledgeable fisherman. His sportsman's camp at Homosassa Springs in Florida enabled him to lead the kind of life that appealed to him as well as providing a modest living for his family.

Came February 15, 1961, Ken Smith, driving south to cover the Yankees at St. Petersburg for his paper, stopped off at Homosassa to spend an afternoon with the old Dazzler.

"We had a hundred laughs as we recalled the old days and Daz said he was, and looked to be, in the best of health and spirits," said Smitty, immeasurably shocked to read next morning that Vance had died of a heart attack in his sleep.

ARTHUR CHARLES VANCE

Born, March 4, 1891, Adair County, Iowa.
Died, January 16, 1961, Homosassa Springs, Florida.
Height 6'1". Weight 200. Threw and batted right-handed.

Year	Club	League	G	IP	W	L	Pct.	H	SO	BB	ERA
1915	Pittsburgh	Nat.	1	3	0	1	.000	3	0	5	6.00
1915	New York	Amer.	8	28	0	3	.000	22	18	16	3.54
1918	New York	Amer.	2	2	0	0	.000	9	0	2	13.50
1922	Brooklyn	Nat.	36	246	18	12	.600	259	134	94	3.70

ARTHUR CHARLES VANCE (*Continued*)

Year	Club	League	G	IP	W	L	Pct.	H	SO	BB	ERA
1923	Brooklyn	Nat.	37	280	18	15	.545	263	197	100	3.50
1924	Brooklyn	Nat.	35	309	28	6	.824	238	262	77	2.16
1925	Brooklyn	Nat.	31	265	22	9	.710	247	221	66	3.53
1926	Brooklyn	Nat.	24	169	9	10	.474	172	140	58	3.89
1927	Brooklyn	Nat.	34	273	16	15	.516	242	184	69	2.70
1928	Brooklyn	Nat.	38	280	22	10	.688	226	200	72	2.09
1929	Brooklyn	Nat.	31	231	14	13	.519	244	126	47	3.90
1930	Brooklyn	Nat.	35	259	17	15	.531	241	173	55	2.61
1931	Brooklyn	Nat.	30	219	11	13	.458	221	150	53	3.37
1932	Brooklyn [1]	Nat.	27	176	12	11	.522	171	103	57	4.19
1933	St. Louis [2]	Nat.	28	99	6	2	.750	105	67	28	3.55
1934	Cincinnati [3]-										
	St. Louis [4]	Nat.	25	77	1	3	.250	90	42	25	4.56
1935	Brooklyn	Nat.	20	51	3	2	.600	55	28	16	4.41
American League Totals			10	30	0	3	.000	31	18	18	4.20
National League Totals			432	2937	197	137	.590	2777	2027	822	3.22
Major League Totals			**442**	**2967**	**197**	**140**	**.585**	**2808**	**2045**	**840**	**3.23**

[1] Traded with Shortstop Gordon Slade to St. Louis for Pitcher Owen Carroll and Infielder Jake Flowers, February 9, 1933.
[2] Sold to Cincinnati, February 6, 1934.
[3] Released to St. Louis on waivers, June 25, 1934.
[4] Released by St. Louis and signed by Brooklyn, April, 1935.

WORLD SERIES RECORD

Year	Club	League	G	IP	W	L	Pct.	H	SO	BB	ERA
1934	St. Louis	Nat.	1	1⅓	0	0	.000	2	3	1	0.00

* key
G = games
IP = innings pitched
W = won
L = lost
Pct. = percentage of games won
H = hits given up
SO = strikeouts
BB = bases on balls or walks
ERA = earned-run average

10

JAMES HOYT WILHELM
Relief Specialist

UNFORTUNATELY FOR James Hoyt Wilhelm, voting for admission to the Hall of Fame is not conducted by active ballplayers. If it were, the relief specialist would probably be firmly ensconced in the Cooperstown shrine by now.

The list of outstanding relief pitchers includes several names romanticists will insist had more on the ball than Wilhelm.

Hugh Casey could still win enough votes to get elected to public office in Brooklyn. Johnny Murphy more than helped the Yankees to several pennants. And who can forget Joe Page's dramatic contributions to the Yankees' pennant of 1949?

With more and more night games and shorter series, because of expansion travel schedules, solid relief pitchers are worth much more than their weight in baseballs.

Of the current crop, Elroy Face made things much easier for Pittsburgh's 1960 world champs. And, as important as starter Sandy Koufax was, could the Dodgers have won in 1963 without reliever Ron Perranoski?

Regardless of how impressive and extensive a list of premier relief pitchers is compiled, however, only one name belongs at the top . . . James Hoyt Wilhelm, who at times during his distinguished career has pitched as if he held some of the original patents in the business.

Wilhelm's career statistics read as interestingly as those of a well-stacked beauty queen's but that's not all the master moundsman has going for him. His biggest recommendation is consistency. To put it simply, Wilhelm has been a good man to have around since the Giants gave him a regular job in 1952.

As a comparatively old rookie of 26, Wilhelm was the first freshman to lead the National League in both earned-run average (2.43) and winning percentage (.833). The slender right-hander answered manager Leo Durocher's call for help 71 times, working 159 innings and winning 15 and losing three as the Giants slipped from their 1951 championship standing.

Perhaps just to prove he hadn't lost his touch, seven years later Hoyt led the American League in ERA, posting a 2.19 figure to become the only pitcher to accomplish the feat in both leagues. Oddly, in 1959, Wilhelm also matched his rookie winning figure, chalking up 15 as the Orioles gave the Yanks a run for the pennant money right down to the wire.

The 1959 ERA title, though, was a little like offering a handout to a millionaire since Hoyt had been in the chips all season after having hit big casino the year before when he tossed a no-hitter at the Yankees, outdueling the Bombers' Don Larsen and Bobby Shantz, 1–0, on September 20, in the rain, at Baltimore.

The no-hitter was doubly important to Wilhelm in that it just may have saved his major league life. The '58 season must have seemed extra long and disappointing to the serious, slender North Carolina native. Turned into a starter for the first time, victories were few and far between and the no-hitter was only Hoyt's third win of the season, against 10 losses.

He and the Baltimore brass may have been thinking the same thing: What future was there for a much traveled knuckle-ball specialist of 32 who certainly didn't have the glamour to match the rest of Baltimore's young flamethrowing staff?

Inevitably, during the 1958 season, Wilhelm must have thought of calling it a career after several minor league stops and disappointing seasons with the Cardinals (1957) and Indians (1958, until the Orioles purchased him).

The Giants had dealt Hoyt to the Cards following the 1956 season and he was only 1–4 in St. Louis for 1957. He didn't get much work with Cleveland, which picked him up on waivers from the Cards, during the early part of 1958 but moved into the Orioles' regular rotation after they acquired him for the $20,000 waiver fee.

Things didn't go much better with the Birds until the no-hitter, but Hoyt kept knuckling down and an innovation of manager Paul Richards kept him going strong through the 1963 season before Baltimore dealt him to the White Sox.

Until Richards' brainstorm Hoyt, oddly, always had more trouble with his own catchers than he did with opposing batters. It wasn't that he was hard to get along with, it was just that his receivers had trouble handling his bread-and-butter pitch . . . labeled the butterfly by a romantic sportswriter but more commonly known as the knuckler.

Hoyt always had been tough on his catchers. His knuckler was a natural he picked up while in high school at Huntersville, North Carolina. Signed by the Braves and sent to Mooresville, N. C., he was sent home quickly—after his manager took one look at Hoyt's big pitch, which he throws with an unusual grip. Wilhelm holds the ball with his fingernails rather than his knuckles to produce a dipsy-doodle effect by taking the natural spin off the ball.

There are enough major league batters who wish Wilhelm had stayed home, but he was back in uniform, winning 10 and losing three before entering the Army in 1942. He returned to baseball with a Purple Heart in 1947 and started the long climb to the Giants.

Hoyt's road to the majors is easy to follow, it was a trail of broken fingers, all belonging to his battery-mates. And things weren't much better in the majors.

Right from the very beginning, Hoyt had trouble finding a catcher who could handle his baffling butterfly without a net. It was an exasperating experience for catchers, veterans and rookies alike.

The first time rookie catcher Sal Calderone worked with Wilhelm in the spring of 1952 he hurt a finger. The second time he hurt another finger and groaned, "Here I got two fingers gone and I haven't even caught this guy in a game."

Hoyt's problem became more serious during the 1959 season. While Wilhelm was leading the league and winning 15 games, the Orioles' catchers were establishing a record in passed balls, 49—38 chalked up with Hoyt pitching.

"Except for those passed balls," manager Paul Richards remarked at the time, "Hoyt might have won 20 or more." This set the manager to thinking about the problem and he dreamed up a cure for the pitcher who has caused more passed balls than Abner Doubleday.

At times it might have seemed more sensible for Wilhelm to discard the knuckler, but it wouldn't have been very practical. Gus Triandos, who knew many an embarrassing moment behind Baltimore's home plate, grinned. "The knuckler is his only pitch."

Wilhelm didn't see quite eye-to-eye with Triandos on that count and shrugged the catcher's evaluation off as an exaggeration. "Only 98 per cent of my pitches are knucklers," he said. "I throw a slider, curve, and fast ball, too, but I'm not kidding anybody if I think I can get by on them alone. I've got to have my knuckler."

Richard's remedy was a special catcher's mitt 50 per cent larger than what was then in general use. A sports manufacturer provided the finished product for a cost of $300 and the new mitt was first put to use in Yankee Stadium on May 27, 1960, as Hoyt beat the Yanks and Art Ditmar, 3–2.

Of greater significance, however, was the fact that catcher

Clint Courtney didn't have one passed ball. And from that point on, Wilhelm pitched 109⅓ innings and his catchers were charged with only three passed balls as he won ten, lost six, and saved seven for an ERA of 2.66.

The oversized mitt had a couple of other repercussions, though. Although perfectly legal since rules didn't restrict a mitt's size, it caused some managers to holler "foul," and eventually brought about a rules change for 1965 which will limit the size of a catcher's mitt.

Through all the bitter and sweet and fat and lean years, Wilhelm has remained completely unaffected and is not even given to small talk. His life revolves around baseball and his wife and three children. With Hoyt actions speak louder than words . . . and he only has a lot to say when he's on the mound.

JAMES HOYT WILHELM

Born, July 26, 1923, Huntersville, North Carolina.
Height 6'. Weight 190. Throws and bats right-handed.

Year	Club	League	G	IP	W	L	Pct.	H	SO	BB	ERA
1952	New York	Nat.	71	159	15	3	.833	127	108	57	2.43
1953	New York	Nat.	68	145	7	8	.467	127	71	77	3.04
1954	New York	Nat.	57	111	12	4	.750	77	64	52	2.11
1955	New York	Nat.	59	103	4	1	.800	104	71	40	3.93
1956	New York [1]	Nat.	64	89	4	9	.308	97	71	43	3.84
1957	St. Louis [2]	Nat.	40	55	1	4	.200	52	29	21	4.25
1957	Cleveland	Amer.	2	4	1	0	1.000	2	0	1	2.25
1958	Cleveland [3]-										
	Baltimore	Amer.	39	131	3	10	.231	95	92	45	2.34
1959	Baltimore	Amer.	32	226	15	11	.577	178	139	77	2.19
1960	Baltimore	Amer.	41	147	11	8	.579	125	107	39	3.31
1961	Baltimore	Amer.	51	110	9	7	.563	89	87	41	2.29
1962	Baltimore [4]	Amer.	52	93	7	10	.412	64	90	34	1.94
1963	Chicago	Amer.	55	136	5	8	.385	106	111	30	2.65
National League Totals			359	662	43	29	.597	584	414	290	3.09
American League Totals			272	847	51	54	.486	659	626	267	2.47
Major League Totals			**631**	**1509**	**94**	**83**	**.531**	**1243**	**1040**	**557**	**2.74**

[1] Traded to St. Louis for outfielder-first baseman Whitey Lockman, February 26, 1957.

93

² Sold to Cleveland, September 21, 1957.

³ Sold to Baltimore, August 23, 1958.

⁴ Traded with Shortstop Ron Hansen, Outfielder Dave Nicholson, and Infielder Pete Ward to Chicago for Shortstop Luis Aparicio and Utilityman Al Smith, January 14, 1963.

WORLD SERIES RECORD

Year	Club	League	G	IP	W	L	Pct.	H	SO	BB	ERA
1954	New York	Nat.	2	2⅓	0	0	.000	1	3	0	0.00

* key
G   = games
IP = innings pitched
W   = won
L   = lost
Pct. = percentage of games won
H   = hits given up
SO = strikeouts
BB = bases on balls or walks
ERA = earned-run average

11

BILL DICKEY

Stylist from Arkansas

So FAR, this effort to select an all-time, all-star squad of major league ballplayers has produced three right-handed starting pitchers, any one of whom would gladden the heart of a manager.

It seems high time to change the pattern and nominate a man to throw the ball back to the box. A tall, limber ex-Yankee is first choice here for that assignment.

There will be differences of opinion. An old Chicago Cub named Johnny Kling is credited with having invented many modern catching techniques. A little later, Roger Bresnahan, a talented all-around performer, earned the gratitude of generations of catchers when he actually did invent shinguards.

For many years, the White Sox had a little guy named Ray Schalk, so catlike and sure-handed behind the plate that he reached the baseball Hall of Fame although strictly a banjo hitter.

A latter-day Cub had real power and Gabby Hartnett played with a lighthearted aggressiveness that delighted his fans.

Mickey Cochrane was a great catcher with the Philadelphia Athletics and later a successful catcher-manager for the Detroit Tigers. And Black Mike had achieved a lifetime batting average of .320 when the playing side of his career ended with a bean ball that almost killed him.

Cochrane would have plenty of support and so would the

inimitable Yogi Berra, who hit more home runs than any catcher who ever lived.

Then there was Roy Campanella, Yankee Berra's National League counterpart through most of the '50's until a tragic auto crash ended his career.

The credentials of Bill Dickey seem a mite stronger than any of the rest. He was a left-handed batter and a good one. Cochrane's batting average topped his, but Dickey hit .313 over 17 American League seasons. Berra, Campanella, and Hartnett hit more home runs, but Dickey's total of 202 in the majors is a highly respectable figure.

And you never saw a better catcher.

"He is," Bucky Harris once remarked, "the only man I ever saw who could make that tough job look easy. The true gauge on Dickey's ability is the way his performance was taken for granted. The man in the stands is prone to notice only a catcher's mistakes and Bill made darned few."

Dickey came out of the South to join the Yankees late in the 1928 season. The following spring, at the age of 21, he became first-string catcher and began a string of 13 consecutive seasons in which he appeared behind the plate in more than 100 games. In six of those seasons, he led the catchers of the American League in fielding percentage. In 1931, he caught 125 games and was not charged with a single passed ball.

It was Miller Huggins who gave Dickey the job and Joe McCarthy who kept him there as Bill bridged the gap between the New York's Murderers' Row of the '20's and the Bronx Bombers, who operated into the '40's.

It was only the year before Dickey joined the Yankees that Babe Ruth had hit 60 home runs for the major league record. As a wide-eyed youth on the bench, Bill saw the mighty Babe hit three out of Sportsman's Park in one game as the Yankees demolished the Cardinals in a four-straight World Series.

Came the following year and Dickey was catching practically

96

every day on the same team as Ruth and his powerful supporting cast, which included the strong and ill-starred Lou Gehrig, Tony Lazzeri, Bob Meusel, Jumping Joe Dugan, and Earle Combs.

Dickey, of course, was there after all of these were gone and an entire new wave of Yankee stars had come up and, in some cases, gone down again. He operated side by side with Joe DiMaggio and Charley Keller, Frankie Crosetti and Tommy Henrich, Joe Gordon and Red Rolfe. He was still first-string Yankee catcher when Crosetti became a Yankee coach, having been displaced at shortstop by chunky little Phil Rizzuto.

He was still a catcher for the Yankees after World War II, but by 1946, his skills had been dulled by two years in the Pacific theatre and he was approaching the end. He became manager of the Yankees in May of that season when the hard-nosed McCarthy and the highly inflammable Larry MacPhail came to the parting of the ways.

But the easygoing, mild-mannered Dickey and the fiery executive then running the Yankee front office did not make a good combination either and Dickey, too, was gone in September as Johnny Neun took over as stop-gap manager for the final month.

Actually, Dickey had no real interest in managing although he tried it again at his hometown of Little Rock in 1927, resigning and retiring after his club finished in the Southern Association cellar. He was keen for coaching and returned to serve in that capacity for more than a decade after, of course, MacPhail had departed from the scene.

The Yankees won eight pennants when Dickey was playing and seven of the eight World Series they played over this stretch. It is worth noting that Bill caught every inning in each of these World Series and that the Yankees won 29 Series games and lost only nine with Dickey behind the bat.

The list of Yankee pitchers he handled and helped is impressive. It includes Waite Hoyt, Herb Pennock, Wilcy Moore, Bob Shawkey, and George Pipgras who properly belong to the turbulent '20's. After them came Red Ruffing and Lefty Gomez, Johnny Murphy, Spud Chandler, Bump Hadley, and Monte Pearson and, still later, Tiny Bonham, Hank Borowy, Marius Russo and Atley Donald. Some of these never threw to another Yankee catcher.

There is no record that Bill ever had trouble handling any pitcher's delivery with a single exception that was a bit of a freak. In 1934, Burleigh Grimes caught on for a couple of weeks with the Yankees at the tail end of his pitching career.

"Old Stubblebeard" not only was the last of the legally recognized spitball pitchers but threw the widest-breaking spitter ever seen.

Grimes relieved in a ball game and, at a proper moment, Dickey signaled for the spitball he had never seen before. The pitch got away to the backstop and a runner on first moved down to second.

Bill signaled for another spitter and again the pitch went through and the runner moved on to third. When Dickey flashed the sign for a third spitball, Grimes called him out to the mound.

"Are you sure you know what you're doing?" growled Grimes.

"Of course," grinned Bill, cheerfully, "but I guess you'd better be prepared to rush in and cover the plate after you let the ball go."

It turned out that wasn't necessary. Bill managed to block the next pitch, they eventually got the batter out and the runner died on third.

Somebody once called Dickey an outstanding "quarterback" behind the plate. He had not only a comprehensive grasp of the ability of his own pitchers but an invisible card index in his own mind on the hitting likes and dislikes of every batter he ever saw.

Joe Gantenbein, who had played briefly for the Athletics,

98

told a story about running into Lieutenant Commander Dickey during a wartime baseball tournament for servicemen in Hawaii.

Gantenbein saluted smartly and said, "Do you remember me, sir?"

"I apologize for not remembering your name," answered Dickey, "but we pitched you fast balls, high and away."

Dickey was born at Bastrop, Louisiana, June 6, 1907. His father had played some baseball in his youth and then became a railroad man with the Missouri Pacific. The family moved to Kensett, Arkansas, not far from Little Rock and that's where Bill grew up to a gangling six feet one and a half inches, later padded with 185 pounds. After maturity, weight never was one of Dickey's problems.

He went through grade school and high school, then started on the sandlots as a pitcher. He soon found out that other pitchers in that limited orbit were just about as good, but he could catch better than any youth in the area.

He signed with Little Rock in 1925 and was the property of that club for the next three years although he had side trips to Muskogee, Jackson, and Buffalo. He had the benefit of teaching in the minors from Lena Blackburne and Joe Cantillon, two wise old managers.

Oddly enough, Little Rock had a working agreement with the White Sox but, through a front-office slipup, the Chicago club failed to exercise its rights and the Yankees were able to buy him at a modest price. Johnny Nee was the scout who touted him in superlatives to Ed Barrow, then general manager of the New York club.

The deal was made late in the 1928 season and Dickey reported to Yankee Stadium for a September "look." After that, the component elements that combined to create his manifest destiny slipped neatly and swiftly into place.

It was in the Yankee clubhouse that a bit of traditional advice for young ballplayers was coined, probably by Joe McCarthy. It is: "To be a big leaguer, dress like a big leaguer."

That was no hardship for young Bill. He is a neat man and clothes hung well on his tall, lean frame. He had young teammates of the same personable appearance.

There was the delightful Vernon Gomez, Lyn Lary, an infielder with the manner and poise of a young Wall Street man, and Sammy Byrd, a fine golfer who eventually became a pro and was thoroughly at home with the country club set.

Along about the same time—1932—Gomez married June O'Dea and Lary was wed to Mary Lawlor. Both girls were musical comedy stars. Byrd dated a girl from his hometown who was with Earl Carroll's Vanities and this young lady introduced Dickey to Violet Arnold, who sang and danced in the same show.

Right after the World Series of that year, Bill and Vi were married and it is worth noting that all three of Yankee "stage" matings that year turned out to be enduring and happy.

Yet Dickey remained essentially a country boy. Season's end invariably found him back in Arkansas, playing some golf, fishing and trailing his bird dogs in search of game. And that's his life, more or less, today. His long period as Yankee coach under Casey Stengel ended because certain health problems developed and his doctors prescribed a quieter life than the hectic baseball beat.

An isolated incident of extracurricular trouble in Dickey's career was the result of a complete misunderstanding. In 1932, there was a jarring collision at home plate as Carl Reynolds of the Senators barreled in, trying to score. Both players picked themselves out of the dirt and Reynolds, who had been knocked a few yards off line, rushed at the plate and Dickey again.

It developed later that Reynolds was trying to reach home plate which he thought he had missed, but Dickey, thinking the Washington player was launching an assault, cut loose with a right hand swing. The result was a broken jaw for Reynolds and a $1,000 fine and 30-day suspension for Dickey.

Through the years, Dickey's performance was so smooth and consistent that there seem to be few high spots. One game that he must remember was the opener of the 1938 World Series when he went four-for-four at the plate and Ruffing, although allowing nine hits, beat the Chicago Cubs, 3 to 1.

But Bill's most glorious memory, he'll tell you, was the last World Series game he ever caught. That was the finale of the five-game series of 1943 between the Yankees and the Cardinals.

The Cards had upset the Yankees the autumn before and now World War II was in full blast and the drainage of talent to the armed forces had created conditions that made baseball form highly unpredictable to say the least.

The Yankees jumped into a lead of three to one in games and were trying to wrap it up in the fifth contest with Chandler facing Morton Cooper of the Cardinals.

Came the sixth inning and Keller ripped a single through the infield after two were out. Dickey came up and waited for Cooper's fast ball and got it.

"I wasn't trying to overpower it," Dickey said later, "merely going for a base hit and I had no idea I had a home run until I rounded second and saw Art Fletcher, coaching at third, throwing his cap in the air.

"As I got back to the bench, I was still concerned with how I could help Chandler continue pitching at his shutout pace. Spud came through although I was sweating golf balls at the finish. He gave up ten hits and the Cardinals left eleven on base, but we won, 2 to 0.

"In the clubhouse celebration I was so happy about Chandler's great clutch pitching and whatever part I had in it that the full impact of what had happened didn't hit me for hours. It wasn't until I went to bed that night that I realized the two teams might still have been struggling if I hadn't hit Cooper's fast ball just right."

WILLIAM MALCOLM DICKEY

Born, July 6, 1907, Bastrop, Louisiana.
Height 6'1½". Weight 185. Batted left and threw right-handed.

Year	Club	League	Pos.	G	AB	R	H	2B	3B	HR	RBI	BA
1928	New York	Amer.	C	10	15	1	3	1	1	0	2	.200
1929	New York	Amer.	C	130	447	60	145	30	6	10	65	.324
1930	New York	Amer.	C	109	366	55	124	25	7	5	65	.339
1931	New York	Amer.	C	130	477	65	156	17	10	6	78	.327
1932	New York	Amer.	C	108	423	66	131	20	4	15	84	.310
1933	New York	Amer.	C	130	478	58	152	24	8	14	97	.318
1934	New York	Amer.	C	104	395	56	127	24	4	12	72	.322
1935	New York	Amer.	C	120	448	54	125	26	6	14	81	.279
1936	New York	Amer.	C	112	423	99	153	26	8	22	107	.362
1937	New York	Amer.	C	140	530	87	176	35	2	29	133	.332
1938	New York	Amer.	C	132	454	84	142	27	4	27	115	.313
1939	New York	Amer.	C	128	480	98	145	23	3	24	105	.302
1940	New York	Amer.	C	106	372	45	92	11	1	9	54	.247
1941	New York	Amer.	C	109	348	35	99	15	5	7	71	.284
1942	New York	Amer.	C	82	268	28	79	13	1	2	37	.295
1943	New York	Amer.	C	85	242	29	85	18	2	4	33	.351
1944–1945	(In Military Service)											
1946	New York	Amer.	C	54	134	10	35	8	0	2	10	.261
Major League Totals				**1789**	**6300**	**930**	**1969**	**343**	**72**	**202**	**1209**	**.313**

WORLD SERIES RECORD

Year	Club	League	Pos.	G	AB	R	H	2B	3B	HR	RBI	BA
1932	New York	Amer.	C	4	16	2	7	0	0	0	4	.438
1936	New York	Amer.	C	6	25	5	3	0	0	1	5	.120
1937	New York	Amer.	C	5	19	3	4	0	1	0	3	.211
1938	New York	Amer.	C	4	15	2	6	0	0	1	2	.400
1939	New York	Amer.	C	4	15	2	4	0	0	2	5	.267
1941	New York	Amer.	C	5	18	3	3	1	0	0	1	.167
1942	New York	Amer.	C	5	19	1	5	0	0	0	0	.263
1943	New York	Amer.	C	5	18	1	5	0	0	1	4	.278
World Series Totals				**38**	**145**	**19**	**37**	**1**	**1**	**5**	**24**	**.255**

* key
Pos. = position
G = games
AB = at bat
R = runs
H = hits
2B = two-base hits or doubles
3B = three-base hits or triples
HR = home run
RBI = runs batted in
BA = batting average

12

ROY CAMPANELLA
The Cat

THERE IS NO question that the home run Bobby Thomson streaked into the lower left field stands of the Polo Grounds in the ninth inning of the third play-off game against Ralph Branca will be told and retold as long as baseball is played. It gave the Giants, who had been 13 games behind in mid-August, the 1951 pennant over a bewildered Dodger team.

Historically, Thomson's blow will rank with Babe Ruth's "called-shot" home run against Charley Root and the Cubs in the 1932 World Series; with the failure of Fred Merkle to touch second in 1908, which resulted in the Giants and Cubs being tied for the pennant and the Cubs winning the replay; with Fred Snodgrass' muff of a seemingly simple fly which prevented the Giants from winning the 1912 Series from the Red Sox.

There was anguish on the Brooklyn bench when the ball sailed into the stands to transform a 4–2 Dodger lead into a 5–4 Giant victory—anguish and utter disbelief. There was one man who watched the ball with even more anguish and more disbelief than any of his teammates.

"Sink, you devil, sink," he prayed under his breath. But the ball didn't sink.

The man was Roy Campanella, the Dodger catcher, riding the bench with an injured thigh that day. To all of the Brooks,

Thomson's three-run homer seemed like a bad dream but to Campy it was worse—it was a bad dream repeating itself.

His mind went back to his second season in organized baseball, to 1947 when he played with Montreal, Brooklyn's farm team in the International League. The Royals had a 14-game lead at one stage but Jersey City, then the Giants' International farm team, started to eat it away.

It came down to the final game of the season, with the Jerseys now only percentage points behind. Montreal was at home for a pair with Toronto and Jersey City was playing a single game with Baltimore. Since the Royals had lost a game through rain, they needed both for the pennant.

Montreal led Toronto 5 to 3 going into the ninth, but Jack Van Cuyk ran into trouble. The Leafs got two on with one out and Manager Clay Hopper lifted Van Cuyk and called on Chet Kehn. Chet retired the first man and needed only to get by Len Kensecke to sew up the victory. Kensecke belted the ball over the right field fence for a home run and Toronto won, 6 to 5, and the pennant was gone.

That winter, in a letter to a teammate, Campanella confessed that in his dreams he still saw Kensecke's ball go flying over the screen. "I still don't believe we lost that pennant after being so far in front," he wrote. "There'll never be anything like that game again."

He was to recall that letter on October 3, 1951. History had repeated with a bang and the bang was supplied by Bobby Thomson.

More than one observer has likened Campanella's quickness behind the plate to that of a cat. He can pounce on bunts placed far out in front of the plate and he gets his throws away with no waste motion. He has not only a rifle arm but an accurate one.

Campanella's record against would-be base stealers is phenomenal. It is only since 1950 that the National League has been keeping records of the success of catchers against base stealers and the overall record of the league has held at a steady one-for-two ratio. In other words, the other National League catchers (Campy excepted) are something like the Ancient Mariner "who stoppeth one of three."

This is in direct contrast to Roy's record. He nails two out of three. Allen Roth, the Dodger statistician, has been keeping records of this phase of catching for some time. Through 1952, during which period Campanella caught over 600 games, the squatty catcher has nailed 138 base stealers out of 209. And he has kept to this average closely, too, getting 30 out of 45 in 1951 and 31 out of 46 in 1952. In the 1952 World Series against the Yankees, Campy improved his average, nailing three out of four.

Another of Campanella's catching assets is his willingness to throw. He is one of the very best of the pick-off artists because he has utter confidence in his ability to get the ball where he wants it. No less a judge than Mickey Cochrane raved about the play Roy made to pick Phil Rizzuto off third in the fourth game of the 1949 World Series.

In the same game against the Yankees, Campy averted disaster in the very first inning when he had Rizzuto trapped between third and home in a run-down play and not only tagged Phil but alertly threw the ball to Jackie Robinson at second to nip Tommy Heinrich who had rounded the bag on the play.

Since Campanella came to the Dodgers he has been a real home-run threat. In four full seasons he batted a total of 111 round-trippers, an average of better than 27 a season which is unusually high for a catcher.

Campanella's home runs, like bananas, seem to come in bunches. Roy, in 1950, hit six in six games, just one short of the record. The next year he hit seven homers in eight games. Roy will go a week or ten days without a homer and then suddenly he'll lower the boom. Incidentally, the majority of Roy's homers come with men on base and account for a great many of his runs batted in.

Since he came into baseball from the Negro leagues, Campanella has improved as a hitter. When Branch Rickey, at that time president of the Dodgers, first heard of Campy he personally scouted him, although Roy didn't know it.

"In those days," declared Rickey, "Campanella had a blind swing. He would turn his head at the last second, taking his eyes off the ball. In that way he would strike out a lot and it wasn't easy to see his potentialities as a hitter."

Somewhere between Walter Alston, who managed Campanella at Nashua, New Hampshire, in the defunct New England League, and Clay Hopper who had him at Montreal the next year, Roy found the home-run range. He hit thirteen at Nashua in 1946 and the same number at Montreal, but when he was optioned to St. Paul in 1948, he broke loose with 13 homers in 35 games before he was recalled to Brooklyn.

One of the toughest pitchers for the Dodgers was Ken Raffensberger, the veteran southpaw of the Reds. The Brooks beat him fairly frequently, which is only natural considering the disparity between the clubs, but Ken always made it rough for them. Oddly enough, Campanella hit him freely.

In a night game in Cincinnati in 1950, Campanella tore into Raffensberger for three home runs. All cleared the left field fence at Crosley Field, the first landing on the roof of a laundry behind the barrier, the second hitting the second-story window and the third just disappearing from sight, clearing the laundry, the sign atop its roof and all. Tom Swope, veteran baseball writer of the Cincinnati *Post*, couldn't recall any longer drives, although he cautiously admitted that perhaps Ernie Lombardi and Walker Cooper, both catchers, by the way, might have hit drives as far.

"That Raffensberger," grinned Campy after the game, "I'd get up at six-thirty in the morning to hit against that guy!"

No Dodger is any more popular with his teammates than Campanella. Despite his fine competitive fire, Roy is affable and easy going, no more complex than any one of his five young children. His disputes with umpires are infrequent—the Frank Dascoli incident in Boston in the waning days of the 1951 season was exceptional—and he never tries to show up an umpire as some catchers will.

Because Campanella began playing in the Negro leagues when he was only 16, he developed a religious streak unusual in ballplayers. Ballplayers, as a group, are no more irreligious than bankers or grocers or cops or sports writers, but Campanella has probably read the Bible more often than any ballplayer I know since Pepper Martin of the Cardinal Gas House Gang.

Roy's mother, Mrs. Ida Campanella, gave him a Bible for his first trip away from home because he was to be away from parental guidance so young and counseled him to read it. It has been Roy's constant traveling companion ever since, no matter where he has gone.

Campanella has great faith in the efficacy of prayer. Three times during that feverish final playoff game with the Giants in 1951, Roy sneaked off to the closet at the end of the visitors' dugout in the Polo Grounds to pray for the cause of the Dodgers. That his prayers were in vain in that particular instance didn't weaken his faith.

"God has been good to me more often than not," he says.

On a cold night in October, 1945, Campanella was catching at Ruppert Stadium in Newark, New Jersey, for the Negro All-Stars against the major league All-Stars, the latter team organized by Charley Dressen, then the Dodger coach.

The major leaguers had a pretty good club, Eddie Stanky, Whitey Kurowski, Buddy Kerr, Tommy Holmes among others. On this particular night, Ralph Branca was breezing his fast one by Campy and his mates and the score was 11 to 0.

As Dressen walked past Campanella to coach at third, he asked Roy to meet him after the game.

"Where?" asked the catcher.

"Outside the park," said Chuck.

When Campanella and Dressen met outside the park after the game, Charley told him simply that Branch Rickey, the Dodger president, wished to see him in the Brooklyn offices at ten the following morning. That was all Dressen had to tell him because that was all Dressen knew—he wasn't privy to the Mahatma's plans.

"Take an 'A' train on the Independent line and get off at Borough Hall. Anybody'll tell you where Montague Street is. The number is 215," instructed Dressen.

About all that could be said about Campanella's meeting with Rickey is that the catcher was flattered and bewildered. It meant a lot that his reputation in the Negro League should have reached the ears of a man placed as highly in baseball as the Mahatma, but on the other hand, Roy couldn't see it leading to any advancement.

Campanella was neither the first nor the last to listen to Rickey and leave, hours later, in a state of pleasant befuddlement. He was amazed at how much the Dodger president knew of his background, how much he knew about other players in the Negro League. Roy had read that a new Negro League was to be formed, the United States League, which was to be more or less subsidized by major league clubs. Brooklyn was to back an entry in this league, the Brown Dodgers, who were to play at Ebbets Field.

It was easy for Roy to assume that this was the purpose of the meeting with Rickey. There were two Negro leagues at the time, the National, to which Campanella's Baltimore Elite Giants belonged and the American, which operated in the Middle West. There had been a lot of talk among Negro players about the United States League. It opened up new fields of employment and therefore the possibilities of more money.

When Campanella left Rickey that October afternoon in 1945, he felt that an offer for the Brown Dodgers would be forthcoming, but he wasn't particularly excited about it. With Baltimore, he was making about $3000 a season and in the winter months he played with other Negro stars in the Latin-American circuit. The United States League was a new thing and it might blow up, as so many new organizations did.

A week or so later, Campanella was in Harlem's Hotel Woodside where Negro ballplayers from all over the country were gathering for an invasion of Venezuela. They would play against local teams in the South American capital, Caracas. As Dick Young reported the story in his fine biography of Campanella (A.S. Barnes & Co., New York), it was Jackie Robinson who first tipped off Roy to the importance of his meeting with Rickey.

"I hear you were over to Brooklyn to see Mr. Rickey," said Robbie casually as they dealt a hand of gin rummy.

"How did you ever find that out?" asked the surprised Campanella.

"Because I was over to see him myself," was Robinson's answer.

Campanella then launched into a discussion with Jackie, in which he pointed out that whereas it would be all right for him, a newcomer to Negro baseball, to take a chance with the United States League, he, Campanella, couldn't afford to.

"Did you sign?" asked Robbie.

"I didn't sign to play ball for him, no," answered Roy, "but I did sign an agreement that I wouldn't sign with any other team for next season without letting him know. But I don't want to play with the Brown Dodgers."

"Did Mr. Rickey mention the Brown Dodgers?" persisted Robinson.

"Come to think of it, Jackie, he didn't mention any team," said Roy. "He just talked and talked but I couldn't really pin him down on anything he said."

"Well, I signed with him," declared Robinson.

Campanella promptly congratulated the young Negro, who had been the shortstop of the Kansas City Monarchs, and told him he was certain Jackie would make good with the Brown Dodgers.

"But I didn't sign with the Brown Dodgers," said Robbie. "I signed with Montreal."

Then the words tumbled forth as Campy listened first in bewilderment and then excitedly, "I'm going to be the first Negro in organized baseball," said Jackie with rising excitement. "I'm to be signed at a public ceremony in Montreal tomorrow. It means the end of the Jim Crow law in baseball."

It was only then that Campanella realized the full import of Robinson's statement and realized the full import of his meeting with Rickey. He knew then that the Mahatma had tapped him for organized baseball, too.

The first step up was a long one for Campanella. He wrote Rickey from Caracas and eventually, months later, received a telegram telling him to report at the Dodger office on March 10. Roy flew back and was a little upset to find that Branch was in Sanford, Florida, and that his destiny was in the hands of Rickey's assistant, Bob Finch.

Finch tried to place Campanella with the Danville, Illinois, farm of the Dodgers in the Three-Eye League but there was no room there. He finally made arrangements for Roy to join Nashua, New Hampshire, in the New England League, like the Three-Eye, a Class B organization.

It turned out to be the best break Campanella possibly could have gotten. The general manager at Nashua was Emil (Buzzy) Bavasi, an intelligent, understanding young man. Like Campanella, Buzzy was to go right up the ladder of the Brooklyn

Organization and in December, 1950, after Rickey moved to Pittsburgh, Walter F. O'Malley, who succeeded Branch as president, promoted Bavasi to the vice presidency of the parent club.

Class B salary limitations are rigid. Campanella would have to play for $185 a month, a third of what he was receiving in the Negro National League. However, the Dodgers offered him a post-season job at twice his Nashua salary, so he was getting the $3000 he had made with Baltimore. The post-season job turned out to be a detail of scouting the Negro leagues and Campanella is particularly proud of his scouting record. Among the players he recommended to Rickey were Larry Doby, later a Cleveland star, and Monte Irvin, the Giant slugger.

It is not generally known that one of the reasons which cost Leo Durocher his job as Dodger manager in 1948 was his refusal to see eye-to-eye with Rickey on the subject of Campanella's services. The Lip wanted to use Campy with Brooklyn. The Mahatma, taking the long view, wanted to use Roy at the Dodgers' St. Paul farm and thus break the color line which still existed in the American Association.

Rickey, of course, gained his point. Campanella obediently went to St. Paul, where he broke out in one of his famous home-run rashes. He was recalled by the Dodgers, again at the insistence of Durocher, but Leo lasted only a couple more weeks with the club. He went to the Giants when that club released Mel Ott as manager, and Burt Shotton took over the Brooklyn stewardship for the balance of the season.

The Dodgers finished third that year, although they were in first place in September, but Campanella proved he was a major league catcher, maybe the best catcher in the major leagues. He set what probably was some sort of a record in the closing weeks by throwing out a dozen would-be base stealers in succession.

Campanella came into a World Series in 1949 and it was here for the first time that his true worth became generally recognized. His pick-off of Phil Rizzuto—the first time in his life the Yankee infielder had ever been picked off third base—and his amazing agility behind the plate drew raves from those who saw the Series, not merely raves from the press box but raves from baseball people, particularly American Leaguers who never had seen Campy before.

Although he didn't make the World Series in 1950—Dick Sisler's last game home run for the Phils took care of that— nor in 1951, when Bobby Thomson's homer took care of that—Campanella was steadily climbing. He had his reward in 1951 when he was named the most valuable player in the National League, getting all of 24 first-place votes and finishing with a score of 243 against 191 for Stan Musial, the Cardinal slugger who was the runner-up. He was the first National League catcher to be named the MVP since Ernie Lombardi of the Reds in 1938.

Campy tailed off after receiving this award. In 1952, his weight was up and his batting average was down. Then he came back in 1953 with a remarkable performance and Chuck Dressen piloted the Dodgers to their second straight pennant. Roy broke all sorts of catcher's batting records, hitting 41 home runs and leading the National League in runs batted in with 142. He batted .312 and hit a homer in the World Series, which saw the Yanks again down the Brooks, this time in six games.

Once more Campanella was voted the most valuable player in the National League. By being named for the second time, Roy moved into select company. He was to top that, but only after a typical Campy interruption.

A hand injury, sustained when Whitey Lockman of the Giants slid into him at the plate in the closing days of the 1953 season, virtually put Campanella out of action in 1954. There were several operations, including one after the season, and Campy's bat was an empty threat most of the time, although he did hold up his end in the home run department. His average, however, fell off over 100 points from his .312 of 1953.

With the irregularity that any rider on the "A" train could have guaranteed, Roy snapped back with another great year in 1955. His .318 batting average, 32 home runs and 107 RBI's sparked Brooklyn to another pennant and gave Campy his third MVP award, a National League record he shares with Stan Musial. The award was further sweetened when Roy and the rest of the Dodgers brought joy to Brooklyn by winning their first world championship in a seven-game Series with the Yankees.

Campy played his last game in 1957, as a near fatal auto accident that winter left him partially paralyzed. As he lay in the wreckage, only a few blocks from his Long Island home, and futilely tried to move his arm to turn off the ignition, he realized not only that his playing days were over, but he was also going to have to start a new life.

He fought back from paralysis just as he did from those hexing years of famine between MVP awards. Today, he works as a radio announcer, has a prosperous business, and is the same laughing, smiling Campy.

ROY CAMPANELLA

Born, November 19, 1921, Philadelphia, Pa.
Height, 5'9". Weight, 205. Batted and threw right-handed.

Year	Club	League	Pos.	G	AB	R	H	2B	3B	HR	RBI	BA
1948	Brooklyn	Nat.	C	83	279	32	72	11	3	9	45	.258
1949	Brooklyn	Nat.	C	130	436	65	125	22	2	22	82	.287
1950	Brooklyn	Nat.	C	126	437	70	123	19	3	31	89	.281
1951	Brooklyn	Nat.	C	143	505	90	164	33	1	33	108	.325
1952	Brooklyn	Nat.	C	128	468	73	126	18	1	22	97	.269
1953	Brooklyn	Nat.	C	144	519	103	162	26	3	41	142	.312
1954	Brooklyn	Nat.	C	111	397	43	82	14	3	19	51	.207
1955	Brooklyn	Nat.	C	123	446	81	142	20	1	32	107	.318
1956	Brooklyn	Nat.	C	124	388	39	85	6	1	20	73	.219
1957	Brooklyn	Nat.	C	103	330	31	80	9	0	13	62	.242
Major League Totals				1215	4205	627	1161	178	18	242	856	.276

WORLD SERIES RECORD

Year	Club	League	Pos.	G	AB	R	H	2B	3B	HR	RBI	BA
1949	Brooklyn	Nat.	C	5	15	2	4	1	0	1	2	.267
1952	Brooklyn	Nat.	C	7	28	0	6	0	0	0	1	.214
1953	Brooklyn	Nat.	C	6	22	6	6	0	0	1	2	.273
1955	Brooklyn	Nat.	C	7	27	4	7	3	0	2	4	.259
1956	Brooklyn	Nat.	C	7	22	2	4	1	0	0	3	.182
World Series Totals				32	114	14	27	5	0	4	12	.237

* key
Pos. = position
G = games
AB = at bat
R = runs
H = hits
2B = two-base hits or doubles
3B = three-base hits or triples
HR = home run
RBI = runs batted in
BA = batting average

13

YOGI BERRA
The Solid Man

THOSE WHO LAUGHED when he sat down to manage would be well-advised to have second thoughts on the matter, for Yogi Berra is no laughing matter. This doesn't mean that Yogi hasn't provided a generous share of laughs during his career with the Yankees, which stretches all the way back to the tag end of the 1946 season. The point which always should be kept uppermost is that you laugh WITH Yogi, not AT him.

When Berra was named to succeed Ralph Houk as manager of the Yankees for 1964, there was surprise in many quarters. Some, with a Madison Avenue slant, thought the Yankees wished to change their "image," so as to compete on more even terms with Casey Stengel and the New York Mets.

This may have been a minor point in the appointment of Berra as manager. The major factor, however, was that more than one major league club saw managerial talents in Yogi. It was a question of how long Berra, with his active days closing out, could be kept waiting in the wings. Making him a player-coach the year before was an indication of the regard in which the Yankee management held the squatty little catcher.

The list of people who laughed at Berra at first sight is long—and also illustrious. Some of baseball's better minds couldn't see the misshapen Berra as a ballplayer, let alone a major leaguer.

As a kid on The Hill in St. Louis, a predominately Italian

area, Berra and his close pal, Joe Garagiola, were given trials by the St. Louis Cardinals. This was as long ago as 1942, when Branch Rickey was the resident genius at Sportsman's Park. Garagiola was offered a couple of hundred dollars to become a Cardinal vassal. Yogi was told he could sign if he wished, but that he would not receive a bonus. Berra's reaction reflected his principles for the first time, principles to which he has clung ever since. "No money, no deal."

A few months after the twin tryouts of Garagiola and Berra, Rickey, having seen his Cardinals beat the Yankees in the World Series, moved to Brooklyn. The Mahatma sent emissaries to Berra but by then Johnny Schulte, a St. Louis resident and bullpen coach for the Yankees under Joe McCarthy, had signed Yogi to a Yankee contract for $500. It well could have been one of baseball's greatest bargains.

Quite possibly the first baseball man to recognize the full baseball potential of Berra was Mel Ott, then managing the New York Giants. This was in 1945 and the Giants played an exhibition game in New London, Connecticut, against a Navy team with Berra catching for the sailors.

"Why he impressed me so much, I'll never know," related Mel years later. "Berra was a paradox. He seemed to be doing everything wrong, yet everything came out right. He stopped everything behind the plate and hit everything in front of it. He made two hits on two wild pitches."

Ott went to Larry MacPhail, who with Dan Topping and Del Webb had purchased the Yankees before the start of the season. Mel was not a devious man. He said there was a catcher at the submarine base in New London who was Yankee property and that the Giants would like to buy him for $50,000 when he received his Navy discharge. "Fellow name of Berra," said Mel.

MacPhail had never heard of Berra until that minute but Larry was an old hand at the horse-trading dodge. "Oh, yes,

Berra," stalled Larry. "We have some good scouting reports on him. I'd have to talk things over with our scouts before I could consider any sort of deal."

When MacPhail looked into Berra's background, he found precious little. He learned that on Schulte's recommendation he had received a $500 bonus and had played one year at Norfolk, Virginia, in the Piedmont League, where he batted .253, before enlisting in the Navy, in which he served in 1944 and 1945. Larry decided to take a look at the young man who had impressed Ott to the extent of $50,000 on the strength of one exhibition game.

"When he walked into my office, I almost fainted," said MacPhail bluntly. "He was in his sailor blues and looked like the anchor man on an acrobatic troupe. I figured that $50,000 had gone out the window but I suggested he work out with Newark in the International League the next year, in 1946."

In writing off Yogi on the strength of one look, MacPhail became the first to be fooled by Berra. The second man was the clubhouse attendant with the Newark Bears, who attempted to palm off a scrub uniform on Yogi when he reported. "Gimme a regular uniform," said Berra forthrightly. "I ain't here for no tryout. I'm here to play with the ball club."

The third man Berra fooled was no less than Joe DiMaggio. Yogi came up to the Yankees at the tail end of the 1946 season. On successive days, he belted home runs into the right field bleachers at Yankee Stadium, one off a high, inside pitch, the other off a high, outside pitch.

The Yankees, after this demonstration by Berra, left for a brief series in Boston, boarding their special New York Central train at the 125th Street Station. DiMaggio decided the rookie was worth a complete "look" and was studying him unobtrusively as he thought, on the station platform. Suddenly Joe realized that Berra was giving him a complete inspection, too. The dead-panned DiMaggio burst out laughing and Yogi laughed right back at him. "I can hit homers, too," said the rookie.

Bucky Harris was the manager of the Yankees in 1947 and Berra embarked with Bucky on a spring training tour which would have made Gulliver jealous. The club started training in San Juan, Puerto Rico, moved to Caracas, Venezuela, then to Havana, Cuba, and finally to St. Petersburg.

Harris realized Berra's potential but felt Yogi lacked too many of the refinements of the trade to be used as a catcher and tried him in the outfield—thus joining MacPhail and DiMaggio (and maybe Rickey) as sound baseball men who had underestimated the little catcher.

In 1949, Casey Stengel succeeded Harris as Yankee manager and Bill Dickey, who had been fired by MacPhail as manager during the 1946 season, came back as coach. It was understood that Dickey, one of the all-time catching greats, would be Yogi's Svengali.

Dickey was fascinated the first time he saw Berra catch. He studied him with the rapt absorption that a paleontologist might display at his first exposure to Pithecanthropus Erectus. After this first meeting, Dickey was besieged by writers seeking his opinion on the future of Berra as a catcher, if any.

Dickey became the first baseball man of record not to be fooled by Berra. "Berra has the makings of a good catcher," said Bill calmly. "I wouldn't say a great one, although he could be that, too, but certainly a good one."

"Right now," added Dickey, "he does about everything wrong but Casey warned me about that. Nobody told me how quickly he can move behind the plate and that's the main thing. He has speed and agility. His arm is strong enough—his throwing is merely a matter of teaching him where to throw from. I know he can hit. I've seen him pull outside pitches as few batters can."

118

The ugly duckling didn't exactly become a graceful swan overnight but he became Stengel's first-string catcher that season, hitting 20 home runs, the first of ten consecutive seasons in which he was to hit 20 or more for the Yankees.

Berra arrived gradually as a top-notch catcher, almost sneaking up on an unsuspecting public. In a five-year span, 1951–55, he was three times voted the American League's Most Valuable Player. Yogi always claimed it was his soccer training which gave him the gift of agility behind the plate but there was no one quicker in moving out on bunted balls or more deft in tagging a sliding runner.

Because of his "Berraisms," Yogi's intelligence has been vastly underrated. Except by those who have played with him or against him. Front-line Yankee pitchers, men like Allie Reynolds, Vic Raschi, and Eddie Lopat, who antedated Yogi with the Yankees, soon were letting him call all the pitches. When Whitey Ford joined the club, Yogi had become one of the elder statesmen of the Yankees and it was taken for granted that he would call all the pitches from behind the plate.

Whether or not the Yankees deliberately selected Yogi as a manager so that he would counteract the earthy image of Stengel with the Mets is highly debatable, and perhaps improbable, since managers are not selected because of their ability as crowd pleasers. It remains a fact, however, that Berra, the neophyte manager, and Stengel, the grizzled veteran, have much in common.

Bucky Harris won the pennant with the Yankees in his first season, 1947, and was in contention until the final week in 1948 when he was summarily dismissed. Many believed that Stengel was hired as Bucky's replacement because his personal popularity with the metropolitan press would offset what many considered the cavalier treatment of Harris. Casey was the first to set them straight.

"I've known Mr. Weiss since he ran the New Haven club in the Eastern League and I managed Worcester in the same league," said Casey bluntly. "I've known Mr. Del Webb for several years in California. I want to make it plain that I didn't get this job through friendship. You don't get jobs like this through friendship. I was hired because these people thought I could do a job for 'em."

The job Stengel did with the Yankees, ten pennants in a dozen seasons, needs no retelling here but it is a pretty safe bet that Berra could say "Amen" to Stengel's remarks. As popular a ballplayer as ever wore the Yankee pinstripes, he didn't get his job through a mutual admiration society either.

When Stengel was named Yankee manager a national magazine, conscious of the dignity of the Yankees through the years, but unaware of the baseball acumen Casey possessed, sought a story entitled "The Court Jester in Baseball's Royal Box."

Saner heads prevailed and the story was written in a somewhat different manner, yet the first reaction to Casey's appointment as Yankee manager was not unlike that which greeted the announcement on Yogi 15 years later.

Should Berra, the manager, ever approach Berra, the player, all managerial records will fall. As the true greatness of Yogi as a catcher and hitter began to dawn on the general public, there was a disposition to regard him as a self-made ballplayer, which is not entirely accurate.

Berra always had the talent and the potential for baseball greatness. It was merely a matter of harnessing them, of shaping them toward perfection. Yogi had many helpers along the way—Bill Dickey, for one—but the final contribution was made by Berra himself in his determination.

When Dickey was brought in to St. Petersburg to supervise the education of our hero, Yogi was supposed to have said "Bill

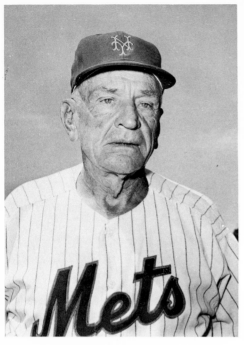

Casey Stengel

Grover Cleveland Alexander

Walter Johnson

Christy Mathewson

Bob Feller

Lefty Grove

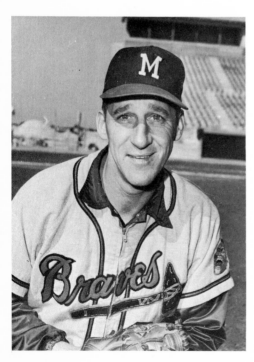

Warren Spahn

Dazzy Vance

Carl Hubbell

Hoyt Wilhelm

Bill Dickey

Yogi Berra

Roy Campanella

Rogers Hornsby

Johnny Mize

Lou Gehrig

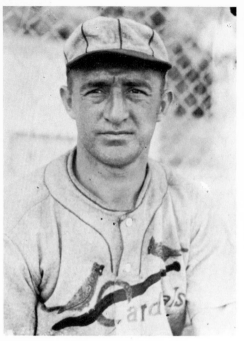

Frankie Frisch

Honus Wagner

Jackie Robinson

Harold "Pie" Traynor

Babe Ruth

Joe Di Maggio

Ted Williams

Ty Cobb

Stan Musial

Willie Mays

is learning me his experience." He may or may not have made that remark, although goodness knows he has perpetrated as many "Berraisms" as Casey has "Stengelese."

Berra is not articulate, principally because he thinks faster than he can speak, a trait of Stengel also. I recall one night when the Yankees made an overnight jump from Tampa to West Palm Beach in an old fashioned sleeper, with uppers and lowers. Yogi had the berth across from me and we awakened at about the same time.

Berra took out his wristwatch and wound it. "What time you got?" he asked sleepily.

"Seven," I answered.

"Seven?" questioned Yogi. "I got six. Time didn't go off anywhere during the night, did it?"

The question was a puzzler, the explanation relatively simple. It happened that Berra's watch had stopped exactly one hour before. Accustomed as he was to rapid switches from one time zone to another during the regular season, he assumed there might have been a difference in time between Florida's west and east coasts.

Berra may have trouble expressing himself but he has no trouble thinking. People who mark him off as a genial clown will find they've made the same mistake they made years ago about Stengel.

Statistics are dry but impressive. Consider some of Yogi's achievements:

Three times the American League's Most Valuable Player.

More home runs than any other catcher in major league history—313. This doesn't count 45 he hit while filling in in the outfield for the Yankees.

More World Series games (75), more World Series hits (71), and more World Series runs batted in (39) than any player in baseball.

First player to deliver a home run as a pinch hitter in World Series history. One of eight players (six of them Yankees) to hit a World Series grand-slammer.

These are merely the cream of Berra's achievements. If he wishes to indulge in his most noted malaprop and thank every one who made this necessary, he'll have to head the list with Lawrence Peter Berra.

LAWRENCE PETER BERRA

Born, May 12, 1925, St. Louis, Missouri.
Height, 5'8". Weight, 191. Batted left and threw right-handed.

Year	Club	League	Pos.	G	AB	R	H	2B	3B	HR	RBI	BA
1946	New York	Amer.	C	7	22	3	8	1	0	2	4	.364
1947	New York	Amer.	C	83	293	41	82	15	3	11	54	.280
1948	New York	Amer.	C	125	469	70	143	24	10	14	98	.305
1949	New York	Amer.	C	116	415	59	115	20	2	20	91	.277
1950	New York	Amer.	C	151	597	116	192	30	6	28	124	.322
1951	New York	Amer.	C	141	547	92	161	19	4	27	88	.294
1952	New York	Amer.	C	142	534	97	146	17	1	30	98	.273
1953	New York	Amer.	C	137	503	80	149	23	5	27	108	.296
1954	New York	Amer.	C	151	584	88	179	28	6	22	125	.307
1955	New York	Amer.	C	147	541	84	147	20	3	27	108	.272
1956	New York	Amer.	C	140	521	93	155	29	2	30	105	.298
1957	New York	Amer.	C	134	482	74	121	14	2	24	82	.251
1958	New York	Amer.	C	122	433	60	115	17	3	22	90	.266
1959	New York	Amer.	C	131	472	64	134	25	1	19	69	.284
1960	New York	Amer.	C	120	359	46	99	14	1	15	62	.276
1961	New York	Amer.	C	119	395	62	107	11	0	22	61	.271
1962	New York	Amer.	C	86	232	25	52	8	0	10	35	.224
1963	New York	Amer.	C	64	147	20	43	6	0	8	28	.293
Major League Totals				**2112**	**7546**	**1174**	**2148**	**321**	**49**	**358**	**1430**	**.285**

WORLD SERIES RECORD

Year	Club	League	Pos.	G	AB	R	H	2B	3B	HR	RBI	BA
1947	New York	Amer.	C	6	19	2	3	0	0	1	2	.158
1949	New York	Amer.	C	4	16	2	1	0	0	0	1	.063
1950	New York	Amer.	C	4	15	2	3	0	0	1	2	.200
1951	New York	Amer.	C	6	23	4	6	1	0	0	0	.261
1952	New York	Amer.	C	7	28	2	6	1	0	2	3	.214
1953	New York	Amer.	C	6	21	3	9	1	0	1	4	.429
1955	New York	Amer.	C	7	24	5	10	1	0	1	2	.417
1956	New York	Amer.	C	7	25	5	9	2	0	3	10	.360
1957	New York	Amer.	C	7	25	5	8	1	0	1	2	.320

WORLD SERIES RECORD (*Continued*)

Year	Club	League	Pos.	G	AB	R	H	2B	3B	HR	RBI	BA
1958	New York	Amer.	C	7	27	3	6	3	0	0	2	.222
1960	New York	Amer.	C	7	22	6	7	0	0	1	8	.318
1961	New York	Amer.	C	4	11	2	3	0	0	1	3	.273
1962	New York	Amer.	C	2	2	0	0	0	0	0	0	.000
1963	New York	Amer.	C	1	1	0	0	0	0	0	0	.000
World Series Totals				75	259	41	71	10	0	12	39	.274

* key
Pos. = position
G = games
AB = at bat
R = runs
H = hits
2B = two-base hits or doubles
3B = three-base hits or triples
HR = home run
RBI = runs batted in
BA = batting average

14

JOHNNY MIZE
The Big Cat

THE MANLY ART of pinch hitting has a history that is almost necessarily vague. Each year there are those who demonstrate an ability to walk out of the dugout cold and do better than fair at the business of whacking a pitch at a most important moment, but their records do not survive except in the most general way.

A good pinch hitter is highly esteemed and yet a good pinch hitter more or less is a product of accident. When the occasion arises, he just happens to be in the right place—on the bench—instead of in the lineup. Usually, he is a part-time player. Sometimes he is available because a minor injury makes it inadvisable for him to play nine innings. He may be a fading veteran.

The player is rare who can make a living with his bat alone. In the old days, perhaps Ham Hyatt and Moose McCormick were exceptions.

Hyatt was with the Pittsburgh Pirates for a few seasons. He was an outfielder and a first baseman, but never won a starting job. But he won ball games as a pinch hitter in 1909 when the Pirates won the pennant. His batting average in 49 games was .299. What was impressive in those days of the dead ball was that he delivered three pinch home runs. This must be considered quite a performance since Red Murray of the Giants led the league in homers that year with only seven.

McCormick served with John McGraw's Giants, and aided New York pennant victories in 1912 and 1913 when he hit .333 and .275, almost exclusively as a pinch hitter.

Some of the better pinch hitters have been pitchers. It was Babe Ruth's success as a pinch hitter with the Red Sox that influenced Ed Barrow to convert a brilliant young left-handed pitcher into an outfielder who set home run records.

One of the best pinch hitters throughout his entire pitching career in the American League was Red Ruffing. Don New-combe of the Dodgers was highly successful but only against right-handed pitchers. A right-handed pitcher himself, New-combe batted left-handed and with impressive power.

Holder of the record for most pinch hits in the course of his career was a pitcher. That is Red Lucas, who served 15 years in the National League, was a successful rotation starter and a pinch hitter available in all other games. Lucas delivered 107 pinch hits and was used as a pinch hitter in the impressive total of 440 games.

American League record holder was the late Fat Fothergill, a roly-poly outfielder with the Tigers and the White Sox. He pinch-hit in 257 games, got 76 hits.

In 1932, Johnny Frederick of the Dodgers doubled Hyatt's record of three pinch homers by hitting six, two off Carl Hub-bell; but Frederick was a regular in drydock. He was the center fielder of the club and appeared in 118 games. A chronic leg injury kept him out of the lineup for weeks at a time.

In 1943, Joe Cronin, already managing the Red Sox, was on his last set of tires as a player. He appeared in 59 games and whacked five pinch home runs. An American League record for the current American League president.

Certainly one of the most competent of present-day pinch

hitters is Jerry Lynch. A left-handed batter, unfortunately cursed by defensive deficiencies, Lynch started with the Pirates about a decade ago, played with the Reds for six seasons, then returned to Pittsburgh.

A platoon outfielder, Lynch spends much time on the bench waiting for an opportunity to swing at a right-handed relief pitcher in a late-inning pinch. He can be deadly. In the 1963 season, he smote the 15th pinch home run of his career and that is a major league record.

For the purposes of supplying this team with a first-rate pinch hitter though, you probably couldn't do better than Johnny Mize. The records show that he was a better hitter than the others named herein (always excluding Ruth, of course) and he showed an exceptional talent for coming up cold and hitting one for Casey Stengel at the end of his career.

Mize was 36 years old and somewhat washed up as a National League first baseman in late August of 1949. On the other side of the Harlem River, the Yankees were struggling for a pennant and George Martin Weiss thought John was just the man to beef up his ball club for the September stretch. When National League waivers were obtained, he was purchased for $40,000 or twice the waiver price.

Although Johnny had played for some strong clubs in the National League, he never had been with a pennant winner until he reached the Yankees. He lasted for five years more and in each of these years, the Yanks not only won the pennant but the world's championship as well. Mize helped. The Yanks paid him quite a chunk in salary and not because of his southern drawl.

Mize played in 13 games for the Yankees in 1949, in 90 the next season, in 113 games in 1951, in 78 in 1952 and in 81 in 1953, his final year. These figures are deceptive because he rarely played nine innings.

Stengel, over that period, platooned Mize with Joe Collins at first base and usually Johnny Hopp or somebody else. In games Mize started, he usually was relieved in the late innings. Other games in which he pinch-hit found him finishing up in the field.

Johnny's batting averages as a Yankee were not astronomical. His best was .277 in 1950 which is quite a bit south of his lifetime major league average of .312. He also hit 25 home runs in 1950 and a total of 44 in those five finishing years.

His career, interrupted by three years of navy service in World War II, covered 16 seasons. He finished with 359 homers. That's not a record but you don't need all your fingers and toes to count the number of sluggers who have topped that figure.

When Mize hit 51 home runs for the Giants in 1947, he became the first left-handed National League hitter to reach 50 and that distinction still belongs to him after ten years of retirement. As a matter of fact, Babe Ruth was the only left-handed American League hitter to reach 50 until Roger Maris went wild and hit 61 in 1961.

Six times in his career—the last as a Yankee in 1950— Johnny hit three home runs in one game and that is a major league record.

Twice Johnny led the National League outright in home runs with 28 in 1939 and 43 in 1940. On two other occasions, he shared the home run leadership with Ralph Kiner—at 51 in 1947 and 40 in 1948.

Arriving in the majors with the Cardinals in 1936, Mize was a better than .300 hitter in each of his first nine seasons. His top average was a resounding .364 in 1937, but his St. Louis teammate, Joe Medwick, topped him by ten points for the batting championship. In those days, the most dreaded

127

slugging combination in the league was the duo of Medwick and Mize.

In 1939, Mize hit .349 and this time won the league batting title.

John Robert Mize was born at Demorest, Georgia, January 7, 1913, and grew up to be a massive man. He stood six feet, two inches, weighed around 210 pounds in the early years of his career and possibly 15 pounds more than that toward the end of the line.

In his late years, they called him "the Big Cat" and the nickname seemed singularly apropos although his movements on or off the ball field could scarcely be described as feline. But he did rather look like a tiger with his reddish-brown hair, his ruddy round face and white teeth that flashed out of a broad grin.

Here was a left-handed hitter with the brawny construction to have challenged Ruth's records and Johnny would probably have come close had he been as physically sound as he looked. The fact is that a delicate and risky operation was necessary to fit Mize for baseball at all.

His apprenticeship started in the Cardinal chain in 1930. He played in Greensboro for a year and a half, then in Elmira for a season. It was back to Greensboro and then two and a half seasons with Rochester, the big Cardinal farm in the International League.

He hit wherever he went but he was a full-time ballplayer nowhere. From time to time, he was forced to lay off because of an agonizing pain in the pelvic area. It seems that he had a bone spur high on the inside of the leg which raised all kinds of mischief with an important nerve.

Branch Rickey ran the Cardinals of that era and Mr. Rickey preferred to have the other fellow take the gamble or, as he himself would put it, "the calculated risk." And so, Rickey sold

Mize to Larry MacPhail, the bright new general manager of the Cincinnati Reds, before the spring training season of 1935.

This was a conditional deal. If MacPhail were satisfied with Mize, he might have him at a price well up in five figures. If not, Johnny was to be returned to the Cardinal organization. Although Mize hit some memorable shots that spring, Mac-Phail turned him back.

Reassigned to Rochester, Johnny broke down again after playing 65 games and Rickey reluctantly assumed the calculated risk himself.

Dr. Robert F. Hyland, the famed St. Louis surgeon, performed the operation.

"Before I started," said Dr. Hyland, "it was my duty to warn Mize. There was a 50–50 chance of success. If the operation was unsuccessful, Johnny probably would never play ball again."

"Cut away," answered Mize without blinking.

Doc Hyland's skill prevailed. In six minor league seasons, Johnny had been able to play as many as 100 games just once. In his next 11 campaigns in the National League, he rarely was out of the lineup, playing more than 150 games in four of those years.

A right-handed thrower who spent some of his minor league time in the outfield, Johnny settled down at first base for the rest of his career. He never had blinding speed, but he wasn't a tanglefoot either. If he couldn't cover ground like Bill Terry or Dolph Camilli, he at least could handle everything he could reach.

If one were thinking of merely another first baseman for this squad, Terry or George Sisler would rank ahead of Mize. But it is taken for granted here that Lou Gehrig would play first base every day for this team just as he did for so many years with the Yankees.

And Mize, a valuable pinch hitter in his final seasons, probably would have been as good or better at this task if he had concentrated on occasional play throughout his career.

Maybe the part-time duty forced by his ailment in his early years helped him to come up cold and hit. Certainly, his application to the hitting art was a great factor. He was as great a student of batting as Ty Cobb or Ted Williams.

In his earlier years, Mize hit tremendous home runs that rang out like the crack of doom. As he finished up, the Yankees kidded him because so many of his homers dropped about two rows back in the seats.

Tommy Henrich still swears Mize knew the distance to every wall in the American League and just how hard he had to hit the ball to strike paint.

Johnny shrugged that off, but admitted, "Overswinging only gets you into trouble and a home run into the seats counts as much as a home run over the roof."

Taking a pitch, Mize actually followed the ball with his eyes right into the catcher's mitt and he maintains that he actually could see his bat hit the ball.

In his part-time service in five straight World Series, Johnny hit .286—a dozen hits in 42 times at bat. He pinch-hit twice against the Dodgers in 1949 and delivered two singles, each of which drove in an important run.

He practically ruined the Dodgers in 1952 when one of the closest and most exciting seven-game series occurred. He got six hits in 15 trips, driving in six runs, getting one double and three crushing homers.

Against the Giants in 1951, he ostensibly did nothing remarkable to bring victory to the Yankees, but Chub Feeney, the young vice president of the National League Champions, blamed John for the defeat of the Giants.

In the sixth game, Mize was purposely passed with first base open and Gil McDougald followed with a grand-slam homer. In the seventh game, Mize was walked in the same situation and Hank Bauer blasted a three-run triple.

"Two walks to Mize meant seven runs," moaned Feeney. "Did they think he was Ruth?"

Johnny is out of baseball now. He was part of a radio sports show for a while around New York and tried his hand as a batting coach for the Giants. Finally, he retired from the game entirely in good shape physically and financially.

He has lived for years in Deland, Florida, where his vested interests include a collection of orange groves.

JOHN ROBERT MIZE

Born, January 7, 1913, Demorest, Georgia.
Height 6'2". Weight 215. Batted left- and threw right-handed.

Year	Club	League	Pos.	G	AB	R	H	2B	3B	HR	RBI	BA
1936	St. Louis	Nat.	1B	126	414	76	136	30	8	19	93	.329
1937	St. Louis	Nat.	1B	145	560	103	204	40	7	25	113	.364
1938	St. Louis	Nat.	1B	149	531	85	179	34	16	27	102	.337
1939	St. Louis	Nat.	1B	153	564	104	197	44	14	28	108	.349
1940	St. Louis	Nat.	1B	155	579	111	182	31	13	43	137	.314
1941	St. Louis [1]	Nat.	1B	126	473	67	150	39	8	16	100	.317
1942	New York	Nat.	1B	142	541	97	165	25	7	26	110	.305
1943–1944–1945	(In Military Service)											
1946	New York	Nat.	1B	101	377	70	127	18	3	22	70	.337
1947	New York	Nat.	1B	154	586	137	177	26	2	51	138	.302
1948	New York	Nat.	1B	152	560	110	162	26	4	40	125	.289
1949	New York [2]	Nat.	1B	106	388	59	102	15	0	18	62	.263
1949	New York	Amer.	1B	13	23	4	6	1	0	1	2	.261
1950	New York	Amer.	1B	90	274	43	76	12	0	25	72	.277
1951	New York	Amer.	1B	113	332	37	86	14	1	10	49	.259
1952	New York	Amer.	1B	78	137	9	36	9	0	4	29	.263
1953	New York	Amer.	1B	81	104	6	26	3	0	4	27	.250
National League Totals				1509	5573	1019	1781	328	82	315	1158	.320
American League Totals				375	870	99	230	39	1	44	179	.264
Major League Totals				**1884**	**6443**	**1118**	**2011**	**367**	**83**	**359**	**1337**	**.312**

[1] Traded to New York for Catcher Ken O'Dea, Pitcher Bill Lehrman, First Baseman Johnny McCarthy and $50,000, December 11, 1941.
[2] Sold to New York Yankees, August 22, 1949.

WORLD SERIES RECORD

Year	Club	League	Pos.	G	AB	R	H	2B	3B	HR	RBI	BA
1949	New York	Amer.	1B	2	2	0	2	0	0	0	2	1.000
1950	New York	Amer.	1B	4	15	0	2	0	0	0	0	.133
1951	New York	Amer.	1B	4	7	2	2	1	0	0	1	.286
1952	New York	Amer.	1B	5	15	3	6	1	0	3	6	.400
1953	New York	Amer.	1B	3	3	0	0	0	0	0	0	.000
World Series Totals				18	42	5	12	2	0	3	9	.286

* key

Pos. = position
G = games
AB = at bat
R = runs
H = hits
2B = two-base hits or doubles
3B = three-base hits or triples
HR = home run
RBI = runs batted in
BA = batting average

15

LOU GEHRIG

The Iron Horse

MIGHTY MEN have played first base in the major leagues.

Two who can be properly classed in the modern era attained .400 batting averages. In fact, George Sisler topped that figure twice for the old St. Louis Browns and Sisler's .420 in 1922 still is the American League record. Bill Terry of the Giants is the last National Leaguer to hit that mark with .401 in 1930.

Two other first basemen came closest to Babe Ruth's season record of 60 home runs in the years of the 154-game schedule. Jimmy Foxx crashed 58 home runs for the Philadelphia Athletics in 1932. Six years later, Hank Greenberg hit 58 for the Detroit Tigers.

Moreover, Foxx closed out his career with 534 home runs and the only man to have exceeded this total was the incomparable Ruth.

Nevertheless, the first man to be named as a first baseman on this mythical club is Lou Gehrig, another of the Yankee all-time greats. And Gehrig never hit .400 nor did he ever hit as many as 50 home runs in a single season.

Actually, Gehrig was the most consistent and dangerous hitter of the quintet. He had far greater power than Terry and Sisler and he outhit Foxx and Greenberg on average. In his career, he drove in 1,991 runs and the one man who topped that figure was the aforementioned Ruth, who stands alone as having batted in more than 2,000 runs.

133

He was called the "Iron Horse" because of his durable strength and apparent invulnerability to aches and pains, and one record he holds is of awesome proportions.

On June 1, 1925, Gehrig replaced Wally Pipp as first baseman of the Yankees. The next time the Yankees played an American League game without him was on May 2, 1939.

It is unlikely that Gehrig's string of 2,130 consecutive appearances will ever be topped for, until now, no ballplayer has ever remotely approached it.

The millions of baseball fans who have sprung up since the tragic end of Gehrig's career and his subsequent death probably do not realize that Lou was as great as he was durable.

As a matter of fact, the fans of Gehrig's own era seemed to lack a proper appreciation of Lou's ability. He was a quiet and diffident man. If he did not precisely shun the spotlight, it might be said that the spotlight seemed to shun him.

In the beginning, he was the junior partner of Babe Ruth in the strongest one-two punch ever contained in a single batting order. At the end, or almost up to the end, he was still a methodical, consistent slugger outglamorized in the eyes of the crowds by the remarkably graceful and dramatically appealing Joe DiMaggio.

He spent all or parts of 17 seasons with the Yankees, but the long prime of his career covered 12 years, starting with 1926, his second season as a regular.

His batting averages from that point through 1937 were .313, .373, .374, .300, .379, .341, .349, .334, .363, .329, .354, and .351.

His home run totals over the same 12 years were 16, 47, 27, 35, 41, 46, 34, 32, 49, 30, 49, and 37.

In 1931, he drove in 184 runs, still an American League record. He led his league in runs batted in five times. He was batting champion in 1934. He tied Ruth for the home-run leadership in 1931, led the league in homers in 1934 and 1936

134

and was runner-up to the home-run leader in five other seasons.

At the finish his lifetime batting average was .340 and, numbered in his 2,721 hits were 535 doubles, 161 triples and 494 home runs.

In the matter of lifetime average, the top three first basemen enrolled in Cooperstown would fit under a handkerchief, as the saying goes. Bill Terry has a shade at .341. One must carry the averages out to an extra point to split Sisler and Gehrig. Sisler stands at .3401. Gehrig finished at .3400.

To wind up this explosion of figures, Lou was one of the greatest of World Series performers. He played in seven for a grand average of .361. Ten of his 43 hits were homers. He batted in 35 runs in 34 games.

The Iron Horse grew up as an iron colt on the sidewalks of New York. The son of industrious German immigrants, he was born on June 2, 1903 in the Yorkville section of the town, scarcely more than a line drive from the brewery operated by Col. Jacob Ruppert, who was to become big boss of the ball club Gehrig served so long and so well.

Henry Louis—to give him his full baptismal handle—was a big baby who swiftly grew into a strong boy. There were vacant lots in Manhattan then and, in later years, Lou could not remember when and where he first started to bat, throw, and catch a baseball.

By the time he reached his teens, the Gehrig family had moved to the Bronx and Lou ultimately found himself playing football and baseball for the High School of Commerce. His school won the greater New York P.S.A.L. championship in 1920 and earned, as a reward, a trip to Chicago for an intercity game with Lane Technical High School. That afternoon the 17-year-old Gehrig hit a home run completely out of Wrigley Field with the bases filled.

Actually, the Giants and not the Yankees initiated Lou's professional career but that turned out to be a false start. Arthur

Devlin, an old third baseman for John McGraw, had seen Lou belt that Chicago home run and that led to a proposition offered the following June when Gehrig received his high school diploma.

Gehrig demurred. He had accepted a football scholarship at Columbia, his family was enthusiastic over the idea of a college education and he was a dutiful son.

He was conned into the idea that he could play for Hartford in the Eastern League under an assumed name (with ultimate graduation to the Giants, of course) and that everything would be all right. It didn't turn out that way. A lad called "Lou Lewis" had played only a dozen games before the athletic authorities at Columbia found out what was going on and Gehrig was called on the carpet for a reading of the riot act.

The upshot was that Gehrig was ineligible for athletics as a Columbia freshman. As a sophomore, he played guard for the Lions on the gridiron and then began to attract attention regularly when the 1923 baseball season began.

Andy Coakley, who had been a major league pitcher, was the Columbia baseball coach and, at first, Andy didn't know what to do with this bundle of left-handed talent which stood an inch over six feet and weighed 175 hard pounds. Gehrig was his best left-handed pitcher, but also far and away his best hitter. Obviously, he had to play in every game. He showed no skill as an outfielder and it seemed the lesser of existing evils to play him at first base.

No matter what position Gehrig played he overpowered all the college pitching that opposed him. Paul Krichell, the Yankee scout who ultimately signed him, first watched Lou in a game against Rutgers at New Brunswick and was sold immediately when the kid crashed two prodigious home runs into the New Jersey woods behind the right field fence.

A matter of timing helped the Yankees get Gehrig at this point. His own eagerness and that of his family for a college degree had been somewhat dimmed by academic grades somewhat short of spectacular. Besides, Lou's dad had suffered a long illness and medical bills had mounted. The Gehrigs needed the $1,500 the Yankees paid.

And so, June of 1923 found Lou back at Hartford, this time under his own name, and as a Yankee farmhand. He batted .304 in 59 Eastern League games and was brought back to the Yankee Stadium in September to hit .423 and his first major league home run. That fall, he sat on the bench as the Yankees beat the Giants in the World Series.

Nevertheless, it was back to Hartford in 1924 and this time Gehrig hit .369, then an even .500 in ten Yankee games at the end of the season. In the spring of 1925, there was no doubt that Lou would stay. He had attained his physical maturity and the wide left-handed stance with the short stride that characterized his hitting style.

For all of his superb natural tools, Lou was not a ready-made star. For instance, he always could hit the fast ball but had to learn to hit the curve. He had to learn to play first base. These were problems he tackled with Teutonic thoroughness.

"Lou didn't learn quickly, but he learned methodically," said Wally Pipp.

Pipp was the resident first baseman at the Stadium when Gehrig arrived, a smooth, experienced performer who had been one of the American League's top home run hitters in the era of the dead ball. In later years, Wally's favorite story was how he happened to get himself dispossessed.

"I had a headache one day," said Pipp, "and asked the Yankee trainer for a couple of aspirins. Miller Huggins overheard me and suggested that I take the afternoon off while Gehrig played in my place.

"That was on June 2, 1925. The next time I played first base it was 1926 and I was with the Cincinnati Reds."

The subtitle of Frank Graham's excellent biography of

Gehrig is "A Quiet Hero." That is an entirely fitting description of a modest, somewhat shy man. Actually, he wasn't a loner but he was reserved. In his earlier Yankee years, his mother accompanied him to spring training, which is unusual but didn't seem so to Gehrig who was devoted to her.

At the end of the 1933 season Lou married Eleanor Twitchell, a Chicago girl who helped bring out his social side to a greater extent. At least in public, he began to exhibit an ease and self confidence which hadn't been obvious before. And, on the road, he enjoyed billiards and relaxed easily with Bill Dickey, his roommate for many years.

"But I guess I'll never really be a headline guy," Gehrig once said at the height of his career.

His greatest day on the ball field provided a case in point. On June 3, 1932, Gehrig hit four home runs in a game at Shibe Park, Philadelphia to become the first player to accomplish that feat in the twentieth century.

The four home runs were delivered in successive times at bat. The first three were hit off George Earnshaw, one of the great right-handers of the day, the fourth off LeRoy Mahaffey. On his fifth trip to the plate, Gehrig almost got another, but his line drive hit the top of the scoreboard and bounced back on the field.

But to have learned these details in the next day's papers, you'd have had to read far down on the sports pages of New York. For on the day Gehrig was wrecking the Athletics, John J. McGraw, absolutely without warning, decided to resign as manager of the Giants after 30 years.

The day was to come when Gehrig's name was to figure in big, black headlines and this would be a happier story if that hadn't happened.

Toward the end of the 1938 season, Lou began to slump, a rare occurrence for so consistent a hitter. For the first time since 1925, he fell below .300 to a still respectable .295. He finished with 29 home runs, an impressive number for most players, but a figure well below the Gehrig average.

Still, nobody was alarmed. Even Gehrig believed that his batting swing had been affected by nothing more serious than a temporary loss of timing. He went south for spring training in 1939 as big and as strong as ever so far as his physical appearance was concerned; but suddenly and obviously he was all washed up.

His performance was pathetic in Florida exhibition games. His batting swing still was beautifully grooved but even when he hit the ball it went no place to speak of. His reflexes around first base were uncertain and still the Yankees and Gehrig himself hoped he could snap out of it.

Joe McCarthy, then Yankee manager, was not a sentimental man but he loved Gehrig and gave him every chance as the season began. After the first eight games, Lou had four hits—all singles—in 28 times at bat.

Finally, Gehrig, himself, made the move. As the Yankees opened a western trip in Detroit on May 2, Lou met McCarthy in the hotel lobby before the game and said what was on his mind.

"I'm not helping myself and I'm hurting the club," said Lou. "You'd better let Babe Dahlgren take over."

Afterwards, Lou told intimates that in his 2,130th consecutive game, half a dozen of his teammates had crowded around him and slapped him on the back after he had fielded a routine ground ball to end the inning.

"It was a simple, easy play," said Lou, "and the fact that the boys seemed surprised made me realize that I couldn't go on."

He played in only one more game a few weeks later, appearing for five innings of an exhibition in the Middle West. That night, he went to Rochester, Minnesota for a complete check-up at the Mayo Clinic. The report, made public after a few days, amounted to a sentence of death. He was suffering from a rare ailment called "amyotrophic lateral sclerosis."

This is a type of illness involving the motor pathways and cells of the central nervous system and a form of chronic polio-myelitis.

Gehrig was a brave man. He was captain of the Yankees, stayed with the team, handed the lineup to the umpires at home plate before each game. They gave him a tremendous day on July 4 and there were few dry eyes at Yankee Stadium when Lou stepped to the home plate microphone to deliver a few words of thanks.

"I may have been given a bad break," he said, "but with all this I have a lot to live for. I consider myself the luckiest man on the face of this earth."

Before the summer was over, Lou's gait had developed a halting limp and he no longer took the lineup to the plate. He stayed with the team and watched the Yankees knock off the Cincinnati Reds in four straight World Series games, then took off a baseball uniform for the last time.

The end came on June 2, 1941, the 16th anniversary of the day Wally Pipp had a headache and a tremendous ballplayer took over as Yankee first baseman.

HENRY LOUIS GEHRIG

Born, June 19, 1903, New York, New York.
Died, June 2, 1941, New York, New York.
Height 6'1". Weight 215. Batted and threw left-handed.

Year	Club	League	Pos.	G	AB	R	H	2B	3B	HR	RBI	BA
1923	New York	Amer.	1B	13	26	6	11	4	1	1	9	.423
1924	New York	Amer.	1B	10	12	2	6	1	0	0	6	.500
1925	New York	Amer.	1B	126	437	73	129	23	10	21	68	.295
1926	New York	Amer.	1B	155	572	135	179	47	20	16	107	.313
1927	New York	Amer.	1B	155	584	149	218	52	18	47	175	.373
1928	New York	Amer.	1B	154	562	139	210	47	13	27	142	.374
1929	New York	Amer.	1B	154	553	127	166	33	9	35	126	.300
1930	New York	Amer.	1B	154	581	143	220	42	17	41	174	.379
1931	New York	Amer.	1B	155	619	163	211	31	15	46	184	.341

HENRY LOUIS GEHRIG (*Continued*)

Year	Club	League	Pos.	G	AB	R	H	2B	3B	HR	RBI	BA
1932	New York	Amer.	1B	156	596	138	208	42	9	34	151	.349
1933	New York	Amer.	1B	152	593	138	198	41	12	32	139	.334
1934	New York	Amer.	1B	154	579	128	210	40	6	49	165	.363
1935	New York	Amer.	1B	149	535	125	176	26	10	30	119	.329
1936	New York	Amer.	1B	155	579	167	205	37	7	49	152	.354
1937	New York	Amer.	1B	157	569	138	200	37	9	37	159	.351
1938	New York	Amer.	1B	157	576	115	170	32	6	29	114	.295
1939	New York	Amer.	1B	8	28	2	4	0	0	0	1	.143
Major League Totals				**2164**	**8001**	**1888**	**2721**	**535**	**162**	**494**	**1991**	**.340**

WORLD SERIES RECORD

Year	Club	League	Pos.	G	AB	R	H	2B	3B	HR	RBI	BA
1926	New York	Amer.	1B	7	23	1	8	2	0	0	3	.348
1927	New York	Amer.	1B	4	13	2	4	2	2	0	5	.308
1928	New York	Amer.	1B	4	11	5	6	1	0	4	9	.545
1932	New York	Amer.	1B	4	17	9	9	1	0	3	8	.529
1936	New York	Amer.	1B	6	24	5	7	1	0	2	7	.292
1937	New York	Amer.	1B	5	17	4	5	1	1	1	3	.294
1938	New York	Amer.	1B	4	14	4	4	0	0	0	0	.286
World Series Totals				**34**	**119**	**30**	**43**	**8**	**3**	**10**	**35**	**.361**

* key
Pos. = position
G = games
AB = at bat
R = runs
H = hits
2B = two-base hits or doubles
3B = three-base hits or triples
HR = home run
RBI = runs batted in
BA = batting average

141

16

ROGERS HORNSBY
The Rajah from Texas

IN THE MID-20's, Rogers Hornsby had reached the top of his arch as right-handed slugger extraordinary and the Brooklyn Dodgers had a young pitcher named Leo Dickerman scheduled to work against the Cardinals on a certain afternoon.

Before the game Dickerman approached Jack Fournier, the rugged Dodger first baseman.

"You played with Hornsby in St. Louis," said Dickerman, "so how do you suggest I pitch to him?"

"Keep the ball inside," answered Fournier, immediately and emphatically.

In the first inning, Hornsby hit an inside pitch into the left field bleachers. In the fourth inning, he whistled a shot past the third baseman's ears and down the line for two bases.

"I thought you said Hornsby couldn't hit the inside pitch," Dickerman challenged Fournier on the bench.

"I said nothing of the kind," retorted the first baseman, "but I consider myself too young and handsome to be killed by a line drive."

It was here that Dickerman delivered himself of an observation that has been repeated often enough to have become a semiclassic.

"On this ball club," said the young pitcher, "it is everyone for himself."

Leo Dickerman never found out how to pitch to Hornsby and he had plenty of company.

Hornsby's hitting style was unique. He stood far back in the batter's box and farther away from the plate than any other good hitter before or since.

His stance was easy and relaxed with his feet close together, then the ball was pitched and the Rajah took a tremendous stride as he stepped up to meet the ball.

It is fair to say that any pitcher looking at Hornsby for the first time reached an identical conclusion. "If we keep the ball low and away," they thought, "we'll get him out. I don't see how he can even reach that pitch."

Hornsby not only could reach that outside pitch. He could annihilate it. Many used to say that Rog was a rare type of hitter because, although right-handed, his greatest power was to right center field. This wasn't precisely true. Hornsby hit with great power to all fields, but an unusual number of his long drives went to right center because he got so many outside strikes to hit. He never, or almost never, tried to place his hits, was satisfied to hit the ball "where it was pitched," as they say in the dugouts.

When it was all over, Hornsby had a lifetime batting average of .358, a mark topped only by Tyrus Raymond Cobb, a left-handed hitter with great speed getting down to first base.

And not even Cobb matched Hornsby's performance over a five-year period when the Rajah perhaps was the hottest hitter ever seen.

Those five years started in 1921 and the Rajah's respective batting averages were .397, .401, .384, .424, and .403. In those seasons, Hornsby went to bat 2,679 times and delivered 1,078 hits for an overall average of .402.

The 42 home runs he hit in 1922 was a National League record until Hack Wilson created the present league mark of 56 in 1930. His .424 average in 1924 is still the highest batting average compiled in the 20th century by either a right- or left-handed hitter.

The book tells you that Hornsby's playing career in the majors spanned 23 seasons. That's deceptive because he played little in the last nine of those campaigns. In 1929, the Rajah played 156 games and hit .380 to help the Cubs win the pennant. He was then only 33 but managed to play in as many as 100 games in only one subsequent season.

Hornsby won the batting championship for six consecutive seasons as a Cardinal and later added a seventh batting championship as a member of the Boston Braves. That still left him one short of the eight batting championships hung up by Honus Wagner, his great predecessor and only serious rival to be considered as the best right-handed hitter who ever played in the National League.

If you think Rogers Hornsby makes this ball club because he was the greatest right-handed hitter in the last half-century you have the idea exactly.

There have been other famed second basemen cast in a more classic mold.

Napoleon Lajoie also was a thunderous right-handed hitter and a polished fielder, but he properly belongs in an earlier era. Few are left who saw this handsome French-Canadian from Rhode Island at his best. These never refer to him without mention of the stylish grace of his every move on the ballfield.

Eddie Collins was the greatest individual performer of Connie Mack's $100,000 infield. Remember this was a price tag of 50 years ago. The quartet of Stuffy McInnis, Collins, Home Run Baker, and Jack Barry would be a bargain at ten times that figure today.

A left-handed hitter, Collins was regarded as an infielder as brainy as Cobb and not far below the old Georgia Peach as a hitter. His lifetime batting average was .333 over 25 seasons. He was remarkably steady in the field, a master of position play. He seemed to pop up from a trapdoor in front of ground balls.

Frank Frisch, Hornsby's own contemporary, was a scrambler with greater lateral range than the Rajah. He also was a switch-hitter with two-way power and one of the top baserunners of his time.

Defensively, Charley Gehringer may have been the greatest of second basemen although he could also be called the least exciting of all players of that position who reached the Hall of Fame. Gehringer fielded with such even perfection that he was known as "the mechanical man."

The Rajah is not remembered as a great second baseman but it is a mistake to assume that he wasn't a good one. When he came up he had strong, fast legs and excellent range. His speed did not last and Hornsby became more stationary toward the end of his career. Even then he made one play superlatively well. Covering as pivot man on a double play, he had the knack of throwing sidearm and across his body to first base, scarcely shifting his feet at all. It was a graceful thing to watch and saved split seconds that made the difference in many close plays at first.

Hornsby's weakness on pop flies has been so widely publicized that later generations of fans must think that Rog never caught one. This is incorrect. It is true that catching the pop fly was not one of his major accomplishments. So he let other infielders take over on those hit within the confines of the diamond and never ran off a right fielder charging in for a Texas Leaguer. This was only common sense and Hornsby, so far as playing baseball was concerned, was an extremely practical man.

It is interesting that Hornsby got an early chance with the Cardinals not because anyone suspected that he would develop into a devastating power hitter but because of his teen-age talent as a shortstop.

The legend is that Bob Connery, the scout responsible, got a tip from a railroad conductor while beating the Texas sagebrush in a search for talent. Trainmen and itinerant shoe salesmen were always being credited with miraculous finds in those days. In this case, the tale may have been true.

At any rate, Denison, a Texas city in the Western Association, would be a place far off-beat for a scout of Connery's reputation, but there Connery was and there Hornsby was and a deal was closed for a reputed $500.

Born in Winters, Texas, April 27, 1896, Hornsby had started as an 18-year-old shortstop and batted only .232 in the long-gone Texas-Oklahoma League. Connery acquired him in 1915 when he lifted his average to .277. Before the season was over, he had played 18 games for the Cardinals, hitting .246.

At this time, Hornsby was almost as tall as he ever was to be, but outrageously skinny, weighing under 150 pounds. Still, Miller Huggins, then manager of the Cardinals, was impressed with the kid and advised him to eat plenty of steak and drink plenty of milk and get plenty of rest during the winter in an effort to fill out his gangling frame.

Even Huggins was surprised the following spring when Rog showed up with about 20 added pounds of muscle and strength. The dedication with which the young man followed his manager's advice was typical of the determination throughout his entire career to maintain the best physical condition possible.

Good steaks remained his favorite food and milk his favorite drink. He never smoked and never drank anything alcoholic. To save his eyes, he never attended the movies and, except for brief glances at the sports pages, never read even newspapers. Whenever possible, he spent ten or 12 hours a night in the sack.

In his later playing years and through his post-playing days, the Rajah was a highly controversial character. In his case, this was due to no odd traits of personality but to his glorious independence born of complete self-reliance. He said what he

146

thought to everybody including bosses who did not care to be told by an employee that they were muttonheads.

His confidence is illustrated by his own analysis of his success as a hitter. "I had ability," he said late in his life, "and I never saw the pitcher I didn't think I could hit. To tell the truth, I felt sorry for most of the poor slobs trying to get me out."

He was a horseplayer and made no bones about it, although any association with gambling made Judge Kenesaw Mountain Landis, baseball's first commissioner, quiver with rage and indignation.

Hornsby maintained that betting on horses was his own business and that no more moral turpitude was involved than speculating in the stock market.

"As a matter of fact," he once said, "I lost less money betting on horses than I did in the stock market on tips supplied by club owners."

He became player-manager of the Cardinals in mid-season of 1925, succeeding Branch Rickey, and was acclaimed as a great inspirational leader when the Cardinals brought a pennant to St. Louis and beat the Yankees in the World Series of 1926.

Then before the following winter was over, Hornsby was traded to the Giants for Frank Frisch and an old pitcher named Jimmy Ring, and the more rabid St. Louis fans hanged Sam Breadon in effigy. It seemed that Hornsby had bawled out Breadon for scheduling an exhibition game in the late stages of the pennant race and wanted a $50,000 contract to continue as player-manager.

A complication developed because Hornsby owned 1,000 shares of stock in the Cardinals which had to be transferred before he could play for the Giants. He had purchased it for $45 a share and Breadon screamed to the skies when Hornsby demanded $116,000 for his holdings. He got it, too.

He lasted only one season with the Giants, then was passed

to the Boston Braves in an even more astonishing deal. It seems that John McGraw had a high regard for Hornsby's qualifications of leadership and made the Rajah temporary manager of the team through several periods of illness.

It was in one of these that Charles Stoneham, who owned the Giants, questioned Hornsby's judgment on a bit of ball-field strategy. Hornsby's forceful reply suggested that Stoneham stick to his brokerage office and leave the business of playing baseball to baseball people.

It turned out that the 1926 pennant was the only one attained by a team managed by Hornsby although he bossed the Braves, the Cubs, and the Reds in the National League. He also served two hitches as skipper of the St. Louis Browns and half a dozen clubs in the minor leagues.

In his playing days, Hornsby had few intimates among the other athletes but no outright enemies either. As a manager, the general impression is that he was too exacting and uncompromising to get the best out of the new breed of young ballplayers.

Nevertheless, Hornsby went through his later years uncomplaining and happy with any job connected with the only profession he knew or cared about. In one period of idleness in organized baseball, he was hired by the city recreation department of Chicago to coach playground youngsters and worked long hours with the kids.

In the last year of his life—1962—the Rajah wore a big league uniform again as a batting coach for Casey Stengel's Mets.

The end that winter was entirely unexpected. At 65, he was still a powerful and handsome man, troubled only by an ailment of his once famous batting eyes. At last, he was persuaded to enter a hospital for an operation to remove cataracts.

This probably was the first time in his life that Hornsby was confined to bed for any period of time. While in the hospital, he suffered a stroke. He appeared to be making a nice recovery from that when a sudden and fatal heart attack hit and the Rajah was gone.

ROGERS HORNSBY

Born, April 27, 1896, Winters, Texas.
Died, January 5, 1963, Chicago, Illinois.
Height 5'11½". Weight 200. Batted and threw right-handed.

Year	Club	League	Pos.	G	AB	R	H	2B	3B	HR	RBI	BA
1915	St. Louis	Nat.	2B	18	57	5	14	2	0	0	4	.246
1916	St. Louis	Nat.	2B	139	495	63	155	17	15	6	60	.313
1917	St. Louis	Nat.	2B	145	523	86	171	24	17	8	70	.327
1918	St. Louis	Nat.	2B	115	416	51	117	19	11	5	59	.281
1919	St. Louis	Nat.	2B	138	512	68	163	15	9	8	68	.318
1920	St. Louis	Nat.	2B	149	589	96	218	44	20	9	94	.370
1921	St. Louis	Nat.	2B	154	592	131	235	44	18	21	126	.397
1922	St. Louis	Nat.	2B	154	623	141	250	46	14	42	152	.401
1923	St. Louis	Nat.	2B	107	424	89	163	32	10	17	83	.384
1924	St. Louis	Nat.	2B	143	536	121	227	43	14	25	94	.424
1925	St. Louis	Nat.	2B	138	504	133	203	41	10	39	143	.403
1926	St. Louis [1]	Nat.	2B	134	527	96	167	34	5	11	93	.317
1927	New York [2]	Nat.	2B	155	568	133	205	32	9	26	125	.361
1928	Boston [3]	Nat.	2B	140	486	99	188	42	7	21	94	.387
1929	Chicago	Nat.	2B	156	602	156	229	47	7	40	149	.380
1930	Chicago	Nat.	2B	42	104	15	32	5	1	2	18	.308
1931	Chicago	Nat.	2B	100	357	64	118	37	1	16	90	.331
1932	Chicago [4]	Nat.	2B	19	58	10	13	2	0	1	7	.224
1933	St. Louis [5]	Nat.	2B	46	83	9	27	6	0	2	21	.325
1933	St. Louis	Amer.	2B	11	9	2	3	1	0	1	2	.333
1934	St. Louis	Amer.	2B	24	23	2	7	2	0	1	11	.304
1935	St. Louis	Amer.	2B	10	24	1	5	3	0	0	3	.208
1936	St. Louis	Amer.	2B	2	5	1	2	0	0	0	2	.400
1937	St. Louis	Amer.	2B	20	56	7	18	3	0	1	11	.321
National League Totals				2192	8056	1566	2895	532	168	299	1550	.359
American League Totals				67	117	13	35	9	0	3	29	.299
Major League Totals				**2259**	**8173**	**1579**	**2930**	**541**	**168**	**302**	**1579**	**.358**

[1] Traded to New York for Infielder Frank Frisch and Pitcher Jimmy Ring, December 20, 1926.

[2] Traded to Boston for Catcher Shanty Hogan and Outfielder Jimmy Welsh, January 10, 1928.

[3] Traded to Chicago for Infielder Freddie Maguire, Catcher Doc Leggett, Pitchers Harry Siebold, Bruce Cunningham, and Percy Jones and $200,000, November 7, 1928.

[4] Released August 2, 1932; Signed with St. Louis, October 24, 1932.

[5] Released by St. Louis Cardinals, July 25, 1933; signed to manage St. Louis Browns following day.

WORLD SERIES RECORD

Year	Club	League	Pos.	G	AB	R	H	2B	3B	HR	RBI	BA
1926	St. Louis	Nat.	2B	7	28	2	7	1	0	0	4	.250
1929	Chicago	Nat.	2B	5	21	4	5	1	1	0	1	.238
	World Series Totals			12	49	6	12	2	1	0	5	.245

* key
Pos. = position
G = games
AB = at bat
R = runs
H = hits
2B = two-base hits or doubles
3B = three-base hits or triples
HR = home run
RBI = runs batted in
BA = batting average

17

HANS WAGNER
The Flying Dutchman

THE MAN'S NAME was John Peter Wagner. He was generally known as Honus or Hans and sometimes those poetically inclined referred to him as the Flying Dutchman.

He died in 1955 at the age of 81, leaving a tremendous legend of his baseball skills. Perhaps the scope of his reputation is best illustrated by the fact that he played his last game in the majors in 1917, yet succeeding generations of baseball men never have seriously tried to advance another name as Wagner's superior as an all-around shortstop.

This is particularly significant because historically shortstop is a position manned by fine ballplayers. It is almost axiomatic that a pennant-winning ball club must have a good shortstop. This means there have been many good ones and a few who might even be called great.

But there never has been another Wagner.

John McGraw called Wagner the greatest ballplayer he ever saw. The doughty manager of the Giants knew Ty Cobb well enough to have been involved in a long-standing feud with the famed Georgia Peach. McGraw also lived long enough to have witnessed the peak years of Babe Ruth.

Of course, it is true that Cobb and Ruth were American Leaguers and that McGraw wound up inextricably in the National League. And yet after due allowances for provincial prejudice on McGraw's part, there is evidence to suggest that Wagner might have been as McGraw said he was.

Wagner's National League career covered 21 seasons, the first three in Louisville before the turn of the century when there were ten clubs, the remainder in Pittsburgh. He hit for .300 or better in his first seventeen seasons and won eight batting championships, still a National League record. His lifetime batting average was .329.

For many years, Wagner's name was spread all over the record book. Lately, most of these National League marks have been surpassed by Stan Musial, who, in a duel of longevity, had certain advantages over old Honus. Stan reached the majors earlier in life and spent his career in the outfield or at first base, in positions much less wearing than shortstop.

Honus was a rugged-featured man, unquestionably of great strength. He stood five feet, eleven inches and weighed around 200 pounds. Long arms, ending in immense gnarled hands, dangled from his broad shoulders. His bowed legs were caricatured in thousands of sports page cartoons.

On sheer appearance—he looked sloppy in a baseball uniform, too—he'd have been tossed off the lot if he ever had appeared in Hollywood seeking a job as extra in a baseball picture. No one ever heard his actions described as graceful and, undoubtedly, he was ungainly.

There must have been something curiously deceptive about Wagner, especially about his speed. It is a matter of record that the 720 bases he stole is a total surpassed by only three men in the history of the game—Cobb, Billy Hamilton, a speedster of the 19th century, and Max Carey.

Incidentally, the career of Carey, perhaps the most scientific base-stealer who ever lived, and that of Wagner coincided for six years. And Carey had established himself as a shortstop of rare promise when he first joined the Pirates late in the season of 1910.

"They told me when I joined the club," said Carey, long afterwards, "that the old man couldn't go much further and that I'd surely be the next Pittsburgh shortstop. After watching Wagner in a couple of games I decided that life was too short for me to wait."

By the time Wagner did retire seven years afterwards, Carey was one of the finest of center fielders, a career that carried Max into the Cooperstown Hall of Fame.

Getting back, for a moment, to the larceny that beat in the honest German heart of old Honus. He led the league in theft five times. From 1904 through 1908, he stole 277 bases, an average of slightly better than 55 a season. He stole six bases in the 1909 World Series against the Detroit Tigers.

Modesty and pride were integral parts of Wagner's nature. A couple of incidents that involve him had results which may have surprised him.

In the early years of the century, there was a firm that printed small colored cards of ballplayers for use as insets in various brands of cigarettes. For permission to use his picture, each player received the munificent sum of $10.

Wagner returned the check with a letter. He wrote apologetically that he meant no disrespect to the product because he, himself, smoked. But he realized that kids would wind up as collectors of these cards and he could not, in good conscience, lend his name to a project that might encourage youngsters to smoke.

Never dreaming that Wagner would not give his approval, the printers had gone ahead with preparing a Wagner card. When the letter was received, the plates were destroyed but in the meanwhile a few of the cards had been distributed.

The result: Well, if Wagner's decision ever had much influence upon the smoking habits of the nation's youth, that fact has been well-hidden. But collectors today drive themselves frantic trying to locate one of these Wagner cards which would complete a set of 522 pictures. There are only four known to be in existence. One is in New York's National Museum of Art. The three others are owned by private collectors who would rather mortgage their homes than sell them.

Wagner's loyalty to Barney Dreyfuss, owner of the Pirates, during the brief but bitter baseball war that firmly established the American League also backfired in a strange way.

Ban Johnson was president and an organizing genius of the American League. His path, as he raided National League rosters for good ballplayers, was made easy by the fact that, by agreement, National League clubs had a maximum—not minimum—salary of $2,400 for any player, no matter how distinguished.

Johnson personally signed many good ballplayers and assigned them to various clubs in his fledgling league in order to assure a reasonable distribution of talent. But when he tried to sign Wagner, he ran into a brick wall. For no money in the world would Honus "jump" his contract with the Pirates.

Result: Wagner couldn't possibly have done anything more beneficial to the welfare of the American League.

When he failed to grab Wagner, Johnson had an attack of real inspiration. He laid off the Pittsburgh club entirely while continuing to raid the seven other teams in the National League.

In 1902, the American League had an exciting pennant race while the National League campaign was a farce which Pittsburgh won by the incredible margin of 27½ games. That winter a treaty of peace was signed in which the National League, in effect, acknowledged the new league as a worthy rival and admitted it to equal privileges.

John Peter Wagner was born in Mansfield, Pennsylvania, which is not far from Pittsburgh and which has been renamed Carnegie on February 24, 1874. He was the son of German immigrants, the fourth in a family of six children. His father was a miner and these were hard times. Johannes was big and strong at the age of 12, so he too went underground. He loaded coal cars at 79 cents a ton, and, on a real good day, might load two tons.

It is altogether impossible that the humanitarian impulses of 19th-century mine operators have been somewhat maligned. It appears that they did not permit even large children to work on Sundays.

And so, once a week regularly, Honus got into the open air and on summer Sundays he watched his older brother, Al, play on the town baseball team. And when the Mansfield team played out of town, Honus frequently walked a dozen miles into Pittsburgh to watch the Pirates. He didn't have the price of admission, of course, but he was young and strong and he could climb a tree outside the park.

At 15, Honus was playing on the town team himself but he was past voting age before he ever tied up with a club in organized baseball. In his first season—the year was 1895—he was a member of three different clubs. He played at Adrian in the Michigan State League, Steubenville of the Tri-State League, and Warren of the Iron-Oil League.

Adrian, of course, is in Michigan. Steubenville and Warren are Ohio towns. At this long range, it is impossible to learn just why Honus went from one place to another but it certainly wasn't because he didn't hit. His batting averages, respectively, were .365, .402 and .369.

Ed Barrow, who wound up his long career in baseball as builder and general manager of the Yankees, generally is credited as Wagner's Columbus. The fact is that Honus already had completed this first year in organized ball before Barrow signed him to play for the club he operated in 1897—Paterson, New Jersey in the long-gone Atlantic League. After a season and a half, Barrow did strongly recommend Wagner to his friend, Fred Clarke, manager of Louisville, then in the National League.

There is a legend that Honus hit one to the fence in one of his early National League games against the famed Baltimore Orioles. Joe Doyle gave him the hip as he rounded first, Hughey Jennings backed into his path and caused him to run wide at second and McGraw was waiting at third to jam the ball into his ribs like a bayonet.

Instead of sympathy, the good-humored Wagner got a dressing down from Clarke. "You'll be back in Carnegie in a hurry," barked the manager, "if you don't learn how to take care of them."

Later in the game, Wagner hit another long one. This time he ran over Doyle like a runaway tank, inducing Jennings to move prudently out of the way. Then Wagner's high slide into third knocked McGraw halfway to the grandstand.

As McGraw dusted himself off, he paid Wagner what was intended to be a compliment. "For a dumb Dutchman," he said, "you catch on fast."

When Louisville was dropped after the 1899 season, that club's better ballplayers—including Wagner, Rube Waddell, the oddball pitching genius, and Clarke, a fine outfielder as well as a noted manager—were taken by the Pirates.

The new eight-club National League was dominated by three teams for 13 years. Over that stretch, New York won five pennants, Chicago and Pittsburgh four apiece. It was dog-eat-dog. The Giants were managed by the belligerent McGraw after 1902. Frank Chance, the "peerless leader" of the Cubs would rather fight than eat. Clarke would back away from no man.

Despite a reputation for docility, Wagner had little trouble. The word was around the league—"Let that big guy sleep or you'll be sorry."

In his first year at Pittsburgh—1900—Honus won his first batting championship, hitting .380, the highest mark of his career, but he still hadn't found his proper spot in the lineup.

He could play any position. He had been a shortstop in the

156

minors. He was an outfielder in his first year at Louisville, a first baseman and a third baseman in his second year under Clarke, a third baseman and an outfielder in 1899.

In 1900, he was a Pittsburgh outfielder. The next two seasons, he played both infield and outfield positions.

It was late in the season of 1902 that Honus took over at shortstop, replacing a slender, graceful performer named Bones Ely to the great disgust of the Pittsburgh fans.

They booed the initial efforts of the shambling, bowlegged strong man and wound up erecting a huge bronze statue of Wagner at bat in Schenley Park behind Forbes Field.

Although Honus played on four pennant-winning teams, he appeared in only two World Series because that now traditional classic was not initiated until 1903. In the very first World Series, the Red Sox beat the Pirates in eight games and Wagner was disconsolate because he hit only .222.

Six years later, he more than redeemed himself. The 1909 World Series was widely ballyhooed as a duel between Honus, already an elder statesman of the game, and Ty Cobb, the brash and brilliant young outfielder of the Tigers.

Not only did Wagner outhit Cobb in the series—.333 to .200—but Honus stole six bases and Cobb stole a big, fat zero. A story that Wagner and Cobb clashed personally appears to have been greatly exaggerated. Cobb is supposed to have threatened to cut Wagner with his spikes and Wagner is supposed to have rammed the ball down Ty's throat in making a tag.

Wagner was never mad at anybody and Ty, then and afterwards, expressed nothing but admiration for old Honus.

That very winter Wagner expressed a desire to retire. He was susceptible to rheumatism, a hangover from the dampness of the coal pits in which he had worked as a child. But Barney Dreyfuss persuaded him to stick and he played seven more seasons as a regular, the first four as a .300 hitter.

He finished up in 1917, then set another record. In mid-season, Jimmy Callahan, who had succeeded Clarke as manager two years before, was let out and Dreyfuss prevailed upon Wagner to take over. He lasted exactly three days, an all-time mark for managerial brevity in the majors.

"Is not for me," honest Honus told the Pittsburgh owner.

For another ten years Wagner continued to play ball after a fashion.

He managed a semi-pro team that played twilight and week-end ball in the Pittsburgh area, playing first base when his bones did not ache too much and taking an occasional swipe as a pinch hitter. He was well past 50 before he stopped altogether.

He also ran a sporting goods house in Pittsburgh which netted him some income until the depression years when he found himself strapped financially. It was then that he came back to the Pirates as a coach, a popular move acclaimed by banquets and civic parades in Pittsburgh and in Brooklyn, of all places.

Now Honus was really old. His duties were light, consisting mainly of sitting on the bench and gabbing with visitors about old times and guarding the ball bag. Finally came the year that he could no longer travel with the team and not too long after that the end of his life.

The legend he left contains enough truth that is historic to prove that although he started out in the last century John Peter Wagner could have played baseball with distinction at any time including the modern era.

JOHN PETER WAGNER

Born, February 24, 1874, Carnegie, Pennsylvania.
Died, December 6, 1955, Carnegie, Pennsylvania.
Height 5'11". Weight 200. Batted and threw right-handed.

Year	Club	League	Pos.	G	AB	R	H	2B	3B	HR	RBI	BA
1897	Louisville	Nat.	OF	61	241	38	83	17	4	2	...	.344
1898	Louisville	Nat.	1B-3B	148	591	80	180	31	4	10	...	.305
1899	Louisville	Nat.	3B-OF	144	549	102	197	47	13	7	...	.359

JOHN PETER WAGNER (*Continued*)

Year	Club	League	Pos.	G	AB	R	H	2B	3B	HR	RBI	BA
1900	Pittsburgh	Nat.	OF	134	528	107	201	45	22	4	...	.381
1901	Pittsburgh	Nat.	LF-OF	141	556	100	196	39	10	6	...	.353
1902	Pittsburgh	Nat.	LF-OF-SS	137	538	105	177	33	16	3	...	.329
1903	Pittsburgh	Nat.	SS	129	512	97	182	30	19	5	...	.355
1904	Pittsburgh	Nat.	SS	132	490	97	171	44	14	4	..	.349
1905	Pittsburgh	Nat.	SS	147	548	114	199	22	14	6	...	.363
1906	Pittsburgh	Nat.	SS	140	516	103	175	38	9	2	...	.339
1907	Pittsburgh	Nat.	SS	142	515	98	180	38	14	6	91	.350
1908	Pittsburgh	Nat.	SS	151	568	100	201	39	19	10	106	.354
1909	Pittsburgh	Nat.	SS	137	495	92	168	39	10	5	102	.339
1910	Pittsburgh	Nat.	SS	150	556	90	178	34	8	4	84	.320
1911	Pittsburgh	Nat.	SS	130	473	87	158	23	16	9	108	.334
1912	Pittsburgh	Nat.	SS	145	558	91	181	35	20	7	94	.324
1913	Pittsburgh	Nat.	SS	114	413	51	124	18	4	3	55	.300
1914	Pittsburgh	Nat.	SS	150	552	60	139	15	9	1	46	.252
1915	Pittsburgh	Nat.	SS	156	566	68	155	32	17	6	78	.274
1916	Pittsburgh	Nat.	SS	123	432	45	124	15	9	1	38	.287
1917	Pittsburgh	Nat.	SS	74	230	15	61	7	1	0	22	.265
Major League Totals				**2785**	**10427**	**1740**	**3430**	**651**	**252**	**101**	...	**.329**

WORLD SERIES RECORD

Year	Club	League	Pos.	G	AB	R	H	2B	3B	HR	RBI	BA
1903	Pittsburgh	Nat.	SS	8	27	2	6	1	0	0	4	.222
1909	Pittsburgh	Nat.	SS	7	24	4	8	2	1	0	5	.333
World Series Totals				**15**	**51**	**6**	**14**	**3**	**1**	**0**	**9**	**.275**

* key
Pos. = position
G = games
AB = at bat
R = runs
H = hits
2B = two-base hits or doubles
3B = three-base hits or triples
HR = home run
RBI = runs batted in
BA = batting average

18

JACKIE ROBINSON

The Dark Comet

JACKIE ROBINSON called it a baseball career after the 1956 season. That made it 1962 before he was eligible to be placed on a baseball writer's ballot for election to the Hall of Fame.

Election time approached and with it considerable speculation as to whether or not Jackie would be sent to Cooperstown. The then vice-president of the Chock Full o' Nuts Company was asked his opinion and delivered it without pulling punches.

He said, in effect, that he would feel deeply honored if he were elected on the basis of his skills as a ballplayer. But if anyone intended to vote for him primarily because he was a Negro, he'd be pleased if they'd forget all about it.

Robinson, of course, was elected on the very first try and accepted the honor graciously.

The matter is brought up now because of a haunting question.

Was Jackie elected on his own terms?

No one ever will really know. Robinson can't find out and neither can anyone else. The question must remain unanswered because many of the baseball writers who voted for him enthusiastically cannot answer the question even to their own satisfaction.

It is the plain and simple truth that Robinson had great talents on the ball field. It is also the truth that circumstances called upon him to play a vital and historic role in the baseball profession.

These are facts and important component parts of the image of a vibrant, forceful and successful man.

But for the purposes of this piece, you can toss all other considerations to one side. You have left a truly accomplished ballplayer, one uniquely qualified for a place on this mythical team.

His career covered ten eventful years with the Brooklyn Dodgers. The obvious reason why he lasted only a decade is that he was 28 years old before it was possible for him to play at Ebbets Field.

He was the National League's rookie-of-the-year in 1947, its batting champion and most valuable player in 1949.

He was a star of six pennant-winning clubs. Two other Brooklyn teams of his time were beaten in extraordinary fashion. In 1950, the Dodgers lost the pennant to the Phillies in the tenth inning of their last game of the season. In 1951, Bobby Thomson's home run won for the Giants in the ninth inning of the final play-off game.

In six World Series, Robinson played four different positions. He was a first baseman in 1947, a left fielder in 1953, a second baseman in 1949 and 1952 and a third baseman in 1955 and 1956.

His bunting skill and his great speed made it logical to use him as a second-place hitter. He did bat second his first season —and batted in 85 runs. That convinced all hands of his ability as a clutch hitter, so he was dropped to fourth and batted clean-up for most of his later career.

Although his hitting tailed off in his last two seasons, he finished with a lifetime batting average of .311. When he checked out, only Stan Musial and Richie Ashburn among active National Leaguers had higher career averages.

At that point, Jackie had the highest average of any right-handed hitter in the league. He topped Hank Aaron by one point and Willie Mays by five.

He had good power. His 137 home runs represent an adequate figure for one with his line-drive hitting style. He held his bat uncommonly high with his wrists not far from his right ear and rarely uppercut the ball.

He had 273 doubles and 54 triples. Some of these doubles would have been singles and some of these triples would have been doubles for a less fiery performer.

A daring and imaginative baserunner, Jackie did some amazing things. Once in Brooklyn he wound up with a triple on a fly ball that landed not more than 120 feet from home plate.

Almost anyone else would have stopped at first, thankful that the ball hadn't been caught. Robinson was flying low toward second when the second baseman recovered the ball close to the right field line and logically decided that a throw into second was useless.

Then Jackie roared around second and slid into third safely when the second baseman's throw was just a bit off line.

He was the most exciting base-stealer of his time. He finished with 197 thefts, but his average of better than 19 a season reflects only a part of his nuisance value in this respect. A constant threat to steal at all times, Robinson upset the poise of opposing pitchers and disturbed the defensive concentration of opposing infields with his long leads and sudden feints in the direction of the next base.

At least a dozen and probably more of his thefts were steals of home and once he stole home in a World Series. The individual steal of home to differentiate it from the scoring end of a double steal is a rare and exciting thing.

Jackie never matched the record of Pete Reiser, who stole home seven times in one season, but he may have stolen home more often than any other player in the game. There are no records to prove or disprove it.

No one can say how often Robinson rose to an occasion or

how many great games he played. His performance in the final game of the Dodger schedule in 1951 never will be forgotten.

The day started with the Giants and Dodgers tied for first place. The Giants won their game in Boston early and the Dodgers were involved in a wild one at Philadelphia.

In the last of the tenth inning, Robinson saved the game with a diving catch of a line drive described by many as one of the most sensational fielding exploits ever seen. In the gloom of the 14th inning, Jackie lined a home run into the left field seats to project Brooklyn into a playoff.

Under the rules of that time, a tie for the Dodgers would have given the Giants the pennant right there. The Philadelphia Sunday curfew was closing in and there wasn't time for another inning. Ironically, the most conspicuous result of what may have been Robinson's greatest game was that it paved the way for Bobby Thomson's play-off heroics.

Without doubt, Robinson makes a great man for this imaginary ball team. He has all of the qualifications of a fine right-handed pinch hitter, a pinch runner, a utility man of varied talents who could step in and do a job in at least four positions. Maybe more, if he tried.

Everything in the way of sports he ever attempted he did well. He had the size, the strength, the speed and the competitive spirit from the start.

As he grew up in California, he made his first headlines as a football player. In 1938, he led the forces of Pasadena Junior College to 11 straight victories, gained 1,500 yards and scored 131 points. In 1939, he was at U.C.L.A., teamed in the backfield with Kenny Washington, another great colored athlete. U.C.L.A. was unbeaten that year although tied four times and Robinson's rushing average was better than 12 yards.

He was the leading scorer of the southern division of the Coast Conference in basketball. In track, he won the N.C.A.A. broad jump. And, of course, he played baseball.

163

Jackie, although a good student, failed to finish school, leaving in 1941. His mother—a remarkable woman who moved to California from Georgia when Jackie was two and was trying to raise five children on her own—needed income. He took a job, was soon in the army and rose from private to second lieutenant. When mustered out in 1945, he played ball as a shortstop for the Kansas City Monarchs.

The oft-repeated statement that Robinson broke the noxious color line in organized baseball isn't precise. The man who actually broke it was Branch Rickey. Robinson was his chosen instrument and it is difficult to see how the old Mahatma of the Dodgers could have selected a better one.

The story often has been told how Rickey, after his scouts had intensively surveyed the field of Negro baseball talent, sent for Robinson, explained his plan and emphasized the importance of not fighting back when things got rough.

Robinson agreed with Rickey's principle and nobody knows how much it cost him to consent to turn the other cheek. For this was a young man of pride and determination who already had suffered from the slings and arrows of racial discrimination.

There had been California incidents and, even as an army officer, he had been the victim of a ridiculous court martial because of a brush with the Jim Crow laws of the South. He was cleared, but still filled with resentment.

Now Rickey announced that he had signed Robinson to play for the Dodger farm at Montreal and touched off a storm of controversy. There isn't much doubt that the vast majority sided with Rickey and Robinson, but, just as ten people booing in the grandstand drown out 100 who applaud, you wouldn't have thought so.

As an example, the reaction of William G. Bramham stands as perhaps the most ill-considered comment ever delivered by anyone in a position of baseball authority.

"Father Divine will have to look to his laurels," said the commissioner of the minor leagues, "for we can expect Rickey Temple to be constructed in Harlem soon.

"It is those of the carpetbagger stripe of the white race, under the guise of helping, but in truth using the Negro for their own selfish ends, who retard the race. If the Negro is left alone and aided by his own unselfish friends of the white race, he will work out his own salvation."

With that sort of reaction from a highly placed official, you can easily imagine the resentment of some less articulate in the ranks.

In the spring of 1946, Robinson went to training with the Montreal Royals at Sanford, Florida. He was permitted to practice at Sanford, but not to live there and had to commute from Daytona. In Deland, Florida, a local policeman ordered him off the field under penalty of arrest. Several exhibitions were called off. Twice the Royals traveled to Jacksonville for a game and found the park locked when they arrived.

Still, Robinson easily made the Montreal team—as a second baseman because his throwing arm didn't measure to a shortstop's specifications. The verbal abuse he took from opposing benches was scandalous. On the physical side, there was the beanball.

"You never saw anything like it," said Dixie Howell, the catcher who was Robbie's teammate at Montreal and later in Brooklyn. "Everytime he came up, he'd go down."

Still, Jackie hit .349, won the batting championship and the league's Most Valuable Player award. He earned promotion to the Dodgers but Rickey delayed the move. Jackie was on the Montreal roster when 1947 spring training began because Rickey wanted manager Leo Durocher to ask for him.

Durocher had other troubles. This was the spring he was suspended by Commissioner Happy Chandler. So Rickey was forced to make the move on his own. Robinson became a Dodger just before the season started—as a first baseman because that's what the team needed.

There were other complications designed to embarrass Robinson. Certain Dodgers made little effort to conceal their displeasure. Dixie Walker asked to be traded and was accommodated after the season. Others who started out bearing resentment were reconciled and some became more than that, eventually happy that Jackie was on their side.

Peewee Reese and Gil Hodges were among those who did their best to make Robbie feel at home, but Jackie developed no really intimate friends in baseball and perhaps the very nature of the situation made this impossible. By preference Robinson walked alone. As Rickey put it in a flurry of Churchillian rhetoric, "Here was a man whose wounds you could not feel or share."

There were times when Robinson could not stay with the team in hotels around the circuit. In some other cities, he had what might be called limited hotel privileges. There were numerous other annoying incidents on and off the ball field.

The nature of the riding he took from opposing benches was shameful. Ben Chapman, manager of the Phillies, had to be publicly warned by the league to stop the racially-tinged abuse directed at Robinson from his bench.

The St. Louis Cardinals seriously considered a player strike rather than appear at Ebbets Field. Ford Frick, then president of the National League, threatened stern punishment if such a thing occurred.

There was no strike but Cardinal players spiked Robinson four times that first season. And, of course, the stream of beanballs continued.

This went on long after it was evident that Jackie positively would not be intimidated and subsided only somewhat after other colored players reached the majors and a Negro ball-player no longer was a novelty.

By that time, Robinson was firmly established as a star and had veered away from the original "other cheek" policy. He asserted himself in no uncertain terms. He met invective with counter-invective, equally sulphuric. After years of repression, he argued with umpires like other aggressive players and more so than most. He backed away from no man and no situation.

As the years passed, he earned the admiration, however grudgingly, of almost everyone in baseball although his unpopularity grew among certain segments of the public and the day came when he was booed more loudly in Brooklyn than anywhere else. This he proudly ignored. He was satisfied in the knowledge that the people of his own race regarded him as their champion in the lists.

By the end of the 1956 season, Robinson already had established himself with his wonderful wife, Rachel, and their children in a comfortable home in Greenwich, Connecticut. He was having trouble with his legs and had already decided to retire when the Dodgers sold him to the Giants. So the deal was canceled and an eminently successful career in business began.

His fight hasn't ended and it never will. He continues his battle against racial intolerance as an influential member of the N.A.A.C.P. and his voice is heard whenever a new crisis in this area develops.

His contribution already has been great.

His triumph over rough experiences as a trail-blazer made it certain that the way would be easier for all the colored players who followed him and all the colored players who are to come.

No one suggests that baseball has entirely solved its integration problem but the progress in that direction would have seemed unbelievable twenty years ago.

JACK ROOSEVELT ROBINSON

Born, January 31, 1919, Cairo, Georgia.
Height 5'11½". Weight 225. Batted and threw right-handed.

Year	Club	League	Pos.	G	AB	R	H	2B	3B	HR	RBI	BA
1947	Brooklyn	Nat.	1B	151	590	125	175	31	5	12	48	.297
1948	Brooklyn	Nat.	1B	147	574	108	170	38	8	12	85	.296
1949	Brooklyn	Nat.	1B	156	593	122	203	38	12	16	124	.342
1950	Brooklyn	Nat.	1B	144	518	99	170	39	4	14	81	.328
1951	Brooklyn	Nat.	1B	153	548	106	185	33	7	19	88	.338
1952	Brooklyn	Nat.	1B	149	510	104	157	17	3	19	75	.308
1953	Brooklyn	Nat.	1B	136	484	109	159	34	7	12	95	.329
1954	Brooklyn	Nat.	1B	124	386	62	120	22	4	15	59	.311
1955	Brooklyn	Nat.	1B	105	317	51	81	6	2	8	36	.256
1956	Brooklyn [1]	Nat.	1B	117	357	61	98	15	2	10	43	.275
Major League Totals				**1382**	**4877**	**947**	**1518**	**273**	**54**	**137**	**734**	**.311**

[1] Traded to New York Giants for Pitcher Dick Littlefield and reported $35,000, December 13, 1956. Robinson announced retirement, January 5, 1957, thus canceling trade.

WORLD SERIES RECORD

Year	Club	League	Pos.	G	AB	R	H	2B	3B	HR	RBI	BA
1947	Brooklyn	Nat.	1B	7	27	3	7	2	0	0	3	.259
1949	Brooklyn	Nat.	2B	5	16	2	3	1	0	0	2	.188
1952	Brooklyn	Nat.	2B	7	23	4	4	0	0	1	2	.174
1953	Brooklyn	Nat.	LF	6	25	3	8	2	0	0	2	.320
1955	Brooklyn	Nat.	3B	6	22	5	4	1	1	0	1	.182
1956	Brooklyn	Nat.	3B	7	24	5	6	1	0	1	2	.250
World Series Totals				**38**	**137**	**22**	**32**	**7**	**1**	**2**	**12**	**.234**

* key
Pos. = position
G   = games
AB = at bat
R   = runs
H   = hits
2B = two-base hits or doubles
3B = three-base hits or triples
HR = home run
RBI = runs batted in
BA = batting average

19

PIE TRAYNOR

A Mild-Mannered Hero

ONE AFTERNOON at Forbes Field, Pittsburgh, some forgotten Dodger lined a single to right and Paul Waner threw to third base in an attempt to cut down a Brooklyn runner trying to move around from first.

The major leagues still used only two umpires in those days and the man in blue calling decisions on the bases this afternoon was Cy Rigler.

Old Cy scurried over as fast as his magnificent embonpoint would permit, which wasn't nearly fast enough. A low-bounding throw into the third baseman's glove and a sliding baserunner arrived practically simultaneously and Rigler had to call a close play from 50 feet away.

As soon as Cy could chug to a stop, he spread his hands outward and downward to indicate the runner was safe whereupon the third baseman indignantly threw his glove into the dirt.

Before the dust had settled, Pie Traynor—for it was he—had been put out of a ball game for the first and only time in his life.

Chilly Doyle, the *Sun-Telegraph* baseball writer and Traynor's close friend, was visibly upset. He visited Rigler after the game and told the umpire, "You shouldn't have bounced Pie just because he threw his glove in a moment of pique."

"That wasn't anything," said Rigler. "It was the language he used."

"But Pie never uses profanity," protested Doyle.

"This was worse than profanity," declared Rigler, but the umpire's eyes were twinkling.

"What did he say?" pressed Doyle.

"He said, 'I am sick and tired of your rotten decisions, Mr. Rigler,' " answered his majesty, the ump.

That was Traynor, a mild-mannered man who nevertheless was a tremendous competitor. He was so accomplished in his chosen profession that all third basemen who have followed him are compared to him if they display uncommon defensive talent.

There have been fine glove men at that position—Red Rolfe, Billy Cox, the Boyer brothers and Brooks Robinson, to name a few. But Traynor also had a lifetime batting average of .320 in the National League.

And defensively, he had it all. Pie could range far to his left and dive to his right to knock down potential shots for extra bases hit over the bag. He could go out for Texas Leaguers and long fouls and throw bunts to first base before the hitter dropped his bat.

He had one of the strongest and most accurate of throwing arms and, if he had a weakness, it was the fact that his first baseman had to be on the alert.

"You had to get there in a hurry," said Charley Grimm, who played first base when Traynor reached the Pirates. "Pie couldn't hold the ball, was afraid of throwing wild if he took time to aim. Picking it up and firing it, he flipped it over as light as a feather and right at your belt buckle and sometimes he threw hitters out by 40 feet."

Pie was a rangy ballplayer—six feet tall and 175 pounds— but although gifted with strength he hit only 58 home runs in the majors, a relatively small total for a good hitter in the era of the lively ball. He cracked the ball on the line and his hard shots lacked the trajectory to sail out of the ball parks.

Only four players named to the baseball Hall of Fame have been third basemen and one of these outhit Traynor.

You may be surprised to know that this was the truculent John J. McGraw. McGraw, doing most of his playing for the 19th-century Baltimore Orioles, had a lifetime batting average of .334, nevertheless was installed at Cooperstown not because of his prowess as a player but because of his long and successful career as manager of the New York Giants.

Some of McGraw's fielding percentages dipped below .900, not unusual before the turn of the century when infielders did the best they could with gloves that resembled delicate thin pancakes.

McGraw, himself, called Traynor the best he ever saw.

A plaque at Cooperstown cites Jimmy Collins as having "revolutionized" third base. Just how he did this is a secret safe with us moderns although Collins, who played in the National League in the '90's before becoming a star with the Boston Red Sox, undoubtedly was a fine ballplayer.

And, finally, there is John Franklin (Home Run) Baker, a stalwart performer for the Philadelphia Athletics in the dead ball years when anywhere from eight to a dozen home runs a season was enough to lead a major league.

Baker, an adequate third baseman, owes his principal fame to the World Series home runs he hit off Christy Mathewson and Rube Marquard of the Giants, so Traynor becomes the starting choice for the purposes of this imaginary team.

In one respect, third base is an unusual position. Although often called "the hot corner," it hasn't much glamour in the eyes of American youth. You never heard of a 14-year-old kid whose ambition it was to play third base in the major leagues.

In a very real sense, circumstances and not early training make third basemen. Most are frustrated shortstops. The best way for a big league ball club to come up with a good third baseman is to find two shortstops one of whom can hit.

That's how it was with Traynor, a shortstop in his youth and in the minor leagues. Without doubt, he would have made a fine shortstop in the majors too.

But Pie happened to come up with the Pirates, a team which had a tremendous tradition at shortstop dating from the days of Honus Wagner. After Wagner finished up, the Pittsburgh club floundered for a while and then made a trade with the Boston Braves for Rabbit Maranville.

Maranville, a lively, colorful, and intensely popular performer, was playing shortstop when Traynor was ready. So Pie went to third base and stayed there as an imposing succession of fine shortstops followed Maranville in Pittsburgh.

After the Rabbit, there was Glenn Wright, who was big, strong, and fast, and a tremendous ballplayer for an all-too-brief peak of greatness.

There are those who will tell you that Traynor and Wright formed the greatest defensive left side ever seen in baseball for a period of three or four years. Then Wright's throwing shoulder was injured in an otherwise minor automobile accident and Glenn drifted out of sight within a few seasons.

Arky Vaughan followed and Vaughan, fleet and with enough batting skill to win the batting championship one year, made up another impressive left side with the staid and steady Traynor.

In these years, the Pirates were so strong at shortstop that they turned back Joe Cronin, who became a Hall of Fame ballplayer in the American League and eventually president of that league.

Another Pirate rejectee was fiery little Dick Bartell, a long-time shortstop star with the Phillies and the Giants who couldn't make the Pittsburgh roster.

Harold Joseph Traynor was born in Framingham, Massachusetts on November 11, 1899, and grew up in Somerville, where the family moved when he was five years old. That's

172

practically around the corner from old Braves Field and Fenway Park.

There are two versions of the derivation of his nickname. Traynor liked pie and what kid doesn't? The other involves an incident when young Harold came home, sweating and dirty after a long afternoon on the sandlots and his father said, "You look like pied type." The head of the family was a printer by trade.

A legend without foundation is that Ed Barrow, when manager of the Red Sox, chased Pie out of Fenway Park after young Traynor cut up the infield working out without spikes.

George Stallings, manager of Boston's National League entry, did run Pie out of the playpen of the Braves, but Barrow aided and abetted Traynor in his debut in organized baseball.

In the early summer of 1920, Traynor was the dashing young shortstop of the Somerville Athletic Club when the shortstop of Portsmouth in the Virginia League broke a leg. The Portsmouth manager, Les Bangs, came out of Somerville, knew Traynor and wired Pie an offer.

Traynor took the offer to Barrow, who advised him to accept. "We'll watch you down there," said the boss of the Red Sox, "and bring you up if you do well."

Pie did well, but Barrow waited too long. As the minor league season ended, Barney Dreyfuss, the Pittsburgh owner, purchased Pie's contract for $10,000, a sizeable amount in those days. And Traynor wound up his first season away from home playing 17 games at shortstop for the Pirates and hitting an unprepossessing .212.

That winter Pittsburgh made its deal for Maranville, so Pie was sent down to play shortstop for Birmingham of the Southern Association. There he hit .336, stole 47 bases and was recalled late in the season when the Pirates were cruising along in the National League lead.

George Gibson, then manager of the Pirates, tried his young

shortstop at third base in a game against the Cubs. Traynor helped lose this game with a wild throw in the ninth.

Max Carey, captain and center fielder of the Pirates, always has maintained that this error indirectly cost Pittsburgh a pennant that seemed to be wrapped up.

"Gibson lost confidence in Pie," said Carey, "and put Clyde Barnhart on third base for the stretch drive. We called Barnhart 'Old Wooden-shoes' and you know what happened."

What happened is history. The Pirates blew a seven and a half game lead in September, losing five straight at the Polo Grounds to the Giants, who came on to win.

Traynor earned the third base job in spring training of 1922 and held it for 13 years. By 1923, he was a true star. That year he was the first Pittsburgh player to get 200 hits, bat over .300, drive in more than 100 runs and score 100 runs, a quadruple feat that had evaded even the mighty Honus Wagner.

He was such a consistent performer that one can recall only a few high spots in his career. One characteristic of his hitting was that Pie rarely swung at the first pitch and yet had an unusually low strikeout total. One season he fanned only ten times.

A star of Pittsburgh's 1925 World Champions, he hit one out of the park in his first time at bat off Walter Johnson in the series. Pie's other championship team was the 1927 club which lost a World Series to the Yankees in four straight games. In that one, Traynor's eighth-inning single ruined a no-hit bid by New York's Herb Pennock.

His playing career ended prematurely because of an injury in 1934.

Trying to score in a game against the Phillies, Traynor's slide carried him wide of the plate. Catcher Jimmy Wilson landed on Pie's right arm with both knees. Nothing was broken but something was certainly torn for Traynor's great throwing skill was seriously impaired. He was out for most of the balance of that season, played in only 57 games in 1935, not at all in 1936, and finished up with five games in 1937.

By this time, he had become manager of the Pirates, taking over in mid-season of 1934 when Gibson, back for a second tour of duty in Pittsburgh, was released. Pie lasted as skipper of the bold, bad Buccaneers until the end of the 1939 campaign.

They said—and they were probably right—that Pie was too nice a guy and too easygoing to be a successful manager. He did come close in 1938. That year, the Pirates led most of the way but were caught by the Chicago Cubs in a wild finish featured by Gabby Hartnett's celebrated homer-in-the-dark which completed the sweep of a three-game series at Wrigley Field.

He has never played and never managed since, yet has managed to stick pretty close to the game he loved so well. For years, he has been sports director of a Pittsburgh radio station, active in sandlot operations, and a Pirate scout in the area of a city which never has forgotten him and never will.

HAROLD JOSEPH TRAYNOR

Born, November 11, 1899, Framingham, Massachusetts.
Height 6'½". Weight 175. Batted and threw right-handed.

Year	Club	League	Pos.	G	AB	R	H	2B	3B	HR	RBI	BA
1920	Pittsburgh	Nat.	SS	17	52	6	11	3	1	0	2	.212
1921	Pittsburgh	Nat.	SS	7	19	0	5	0	0	0	2	.263
1922	Pittsburgh	Nat.	SS-3B	142	571	89	161	17	12	4	81	.282
1923	Pittsburgh	Nat.	3B	153	616	108	208	19	19	12	101	.338
1924	Pittsburgh	Nat.	3B	142	545	86	160	26	13	5	82	.294
1925	Pittsburgh	Nat.	3B	150	591	114	189	39	14	6	106	.320
1926	Pittsburgh	Nat.	3B	152	574	83	182	25	17	3	92	.317
1927	Pittsburgh	Nat.	3B	149	573	93	196	32	9	5	106	.342
1928	Pittsburgh	Nat.	3B	144	569	91	192	38	12	3	124	.337
1929	Pittsburgh	Nat.	3B	130	540	94	192	27	12	4	108	.356
1930	Pittsburgh	Nat.	3B	130	497	90	182	22	11	9	119	.366
1931	Pittsburgh	Nat.	3B	155	615	81	183	37	15	2	103	.298
1932	Pittsburgh	Nat.	3B	135	513	74	169	27	10	2	68	.329
1933	Pittsburgh	Nat.	3B	154	624	85	190	27	6	1	82	.304
1934	Pittsburgh	Nat.	3B	119	444	62	137	22	10	1	61	.309
1935	Pittsburgh	Nat.	3B	57	204	24	57	10	3	1	36	.279
1936	(Did not play)											
1937	Pittsburgh	Nat.	3B	5	12	3	2	0	0	0	0	.167
	Major League Totals			1941	7559	1183	2416	371	164	58	1273	.320

WORLD SERIES RECORD

Year	Club	League	Pos.	G	AB	R	H	2B	3B	HR	RBI	BA
1925	Pittsburgh	Nat.	3B	7	26	2	9	0	2	1	4	.346
1927	Pittsburgh	Nat.	3B	4	15	1	3	1	0	0	0	.200
	World Series Totals			11	41	3	12	1	2	1	4	.293

* key

Pos. = position
G = games
AB = at bat
R = runs
H = hits
2B = two-base hits or doubles
3B = three-base hits or triples
HR = home run
RBI = runs batted in
BA = batting average

20

FRANK FRISCH

The Fordham Flash

JOE MCCARTHY, who managed the Chicago Cubs for four and a half seasons before reaching the Yankees, is a man most sparing of praise. Yet he once declared for all to hear that Frank Frisch was the best ballplayer in the National League.

"If I needed one player to do the job of winning the game I most wanted to win," said McCarthy, "that player would be Frisch. He could beat you in so many ways."

Undoubtedly, Burleigh Grimes was of the same opinion although he expressed it in a different way. Grimes, the last of the legitimate spitball pitchers (all since have been illegitimate), was the surly Early Wynn of his time.

Grimes felt that it was his duty to turn Frisch upside down in the batter's box at regular intervals. This undoubtedly was Burleigh's pleasure, as well.

It is not on record that Grimes ever did skull Frisch with a pitched ball. Frankie was agile and caught on fast. He learned to hit Grimes with one eye on the ball and the other on the nearest exit. But whenever Burleigh pitched against him, Frisch could count on going to the clubhouse with a dirty uniform.

Time passed, as time does, and eventually the fortunes of baseball brought Grimes and Frisch together with the St. Louis Cardinals. Then Frank discovered Burleigh didn't actually eat barbecued batters for lunch. They became fairly friendly.

"Tell me something, Burleigh," Frisch said one day. "Why did you throw at me so much?"

"I was only trying to do you a favor," answered Grimes.

"You what!" expostulated Frisch.

"Sure," said Grimes with an indulgent grin. "I wanted to knock all the corners off your head so that it would be round like everybody else's."

Frank Francis Frisch, alias the Fordham Flash, was a ball-player of varied talents. He started life as a shortstop and played third base on championship teams in the majors. But, of course, he is best remembered as a remarkable second baseman.

At second base, his great contemporary was Rogers Hornsby, who happened to be the best right-handed hitter since Honus Wagner and perhaps this should read including Wagner. Frisch didn't have anything like Hornsby's power but he had just about everything else.

The selection of another second baseman for this mythical team is an open invitation to controversy.

A large band of willful dissenters will scream for Eddie Collins, who, without doubt, was a great ballplayer. Collins was a left-handed hitter with a career batting average of .333 for a quarter of a century in the American League. He was a smooth dependable fielder and an imaginative playmaker.

Older old-timers might favor the inclusion of Napoleon Lajoie, from all accounts one of the most graceful ballplayers who ever lived and a right-handed hitter of the Hornsby type in his time, which was a couple of decades earlier.

But Wagner is the lone exception of the general rule covering the makeup of this team.

The tendency to lean toward Frisch is that you know how the old Flash operated under more or less present-day conditions. All of Lajoie's career and the most productive years of Collins' were before the advent of the lively ball.

That leaves Charley Gehringer of the Detroit Tigers. Gehringer started in the majors five years later than Frisch and lasted five years longer. Each played 19 seasons and Gehringer, a left-handed picture hitter, had a lifetime average of .321 to .316 for the switch-hitting Frisch.

Gehringer also was an uncommonly fine defensive second baseman, so smooth and effortless that they called him the mechanical man.

But—put it this way. Gehringer lacked Frisch's color and flair. Frankie, a vibrant, exciting performer, was a strong factor on eight teams which won National League championships— four in New York and four in St. Louis.

Frisch played in 50 World Series games, getting 58 hits in 197 times at bat for an average of .294. Until the career of Yogi Berra coincided with an almost immoral streak of Yankee success, Frisch held more World Series records than you could comfortably count.

A native New Yorker, born September 9, 1898, Frankie was raised in the Bronx. His family was in comfortable circumstances—his father was in the linen business—and his boyhood was a happy one.

The outdoors was strictly for him. When baseball was in season, he was on the playgrounds from morning until night with bat and glove.

That was only part of it. In those days, a basketball player didn't have to be seven feet tall and Frisch starred on the court for Fordham Prep. In cold weather he ice skated. When he reached Fordham University, he made the varsity football team.

In 1918, Frank made Walter Camp's second All-America eleven as a halfback. Granting that college football was subnormal in that war year, he must have been pretty good. Those who saw him say that Frisch was a terror as an open-field runner. He wasn't big but he was fast and wiry. He stood five-ten, weighed 170 pounds.

And, of course, he played baseball—both at Fordham and the New York Athletic Club. Arthur Devlin, an old third baseman of the Giants, was coach of the Rams and tipped off John McGraw on the young shortstop.

Early in the 1919 season, the Giants signed Frisch for $400 a month. They also gave him a $200 bonus and, in those days, a free agent was lucky to get anything.

Years later, Frisch revealed that there was another unusual clause in his agreement with the Giants. If he did not succeed in making the ball club within two years, he was to get an unconditional release. In that case, it was Frisch's plan to return to Fordham and complete his education. It's almost unnecessary to write that he never went back to Rose Hill, except as a visitor.

Through the years, the story has persisted that Frisch was a cross-handed hitter when he joined the Giants. That isn't true, but the tale has just enough substance to keep the legend alive.

Until this time, Frankie had been exclusively a left-handed hitter. In college competition, he didn't have too much trouble hitting a left-handed pitcher's curve.

When Frisch joined the Giants he speedily discovered that a major league left-hander's curve was something else again. He resolved to try hitting right-handed and the first time he stepped up right-handed—in batting practice—he tried it with his left hand above his right hand on the bat handle.

McGraw let out one outraged bellow and that was that. The veteran manager of the Giants agreed with Frisch's ambition to become a switch hitter, but insisted that he take an orthodox grip on the bat.

And Frank speedily became a good right-handed hitter

180

against southpaws. If anything, he had more power swinging right-handed than from the other side of the plate. Figures are unavailable but the impression persists here that he hit better for average when swinging left-handed.

He was a line-drive hitter. He whacked 105 homers in his career and that is a modest figure today but was entirely acceptable then. An interesting footnote on his home run hitting involves his participation in All-Star games.

Frisch already was a veteran when the All-Star game was inaugurated so he played in only the first two. He was a second baseman for the 1933 National Leaguers and a shortstop the following year. He got two hits in each game and hit a home run in each game.

Frankie spent several months with the Giants without attracting much attention. He occasionally was used as a pinch hitter and once in a while as a pinch runner. Frisch was one of the great baserunners of his time although it took him a long while to break himself of the habit of sliding into a bag headfirst.

Came September and the Giants found themselves in a dog-fight with the Cincinnati Reds for the pennant. The Reds came to the Polo Grounds for three successive doubleheaders and everyone felt that the result of these six games would decide the championship. Everyone was right.

When the Reds won the first two games, McGraw executed a characteristically daring move. On the second day, he sent Frisch in to play second base as a replacement for the veteran Larry Doyle. With Frisch hitting the ball hard and fielding in spectacular fashion, the Giants won that second doubleheader.

But the next day the Reds won two and the pennant hopes of the Giants were shattered, but a young man named Frisch was firmly established as a major leaguer.

That winter for reasons which remain mysterious to this day, Heinie Zimmerman, who had been third baseman of the Giants, dropped out of baseball. So McGraw, in 1920, used Frisch to plug the third base gap and reinstated Doyle at second. Frank missed part of the season through a bellyache eventually diagnosed as appendicitis but wound up hitting .280 in 110 games. He was to be a better than .300 hitter for the next 11 years and in 13 of the next 14 seasons.

The Giants won the pennant in four straight years, starting in 1921. Frisch hit .341, .327, .348, and .328 in those seasons. He was McGraw's third place hitter for three years, then moved up to second place in 1924 when Ross Youngs batted third.

Frank was a third baseman in 1921 when Johnny Rawlings played second. Then McGraw got Heinie Groh to play third base and Frisch replaced Rawlings at second. For several years the New York infield of Frisch, Groh, Dave Bancroft and George Kelly was called the best in baseball.

In 1925, Frisch hit .331, but Pittsburgh won the pennant. In 1926, he finished with a .314 average, but St. Louis won the pennant.

It was late in the summer of 1926 that a break came between Frisch and McGraw, a schism which both men later regretted. As captain of the Giants—and believed to be McGraw's ultimate successor as manager—Frisch was the principal target of the irascible invective of the disappointed manager.

The final straw came in St. Louis when Frisch moved to cover second on a hit-and-run play and Tommy Thevenow, a right-handed hitter, singled through the hole. That night Frisch decided that McGraw had called him a dumb Dutchman for the last time and the next day he left the club and returned to New York.

When the Giants got home, Frisch rejoined them and finished the season but he knew his number was up with the Giants and probably was the least surprised person in North America that winter when McGraw traded him to the Cardinals for Hornsby.

Hornsby, it seems, also was in a specially constructed dog-house. In 1926, he had been player-manager of the world champion Cardinals. After the season he blandly stated that he wouldn't put on his baseball pants in 1927 for less than a $50,000 contract, a demand that turned Sam Breadon, owner of the Cardinals, pale with shock.

Irate St. Louis fans hanged Breadon in effigy that winter, but Frisch got his new boss off the hook. In 1927, he had a great season all around and the Mound City subsided.

With Frisch at second base, the Cardinals won pennants in 1928, 1930, 1931, and 1934 and the World Series in the last two of these years.

In 1934, Frisch was player-manager of the Redbirds who came from far behind in September to pass the Giants and win the pennant. This was the rambunctious ball club that became known as the St. Louis Gashouse Gang and Frankie's job couldn't have been all peaches and cream.

The Dean brothers—Dizzy and Paul—were his brightest pitching stars. Other rugged individualists in charge of the Flash included Leo Durocher, Pepper Martin, Ripper Collins, and Joe Medwick.

"It doesn't seem right for an infielder to be telling a great pitcher like me what to throw," Dizzy once told his flabbergasted manager.

A riotous World Series found the Cardinals and the Detroit Tigers all tied at the end of six games. The seventh game, played in Detroit, was the one in which the "bleacherites" threw so much garbage at Medwick that play was impossible until Judge Kenesaw Mountain Landis ordered Medwick removed from the lineup instead of forfeiting the game to the Cardinals.

Fortunately, the Cardinals, at the time, were well ahead. Frisch, personally, put them in front. After two scoreless innings, he doubled to right off Eldon Auker, clearing a packed set of bases.

From then on, it was a downhill pull for the Cardinals but the game continued to have its moments. Hank Greenberg struck out in his first three times at bat. When he came up again, Dean (Dizzy, of course) asked Frisch, "What was it you said not to throw him?"

"A fast ball, high and outside," answered the Flash.

To Frisch's horror, Dean served a fast ball, high and outside, and Greenberg lined it into right field for a single.

"You're right, Frank," said Dean. "I was beginning to think he couldn't hit nuthin'."

"I don't care how great you are," stormed Frisch. "If you don't stop clowning, you're out of this ball game."

"You dassn't do that," answered Dizzy, but from that point he stuck to his pitching and the Cardinals won, 11 to 0.

Frisch managed the Cardinals for four more years. Later, he was manager of the Pirates for seven seasons and skipper of the Cubs for two.

But he never managed to another pennant. Like Hornsby, Mickey Cochrane, Gabby Hartnett, and a few others, Frank seemed a highly inspirational leader as a player-manager but seemed to lack the touch when he tried to manage from the bench.

In spite of their differences, John McGraw remained Frisch's ideal of a manager but, in an autobiography written a couple of years ago, Frank concedes that perhaps he tried to pattern his ideas of managing too closely to those of McGraw. He concludes that the present-day ballplayer can't take it, maintains that the game has changed and definitely for the worse.

Frisch was elected to the Baseball Hall of Fame in 1947. He appears at Cooperstown on important occasions and frequently at other points on the baseball map where he can find old friends and joyful reminiscence.

For a few years, Frank kept bobbing up in radio and television booths as a broadcaster and amazed his friends by keeping his normally salty choice of words out of the microphone. But now he seems to be retired.

After many years of gracious living in New Rochelle, he and his good wife, Ada, have moved to real country. Near a small village with a long name in Rhode Island, the Old Flash tends a flower garden, grows his own vegetables, and professes not to have a care in the world.

FRANK FRANCIS FRISCH

Born, September 9, 1898, New York, N.Y.
Height 5'10". Weight 185. Batted left- and right-handed.
Threw right-handed.

Year	Club	League	Pos.	G	AB	R	H	2B	3B	HR	RBI	BA
1919	New York	Nat.	SS-2B	54	190	21	43	3	2	2	22	.226
1920	New York	Nat.	3B	110	440	57	123	10	10	4	77	.280
1921	New York	Nat.	2B	153	618	121	211	31	17	8	100	.341
1922	New York	Nat.	2B	132	514	101	168	16	13	5	51	.327
1923	New York	Nat.	2B	151	641	116	223	32	10	12	111	.348
1924	New York	Nat.	2B	145	603	121	198	33	15	7	69	.328
1925	New York	Nat.	2B	120	502	89	166	26	6	11	48	.331
1926	New York [1]	Nat.	2B	135	545	75	171	29	4	5	44	.314
1927	St. Louis	Nat.	2B	153	617	112	208	31	11	10	78	.337
1928	St. Louis	Nat.	2B	141	547	107	164	29	9	10	86	.300
1929	St. Louis	Nat.	2B	138	527	93	176	40	12	5	74	.334
1930	St. Louis	Nat.	2B	133	540	121	187	46	9	10	114	.346
1931	St. Louis	Nat.	2B	131	518	96	161	24	4	4	82	.311
1932	St. Louis	Nat.	2B	115	486	59	142	26	2	3	60	.292
1933	St. Louis	Nat.	2B	147	585	74	177	32	6	4	66	.303
1934	St. Lous	Nat.	2B	140	550	74	168	30	6	3	75	.305
1935	St. Louis	Nat.	2B	103	354	52	104	16	2	1	55	.294
1936	St. Louis	Nat.	2B	93	303	40	83	10	0	1	26	.274
1937	St. Louis	Nat.	2B	17	32	3	7	2	0	0	4	.219
	Major League Totals			**2311**	**9112**	**1532**	**2880**	**466**	**138**	**105**	**1242**	**.316**

[1] Traded with Pitcher Jimmy Ring to St. Louis for Second Baseman Rogers Hornsby, December 20, 1926.

WORLD SERIES RECORD

Year	Club	League	Pos.	G	AB	R	H	2B	3B	HR	RBI	BA
1921	New York	Nat.	2B	8	30	5	9	0	1	0	1	.300
1922	New York	Nat.	2B	5	17	3	8	1	0	0	2	.471

Year	Club	League	Pos.	G	AB	R	H	2B	3B	HR	RBI	BA
1923	New York	Nat.	2B	6	25	2	10	0	1	0	1	.400
1924	New York	Nat.	2B	7	30	1	10	4	1	0	0	.333
1928	St. Louis	Nat.	2B	4	13	1	3	0	0	0	1	.231
1930	St. Louis	Nat.	2B	6	24	0	5	2	0	0	0	.208
1931	St. Louis	Nat.	2B	7	27	2	7	2	0	0	1	.259
1934	St. Louis	Nat.	2B	7	31	2	6	1	0	0	4	.194
World Series Totals				**50**	**197**	**16**	**58**	**10**	**3**	**0**	**10**	**.294**

* key
Pos. = position
G   = games
AB = at bat
R   = runs
H   = hits
2B = two-base hits or doubles
3B = three-base hits or triples
HR = home run
RBI = runs batted in
BA = batting average

21

BABE RUTH

The Sultan of Swat

AFTER MORE THAN 30 years they still argue whether or not Babe Ruth called his home run shot in the third game of the 1932 World Series. Charley Root, the pitcher who was his victim, went into retirement growling that this was a lot of hogwash.

On the other hand, the one and only Babe certainly did gesture grandiloquently toward the outfield in response to the razzing bench of Chicago Cubs after Root had slipped two called strikes past him. And Ruth hit a line drive on the next pitch that still seemed on the rise as it cleared the fence in center at Wrigley Field.

It certainly looked like "Casey at The Bat" with a different ending and that night Ruth shook his head and said he ought not to have done it. "What a jackass I'd have been," he said, "if I'd struck out."

Not many are aware that Ruth had called a World Series home run shot four years before in St. Louis, possibly because the incident was unaccompanied by any majestic wave of his right hand.

The circumstances involved the use of a "quick pitch" by Bill Sherdel, the little left-hander of the Cardinals. If called, it would have been a third strike on the Babe. But Commissioner Kenesaw Mountain Landis had specifically instructed the

World Series umpires not to permit the quick pitch and this one was not allowed.

Sherdel stormed in from the mound, catcher Jimmy Wilson took off his mask and yowled, Cardinals poured off the bench to join in the protest. Ruth stood there, his bat tucked under his arm, clapping his hands until the uproar subsided.

"You big baboon," yelled the angry Sherdel, "I'll throw the next one by you."

"Put it in there," grinned Ruth, "and I'll knock it out of the park."

Sherdel did and Ruth did. That was the Babe's third home run of the game and the second time Ruth had hit three in a World Series game. No one else has ever done this once.

This serves to pinpoint another facet of the many-splendored performance of Babe Ruth through the years. No other great star more consistently rose to great occasions.

For instance, Babe hit three homers in a game only four times in his career. He did it twice in World Series before he collected a triple in an American League game in 1930.

The last time was on May 25, 1935 when Ruth, his spindly legs having grown unequal to the task of carrying around his increasing bulk, was involved in a highly unsatisfactory association with the Boston Braves. He couldn't play much and his additional titles of "vice-president and assistant manager" to Bill McKechnie appeared to have upset everybody involved.

But he did play this afternoon and Pittsburgh will never forget it.

The last of his three homers that afternoon completely cleared the right field roof of the Forbes Field grandstand for the first time since the park had been built. It was the 714th home run of his major league career and the final one, for this was the last game he ever played. The following day he quit the Braves and went into restless retirement.

One of the least rewarding projects of recent years is to try

188

to explain George Herman Ruth to present-day ballplayers, none of whom, of course, ever saw him in action. One is greeted will ill-concealed disbelief even though the facts cited are in the record.

His clubhouse nickname with the Yankees was "Jidge," but he also was known as "The Bambino," "The Sultan of Swat," "The Colossus of Clout," etc. Writers of headlines and flamboyant leads had a ball with him. A few that can be recalled are: "Ruth is Stranger than Fiction"; "Ruth, Crushed to Earth, Shall Rise Again," and "Ruth is Mighty and Shall Prevail."

It is impossible to write of Ruth and his works without the use of superlatives. His home run career total not only is a record but tops Jimmy Foxx, his closest rival, by 180. He struck out more times than any player in history and walked more times.

He also had a lifetime batting average of .342. In 1924, he was American League batting champion with .378. The year before, Detroit's Harry Heilmann hit .403 for the batting crown. Ruth was 10 points behind, but his .393 still is an all-time record for a Yankee player.

His 15 World Series home runs was another record. He played in 41 World Series games over ten series and hit .325. His .625 batting average in the four-game series of 1928, still is an all-time high.

He pitched three World Series games and won them all, including a 2 to 1 victory in 14 innings over Sherrod Smith of the 1916 Dodgers, the longest World Series game ever played.

As a left-handed pitcher, Ruth's lifetime record was 92 victories and 44 defeats and his earned run average for 163 major league games was 2.24. Very likely, Ruth could have made the Hall of Fame as a pitcher alone. He was a full-time pitcher for the Red Sox for only three seasons and over that stretch won 64 games.

There is a popular little sports page feature printed widely throughout the country called "This Day in Sports." Last year it cited May 9, 1918, and the legend ran: "Babe Ruth, pitching and batting clean-up for Boston, belted three doubles, a triple and a single against Washington but lost in the 10th inning, 4 to 3, to Walter Johnson."

One wonders how many hitters there were who ever got five hits off Johnson, one of the greatest of pitchers and at his peak in 1918. It was a day like that and some similar ones that led Ed Barrow, then manager of the Red Sox, to conclude that, brilliant as Ruth was on the mound, he should swing a bat every day. And so, in 1919, Ruth appeared in 130 games, but pitched in only 17 of these.

Up to World War I, the major league record for home runs in a season was 24, set by Clifford (Gavvy) Cravath in 1915. Cravath played for the Phillies and, although a right-handed hitter, developed a specialized knack of popping fly balls over the high but ridiculously close right-field wall at Baker Bowl.

Ruth broke the record—Cravath's and three of his own—four times. He hit 29 for the Red Sox in 1919 and that winter was sold to the Yankees for $125,000, a picayune sum today but then a record by far.

In 1920, his first season in New York, the Babe hit 54 homers. In 1921, he hit 59. In 1927, he hit 60. His batting averages for his record breaking years were .322 in 1919; .376 in 1920, .378 in 1921, and .356 in 1927. By way of comparison, the batting average of Roger Maris was .269 in 1961, the year the modern Yankee hit 61 homers over a schedule expanded to 162 games.

So it is plainly evident that Ruth got plenty of hits that weren't homers. It wasn't until the 1963 season that Stan Musial of the Cardinals broke Babe's record for total number of extra base hits and by that time had appeared in about 300 more games than the Babe played.

Furthermore, he wasn't just a man with a big left-handed

swing. He could and did hit to left often enough to keep the defenses honest. If the third baseman played too deep, he could bunt and beat it out. For a slugger with such a flamboyant specialty he had a wide range of adaptability.

When Barrow altered the Babe's profession from pitching, Ruth played a few games at first base and played that position well. Then he became an outfielder, playing in either right or left depending on the construction of the ball park.

For instance, when Ruth first joined the Yankees he played left field because right field was the "sun" field at the Polo Grounds. When the Yankees built their own Stadium, it was constructed at an angle to make left field the "sun" field, so Ruth played right.

It is likely that, when Yankee Stadium was constructed, they actually built it to Babe's specifications. They figured that Ruth's strong, accurate throwing arm made him more valuable in right field than in left.

As a defensive outfielder, the Babe was a mighty good one through most of the '20's when he had speed surprising in a man of his top-heavy build. Later on, he slowed down but remained capable of catching anything he reached.

It was difficult for those who saw him only at the end to realize how well Ruth could run in his earlier years. One season, he stole 15 bases and he wasn't what you'd call larceny-minded. He was rarely thrown out advancing on a hit. Those who watched him day after day say he almost never made a baseball mistake. The claim is made that he never once threw from the outfield to the wrong base.

There shall be no attempt here to dwell at length upon the Babe's joyous character, his enormous appetite for food, drink, and the ball he had for himself as he rollicked along the baseball trail. To try that would be to swell this chapter into the size of a book and books on Ruth have already been done.

He was a huge, gregarious guy who never truly grew up

and had a tough little boy's disdain for authority. In 1922, he was suspended for six weeks for playing exhibition games the autumn before in direct violation of orders from Kenesaw Mountain Landis, then the czar of baseball. Another season he wrangled with Miller Huggins and, in a fit of anger, threatened to throw the little manager of the Yankees off a train. For this he was fined $5,000 and the fine stuck.

It is improbable that the amount of this fine bothered Babe much. By that time, he was in the chips. His Yankee salary ultimately reached $80,000 and this was to remain an all-time high for baseball salaries for more than 20 years.

Only once did his magnificent constitution break down under the unusual treatment Ruth gave it. In the spring of 1925, Babe's first marriage was on the rocks and Babe was on the loose. On a spring barnstorming tour from Florida, Ruth's stomach rebelled in what was called "the bellyache heard around the world."

Babe was seriously ill for a few days and convalescent for weeks. It was June before he could play and the Yankees finished an inglorious seventh.

The following February at the annual dinner of the New York Baseball writers, Mayor Jimmy Walker made an eloquent plea for the Babe to reform. He called Ruth "the idol of all the dirty-faced little kids in the country" and charged Ruth with "letting them down."

Babe took the public rebuke magnificently. Tearful and penitent, he promised to behave himself. Perhaps his conduct in later years was not consistently immaculate. But he at least learned to become more circumspect and tales of his escapades no longer reached the front pages.

Ultimately Ruth married again and found a wife who could help him. Claire Ruth seemed able to understand the Babe as well as any woman could. She handled him better than any of his managers and nursed him throughout the weeks of his final illness. Ruth died on August 16, 1948, never knowing he had cancer.

That ended a journey which began on February 6, 1895, when George Herman Ruth was born in Baltimore. He knew little of his parents or his other relatives and, at an early age, was taken in hand by the Xaverian brothers at St. Mary's Protectorate.

He played his first baseball in that school and the earliest picture of him in a baseball uniform shows him as a left-handed catcher, of all things. Brother Matthias, the head of St. Mary's, remained Babe's friend and not always admiring critic, as long as he lived.

It was Brother Gilbert of St. Mary's who persuaded Jack Dunn, boss of the Baltimore Orioles, to give Ruth a baseball contract at $600. Babe launched himself in organized ball by pitching a shutout against Buffalo in his very first game.

This was 1914. Ruth won 22, lost 9 for Dunn in the International League, was sold to the Red Sox in time to win two and lose one in the American League before his first season was over. From that point until his exit as a player with the Braves in 1935, just about his only serious setbacks were those he created himself.

In retirement, Ruth lived well, played golf and occasionally displayed some bitterness because he wasn't in baseball. There is no doubt that he felt hurt and neglected, but there also is something to be said on the other side. He wanted to manage and his asking price was high. Club owners questioned his ability to manage and these were depression years.

In 1938, he allowed himself to be lured out of retirement by Larry MacPhail of the Brooklyn Dodgers. He served as first base coach of the club but more than earned the $15,000 he received for half a season by drawing crowds all over the National League circuit to see the great man take his swings in pre-game batting practice.

That ended the following winter when Ruth learned that MacPhail had no intention of naming the Babe manager to succeed Burleigh Grimes. The job instead went to Leo Durocher, an old acquaintance but hardly a friend of the Babe's.

You might argue until dawn whether the greatest of all players was Ruth or Cobb or perhaps Wagner, but few can argue that Ruth was the most important ballplayer of all time.

It was popular at one time to call Ruth "the savior" of baseball. The theory was that the excitement he generated with his heavy hitting offset the effects of the 1920 revelations that the World Series of 1919 had been fixed by gamblers.

The chances are that baseball would have survived anyway.

But the Babe and his influence did change the game as it has been changed by no other individual in history.

At the box office, the club owners saw the tangible results of the home runs Ruth hit high and far. So they increased the liveliness of the ball until it became what Babe himself called "a stitched golf ball."

The ballplayers changed as they watched Ruth's salaries soar. Choke hitting became almost obsolete as everyone started swinging for the fences, in some cases with uncommon success.

The home run, as it became the big thing in baseball, increased attendance, influenced the contours of ball parks and ultimately the creation of larger and more spacious baseball playpens.

Were all these changes for the better? By and large they were. Waite Hoyt believes they were and Hoyt was a pitching teammate of Ruth's with the Yankees.

One day in the clubhouse, another player criticized Ruth for something or other.

"Never let me hear you say anything like that again," scolded Hoyt. "Every ballplayer in the country ought to get down on his knees and thank God for the big fellow. The things he has done have helped every man who plays this game."

GEORGE HERMAN RUTH

Born, February 6, 1895, Baltimore, Maryland.
Died, August 16, 1948, New York, N.Y.
Height 6'2". Weight 215. Batted and threw left-handed.

Year	Club	League	Pos.	G	AB	R	H	2B	3B	HR	RBI	BA
1914	Boston	Amer.	P	5	10	1	2	1	0	0	0	.200
1915	Boston	Amer.	P-OF	42	92	16	29	10	1	4	20	.315
1916	Boston	Amer.	P-OF	67	136	18	37	5	3	3	16	.272
1917	Boston	Amer.	P-OF	52	123	14	40	6	3	2	10	.325
1918	Boston	Amer.	P-1B-OF	95	317	50	95	26	11	11	64	.300
1919	Boston [1]	Amer.	P-OF	130	432	103	139	34	12	29	112	.322
1920	New York	Amer.	P-1B-OF	142	458	158	172	36	9	54	137	.376
1921	New York	Amer.	P-OF-1B	152	540	177	204	44	16	59	170	.378
1922	New York	Amer.	OF	110	406	94	128	24	8	35	96	.315
1923	New York	Amer.	OF	152	522	151	205	45	13	41	130	.393
1924	New York	Amer.	OF	153	529	143	200	39	7	46	121	.378
1925	New York	Amer.	OF	98	359	61	104	12	2	25	66	.290
1926	New York	Amer.	OF	152	495	139	184	30	5	47	155	.372
1927	New York	Amer.	OF	151	540	158	192	29	8	60	164	.356
1928	New York	Amer.	OF	154	536	163	173	29	8	54	142	.323
1929	New York	Amer.	OF	135	499	121	172	26	6	46	154	.345
1930	New York	Amer.	P-OF	145	518	150	186	28	9	49	153	.359
1931	New York	Amer.	OF	145	534	149	199	31	2	46	163	.373
1932	New York	Amer.	OF-1B	132	457	120	156	13	5	41	137	.341
1933	New York	Amer.	P-OF	137	459	97	138	21	3	34	103	.301
1934	New York [2]	Amer.	OF	125	365	78	105	17	4	22	84	.288
1935	Boston	Nat.	OF	28	72	13	13	0	0	6	12	.181
American League Totals				2474	8327	2161	2860	506	136	708	2197	.343
National League Totals				28	72	12	13	0	0	6	12	.181
Major League Totals				**2502**	**8399**	**2174**	**2873**	**506**	**136**	**714**	**2209**	**.342**

[1] Sold to New York for $125,000, January 3, 1920.
[2] Released to Boston, February 26, 1935.

WORLD SERIES RECORD

Year	Club	League	Pos.	G	AB	R	H	2B	3B	HR	RBI	BA
1915	Boston	Amer.	P-OF	1	1	0	0	0	0	0	0	.000
1916	Boston	Amer.	P	1	5	0	0	0	0	0	0	.000
1918	Boston	Amer.	P-OF	3	5	0	1	0	1	0	2	.200
1921	New York	Amer.	OF	6	16	3	5	0	0	1	4	.313
1922	New York	Amer.	OF	5	17	1	2	1	0	0	1	.118
1923	New York	Amer.	OF-1B	6	19	8	7	1	1	3	3	.368
1926	New York	Amer.	OF	7	20	6	6	0	0	4	5	.300
1927	New York	Amer.	OF	4	15	4	6	0	0	2	7	.400
1928	New York	Amer.	OF	4	16	9	10	3	0	3	4	.625
1932	New York	Amer.	OF	4	15	6	5	0	0	2	6	.333
World Series Totals				**41**	**129**	**37**	**42**	**5**	**2**	**15**	**32**	**.326**

PITCHING RECORD

Year	Club	League	G	IP	W	L	Pct.	H	SO	BB	ERA
1914	Boston	Amer.	4	23	2	1	.667	21	3	7	3.91
1915	Boston	Amer.	32	218	18	8	.692	166	112	85	2.44
1916	Boston	Amer.	44	324	23	12	.657	230	170	118	1.75
1917	Boston	Amer.	41	326	24	13	.649	244	128	108	2.02
1918	Boston	Amer.	20	166	13	7	.650	125	40	49	2.22
1919	Boston	Amer.	17	133	9	5	.643	148	30	58	2.97
1920	New York	Amer.	1	4	1	0	1.000	3	0	2	4.50
1921	New York	Amer.	2	9	2	0	1.000	14	2	9	9.00
1930	New York	Amer.	1	9	1	0	1.000	11	2	3	3.00
1933	New York	Amer.	1	9	1	0	1.000	12	0	3	5.00
Major League Totals			**163**	**1221**	**94**	**46**	**.671**	**974**	**487**	**442**	**2.28**

WORLD SERIES PITCHING RECORD

Year	Club	League	G	IP	W	L	Pct.	H	SO	BB	ERA
1916	Boston	Amer.	1	14	1	0	1.000	6	3	4	0.64
1918	Boston	Amer.	2	17	2	0	1.000	13	7	4	1.06
World Series Totals			**3**	**31**	**3**	**0**	**1.000**	**19**	**10**	**8**	**0.87**

* key

Pos. = position	**G** = games
G = games	**IP** = innings pitched
AB = at bat	**W** = won
R = runs	**L** = lost
H = hits	**Pct.** = percentage of games won
2B = two-base hits or doubles	**H** = hits given up
3B = three-base hits or triples	**SO** = strikeouts
HR = home run	**BB** = bases on balls or walks
RBI = runs batted in	**ERA** = earned-run average
BA = batting average	

22

JOE DIMAGGIO

The Yankee Clipper

EARLY IN THE baseball season of 1947, Branch Rickey, then the boss of the Brooklyn Dodgers, executed an astounding transaction. He sent half a dozen players, some of formidable repute to the Pittsburgh Pirates for cash and a little outfielder named Al Gionfriddo.

The popular gag at the time was that Gionfriddo, who looked something like a messenger boy at that, was included in the deal only to carry the money to Rickey's bank.

Time passed and finally there came the sixth game of the World Series that year. It was a wild struggle at Yankee Stadium, marked by frequent substitutions and there was Gionfriddo finishing up in left field for the Dodgers.

With a couple of Yankees on base and running with two out a fly ball was hit over Gionfriddo's head and almost to the bullpen in left center. Little Al raced back, turning his head once or twice to check the flight of the ball, then hastening on. As he neared the bullpen rail, he executed a desperate spinning lunge. As his cap fell off, the ball hit the pocket of his glove— and stuck.

Joe DiMaggio, who had hit the ball, was nearing second base as Gionfriddo triumphantly waved it aloft. And as Joe pulled up, he aimed an exasperated kick at the ground, sending up a cloud of dust.

It was a remarkable incident for two reasons. The spectacular

197

catch was the one thing that will make Gionfriddo always re-membered. And it may have been the only time that the great DiMaggio ever displayed his emotions on the ball field.

He was a rare ballplayer, this one. Joe was tall and trim, lean as a whippet and as graceful an athlete as ever played the game. His nickname—the Yankee Clipper—was most appro-priate.

Throughout his great years in the American League, he was a dead-panned and polished performer on the field. In his contacts with the public away from the park, he was soft-spoken and courteous although extremely reserved.

No one knows how much effort DiMaggio put into this cal-culated control of his feelings but his friends and his teammates were constantly aware that Joe and his public image were dif-ferent people.

For there was inner turmoil inside the man no matter how expertly masked. He had what is best described as a squeamish stomach and ulcers that kicked up now and then.

Behind an impassive façade he was a brooder and he had more than the average man's gnawing cares. Professionally, he had a knee injury that threatened to finish him before he even reached the majors and later, a series of bone spurs on one heel that threatened to prematurely end his career.

He came from a large and happy family and essentially his great desire was a family of his own. But two marriages turned out badly for him and left internal scars.

Joe McCarthy, who managed the Yankees when DiMaggio arrived, was a stern disciplinarian. For example, he forbade his players to shave or play cards on the premises. "This is a club-house, not a barber shop or a recreation room," he barked.

Still McCarthy raised no objections because DiMaggio rarely sat on the Yankee bench when he came in from the field. In-stead, DiMaggio usually headed for the runway and lit a cigarette, palming it from the view of the spectators and seeking to ease the strains within him by taking an occasional puff until it was time for him to do something.

Undoubtedly, McCarthy would have chewed out anybody else, but even to a hard-bitten manager, DiMaggio was something special.

No other player in history ever took as long to leave a ball park after a game. Joe would strip off his outer uniform, light a cigarette, sip at a bottle of beer, and cool off for an hour, letting the tensions of the day unwind before he'd even step under a shower.

The story of DiMaggio perhaps is best told in a series of vignettes.

He was just 21 when he first came to the Yankee camp. He had played three seasons for the San Francisco Seals, but that was close to home. Now Joe was going far away and his worried family felt better when he started out with a couple of *paisans* who lived in the same area.

Tony Lazzeri was the veteran second baseman of the Yankees and Frank Crosetti was the club's shortstop and here the three were tooling 20 hours a day cross-country in Lazzeri's new car. With Frank and Tony alternating at the wheel, Joe sat in the rear happily gazing at the landscape when he wasn't comfortably dozing.

They were somewhere in Texas when Lazzeri nudged Crosetti and said, "Don't you think it's about time our honored guest drove us for a while?"

It was then that Joe confessed that he had never owned a car and never had learned to handle one.

"I can laugh about it now," said DiMaggio, "but I really was scared when they threatened to throw me out of the car and make me walk back to California after cursing me in English and at least two Italian dialects."

199

Crosetti grins at the recollection. "The only time," said the Crow, "a Yankee rookie ever went to training camp with two Yankee regulars as chauffeurs. But don't get the wrong idea. If we hadn't liked him, we wouldn't have razzed him so much."

The most spectacular exploit of DiMaggio's career occurred in the 1941 season when he batted safely in 56 consecutive games for an all-time major league record. He already had a string of 36 games and was threatening the old mark when he faced a pitcher of the St. Louis Browns named Bob Muncrief.

Muncrief got him out three times, then DiMaggio singled in his fourth and final time at bat.

Afterwards a reporter said to Muncrief, "You could have made a name for yourself if you had walked DiMaggio that last time."

The pitcher answered, "Don't think I wouldn't like the distinction of stopping DiMaggio. But he's too big a man and too great a ballplayer to be cheated out of his chance."

DiMaggio had departed before Willie Mays arrived in New York. There were and still are arguments as to which was the superior center fielder. One afternoon there was a heated one in the press box and a baseball writer of Mays's persuasion said that DiMaggio had been "a showboat."

"How in the world can you say anything like that?" he was asked.

"Why," came the answer, "Joe deliberately made the difficult catches look easy."

Funniest part of it was that Joe's critic appeared to be sincere as he came up with the strangest definition of grandstand play on record.

In the spring of 1947, they still talked of the World Series the previous fall in which the St. Louis Cardinals beat the Boston Red Sox in seven games. Ted Williams persisted in trying to overcome the extreme defensive shift the Cardinals had borrowed from Lou Boudreau and batted only .200.

DiMaggio sat silent on the bench at St. Petersburg as various baseball writers discussed the pros and cons of the Williams attitude.

Finally one said, "I'd like to see them try a shift like that against Joe."

Here DiMaggio allowed himself a small smile. He said, "I don't think they'd try it more than once."

He made that sound like a promise. In any event, it was as close to a boast as anyone ever heard from DiMaggio.

As a matter of fact, DiMaggio and Williams had much in common in their respective hitting styles apart from the fact that Joe hit right-handed and Ted from the other side of the plate. Both were pronounced pull hitters out of a wide stance.

Joe stood well back in the box, feet dug in and well apart. He gripped the bat at the extreme end, held it practically motionless and his stride into a pitch was no more than five or six inches.

He really could clobber the ball. He wound up his career after the 1951 season. With three years out for Army service in World War II, he had thirteen complete seasons with the Yankees. In eleven of those seasons, he batted over .300. In ten of those seasons the Yankees won the pennant with Joe an unobtrusive leader of the fighting forces on the field.

He won batting championships when he hit .381 in 1939 and .352 the following year. He won the American League most valuable player award three times. His lifetime batting average was .325 and he finished up with 361 home runs. And he did all this playing half of each season in the Yankee Stadium, regarded by most right-handed hitters as a sort of Death Valley.

As his fame grew, he became much sought after socially but he preferred his own friends. He was and is handsome, in a slightly off-beat way because his nose suggests Cyrano. With his build—he still stands six feet two inches and weighs just under 200 pounds—he could wear clothes well.

Once he was named one of the ten best dressed men in America and didn't seem quite sure whether to be amused or embarrassed.

"I'm astonished," he told his good friend, Jimmy Cannon, "but not nearly as astonished as those who put me on the list if they knew that right now I own just three suits and the blue one is so shiny that I'm a little ashamed to wear it."

Most of Joe's reputed shyness is a myth. Modesty is a different thing entirely and he has that as well as great natural dignity. Interviewers dissatisfied with the result of their efforts usually asked him questions about himself. Joe disliked talking about himself.

Joe was good and he knew it and he preferred to let his performance on the field speak for itself.

His background is a heart-warming story. His father was descended from generations of Mediterranean fishermen and was born on Isola delle Femmine, an islet off the coast of Sicily. When a young man, he emigrated to America with his wife and growing family.

The DiMaggios were settled in Martinez, California, in the San Francisco Bay area by the time Joe was born on November 25, 1914. A few years later, the DiMaggios moved into San Francisco and lived close by Fisherman's Wharf, for DiMaggio, Sr., of course, remained a fisherman.

Joe was the eighth of nine children and it seems slightly amazing that three of Papa DiMaggio's sons became good enough ballplayers to play with distinction in the major leagues and a fourth might have made it, given the opportunity.

For Joe will tell you that his oldest brother, Tom, was the best athlete in the family, but, being the oldest, he was called upon to go to work in his early teens. The economic condition of the family had improved to some extent by the time the others were growing up. Tom, incidentally, became a fine businessman and, for many years, has managed "Joe DiMaggio's," now a world famous eating place on the San Francisco water-front.

Vince DiMaggio, two years older than Joe, was built much like him and could hit a ball with as much power. Although Vince lasted in the major leagues for ten years, he had trouble with the curve and his lifetime batting average was a mere .249.

Dominick DiMaggio was four years younger than Joe and was built on a smaller scale than his brothers. The glasses he wore gave him an owlish expression and he was called "the Little Professor" by admiring Red Sox fans. Like Joe and unlike Vince he could hit for average and was a fine center fielder, but he lacked the power of his larger brothers.

Papa DiMaggio was mystified as his sons, one after another, blossomed into ballplayers, but he was a good father who wanted his kids to have fun. From time to time he shook his head and moaned about the wear and tear on clothes and shoes. But he voiced no serious objections as long as the boys did their bit to add to the family income. In Joe's case, this meant running a paper route which netted him $1.00 a day.

As kids, the DiMaggios played ball in what they called the Horse Lot, used by a dairy company to park its milk wagons. It was a soft dirt field. Pieces of concrete served as bases and a flattened garbage can cover served as home plate. Joe's first bat was a sawed-off oar handle.

After that there were kid teams for Joe and his junior high school team and presently he became known as one of the best boy shortstops in the neighborhood. And, by this time, Vince was an aspiring young outfielder with the San Francisco Seals.

Joe was 17 when Vince announced one evening that Ike Caveney, manager of the Seals, wanted to look him over. This was the end of the 1932 season and Caveney used Joe as a shortstop in three games. He hit a triple to the wall in left center in his first professional time at bat.

Next spring, still on trial, he appeared in the training camp of the Seals. Brother Vince was released to continue his march toward the majors with the Hollywood Stars and Ike Caveney, the San Francisco manager, stationed Joe in the outfield in Vince's place with startling immediate results.

All the 18-year-old kid did in his freshman season was to break a Pacific Coast League record by hitting safely in 61 games and finish with a batting average of .340. Charley Graham, the veteran owner of the Seals, fought off all major league offers for the precocious young man. Graham believed that he'd get two or three times as much if he waited another year. Graham had hard luck.

The 1934 season had hardly begun when the first of Joe's long list of ailments struck. He stepped out of a cab one day and his left knee popped, just like that. He was in a cast for six weeks, missed almost half the season, yet hit .341. But, of course, his market value plummeted.

The Yankees, on the advice of Bill Essick and Joe Devine, their California scouts, took the gamble. They offered $25,000 for Joe plus four ballplayers. Moreover, they'd let San Francisco keep the young star through the 1935 season. Graham played it safe and accepted the best bid he could get under the circumstances. This must be accounted a bit of Yankee luck that people talk about. For Joe hit .398 on the Pacific Coast in 1936 and would have cost four times as much had the Yanks not made the deal a year in advance.

Joe's first baseball contract netted him $225 a month from the Seals. Ultimately, he became the first to get an annual salary of $100,000 from the Yankees. He was still drawing that important money in 1951.

He had missed three years because of World War II service in the army. In 1946, the first year of his return, American League pitchers "held him" to a mere .290. In his eleven other seasons, he was above—usually far above—the .300 mark.

But now it was 1951 and his legs were giving him trouble.

He missed many games and wound up with a batting average of .263. And that, Joe decided, was that. Although Dan Topping, the Yankee co-owner who is one of Joe's close friends, urged him to continue and generously offered to maintain his top salary, DiMaggio declined with thanks. The man has the pride of the perfectionist.

For one year Joe operated a post-game telecast after games at Yankee Stadium for a reputed $75,000, but he gave that up too because he couldn't kid himself that he was good. For a long stretch in recent years, he traveled to U.S. Army Posts all over the world as a good will representative for the purchasing agents which supply the post exchanges.

Meanwhile, he married again. The break-up of his first marriage was a severe blow, particularly since he idolized his one son, now grown and, at last reports, in the Marine Corps. His friends believed he'd never fall again but then, after leaving the Yankees, he met Marilyn Monroe—on a blind date, of all things.

There were a few months of happiness ended by the stress and strains of Miss Monroe's profession. DiMaggio was never cut out for the Hollywood pattern of life. There were disagreements and ultimately a divorce.

It is noteworthy that later Miss Monroe regarded Joe as her most trustworthy friend and, after the tragic death of the lady occurred, DiMaggio's conduct as he handled all arrangements won the sympathetic admiration of the nation.

Shortly after that, Joe gave up his globetrotting job and retired. He gets around baseball, maintains his interest in the game, although he never cared to manage. In recent years, he has appeared at the Yankee spring training camp with his great friend, George Solotaire, to serve as a sort of honorary coach for a month or so.

He seems to enjoy that although not nearly so much as the fellows enjoy having him around.

JOSEPH PAUL DiMAGGIO

Born, November 25, 1914, Martinez, California.
Height 6'2". Weight 190. Batted and threw right-handed.

Year	Club	League	Pos.	G	AB	R	H	2B	3B	HR	RBI	BA
1936	New York	Amer.	OF	138	637	132	206	44	15	29	125	.323
1937	New York	Amer.	OF	151	621	151	215	35	15	46	167	.346
1938	New York	Amer.	OF	145	599	129	194	32	13	32	140	.324
1939	New York	Amer.	OF	120	462	108	176	32	6	30	126	.381
1940	New York	Amer.	OF	132	508	93	179	28	9	31	133	.352
1941	New York	Amer.	OF	139	541	122	193	43	11	30	125	.357
1942	New York	Amer.	OF	154	610	123	186	29	13	21	114	.305
1943–1944–1945	(In Military Service)											
1946	New York	Amer.	OF	132	503	81	146	20	8	25	95	.290
1947	New York	Amer.	OF	141	534	97	168	31	10	20	97	.315
1948	New York	Amer.	OF	153	594	110	190	26	11	39	155	.320
1949	New York	Amer.	OF	76	272	58	94	14	6	14	67	.346
1950	New York	Amer.	OF	139	525	114	158	33	10	32	122	.301
1951	New York	Amer.	OF	116	415	72	109	22	4	12	71	.263
Major League Totals				**1736**	**6821**	**1390**	**2214**	**389**	**131**	**361**	**1537**	**.325**

WORLD SERIES RECORD

Year	Club	League	Pos.	G	AB	R	H	2B	3B	HR	RBI	BA
1936	New York	Amer.	OF	6	26	3	9	3	0	0	3	.346
1937	New York	Amer.	OF	5	22	2	6	0	0	1	4	.273
1938	New York	Amer.	OF	4	15	4	4	0	0	1	2	.267
1939	New York	Amer.	OF	4	16	3	5	0	0	1	3	.313
1941	New York	Amer.	OF	5	19	1	5	0	0	0	1	.263
1942	New York	Amer.	OF	5	21	3	7	0	0	0	3	.333
1947	New York	Amer.	OF	7	26	4	6	0	0	2	5	.231
1949	New York	Amer.	OF	5	18	2	2	0	0	1	2	.111
1950	New York	Amer.	OF	4	13	2	4	1	0	1	2	.308
1951	New York	Amer.	OF	6	23	3	6	2	0	1	5	.261
World Series Totals				**51**	**199**	**27**	**54**	**6**	**0**	**8**	**30**	**.271**

* key
Pos. = position
G = games
AB = at bat
R = runs batted in
H = hits
2B = two-base hits or doubles
3B = three-base hits or triples
HR = home run
RBI = runs batted in
BA = batting average

23

TY COBB

The Georgia Peach

THEN THERE WAS Ty Cobb. The only Cobb, combative and controversial. His fiery spirit made him one of the great ones, perhaps the greatest.

No one in this favored land who grew up believing that this mercurial man from Georgia was the best ballplayer of all time is likely to change his opinion now.

Cobb set more records than any player who ever lived. Many of these have been broken in the 35 years that have passed since he retired. Some still stand. Some will always stand.

In a career that covered 24 years, he played in 3,033 games. He got 4,191 hits, scored 2,244 runs, stole 892 bases, had a grand batting average of .367.

He was a scrawny kid of 18 when he first reported to the Detroit Tigers in 1905 and batted .240 in 41 games in the last six weeks of the season. This was the last time he was to bat under .300. He batted over that figure for the next 23 years in the American League.

He was batting champion twelve years, nine years in succession and in twelve seasons out of thirteen. Only Tris Speaker, another of the greats, prevented Ty from making it thirteen in a row. In 1916, Cobb hit .371, but Speaker hit .386.

Ty was a .400 hitter three times, reaching .420 in 1911, .410 in 1912, and .401 in 1922, after the lively ball had been introduced. He hit .350 or better in sixteen seasons.

Cobb was Cobb. There was no other like him, nor is there ever likely to be.

Strong legs, keen eyes, and a quick imaginative brain made Cobb a good ballplayer. His flaming desire made him great.

Tyrus Raymond Cobb was born in Banks County, Georgia, December 18, 1886. He died, perhaps the wealthiest of all the men who ever played baseball, on July 17, 1961.

Shortly after his death there appeared the autobiography he had been working on for several years. *My Life in Baseball— the True Record* is a fascinating story of Cobb's life and times. In it, Ty and his collaborator, Al Stump, did a fine job of presenting Cobb's side of the numerous rhubarbs in which he engaged.

He had numerous fights—on the field, under the stands, in hotel rooms, and in the clubhouses of ball parks. In his early days, he fought not only opposing players but his own team-mates. Cobb's book is a fascinating argument for the defense, but one must guess that he did not give himself any the worst of it.

Say this for him—he picked no setups. He tangled with Charley Schmidt, a Detroit catcher, possibly a dozen times and Schmidt was one of the strongest and toughest men who ever played baseball. Schmidt eventually got bored with beating Cobb regularly like a gong and eventually the pair patched up their differences and became reasonably good friends.

More than any other of the great players in baseball, Cobb would have fascinated a psychiatrist. One wonders what a pro-fessional headshrinker would have deduced from Ty's earlier years. Although a passion for baseball halted Cobb's formal education, his father was a state senator and a county school commissioner.

How much of Ty's psychological problems were due to his father's death—at home, through a shooting accident? He idolized his father and his grief was boundless.

208

Probably he never admitted, even to himself, that such problems existed. He walked tall, as the saying goes, but he walked alone. He married twice and was twice divorced, which further suggests that he was a difficult person in close relationship with others.

His fierce independence made him impatient with authority. He despised Frank Navin, who owned the Tigers for whom Ty played for 22 years.

He never forgave Ban Johnson, the founder and long-time president of the American League who suspended him for climbing into a grandstand and beating up a loud-mouthed heckler. In this case, Cobb was supported by his teammates who maintained that the fan's abuse had been intolerable. The Tigers actually went on strike for three days in protest of Cobb's suspension.

He had nothing but contempt for Kenesaw Mountain Landis, the first and only baseball czar. Near the end of Cobb's playing career, charges were made by Dutch Leonard, a former pitcher and Cobb's personal enemy, that Ty and a handful of other players had set up a gambling coup in an unimportant ball game played years before.

There was absolutely no substantiation of these charges and Landis could do nothing but give Ty and the others accused a clean bill of health. It was Cobb's contention that the public hearing called by Landis was a farce designed only to bolster the reputation for the stern justice of Landis himself.

He left baseball a rich man but an embittered one. The legend that his early investments in Coca-Cola created his wealth is only partly true. "Coca-Cola was good to me," he said in late life, "but I was in General Motors even before that."

What brought this proud man back to a mild association with the game he played so long and so well was his election to the Baseball Hall of Fame at Cooperstown.

Moe Berg, the former catcher, was there the day Ty was

inducted along with others of the first batch of baseball immortals. Berg tells the story of how he and others had to beg Cobb to appear on the platform.

"He wanted to cut and run," said Moe. "He said that he was too filled with emotion to face the ordeal. We pleaded with him. I told him that he would regret it for the rest of his life if he backed out.

"Fifteen minutes later he was on the stand and no one could have known how deeply he was affected. When called upon, he walked to the dais with that old springy step, delivered a brief speech that hit just the right tone and received tremendous applause. Surprising? Not at all. Cobb always could rise to an occasion."

Cooperstown meant much to Cobb in his mellowing years. As long as his health permitted, he appeared there almost annually, coming from California, Georgia, or wherever he happened to be living to welcome new Hall of Fame members as they were inducted.

A memorable tableau occurred the day Home Run Baker arrived for the unveiling of the Cooperstown plaque recording the exploits of the old third baseman of the Athletics.

The old Maryland farmer concluded his expression of thanks and turned back toward his seat. Like a rocketing pheasant, Cobb rushed to meet him and envelop him in a warm embrace. There were genuine tears in Cobb's eyes.

Only a few of those present remembered that a basepath collision between this pair years before had resulted in Baker being badly spiked and had brought on riotous scenes before a big and angry Philadelphia crowd.

"That was sheer nonsense," maintained Cobb. "Baker knows and always has known that his injury was an accident."

Cobb maintained that his ferocity on the basepaths was wildly exaggerated but others who played against him were equally insistent that his tactics were those of a terrorist. There even was a strong disposition among his contemporaries to deny that Ty, in spite of his record, was the greatest of base stealers.

They said Max Carey was far more scientific in his larceny. Carey stole fewer bases than Cobb but was thrown out far less often.

A recital of one of Cobb's greatest days as a player illustrates how the man could rise to meet the challenge of controversy. The circumstances of this one were set up by tragedy. Late in the 1920 season, Carl Mays, an underhand pitcher of the Yankees, hit Ray Chapman, Cleveland shortstop, on the temple with a pitch. The next day Chapman died, the only such fatality in all the years of major league baseball.

New York papers printed a news service story out of Boston, where the Tigers were playing. Inflammatory statements were attributed to Cobb. He was quoted as saying "Mays should be expelled from baseball forever."

Later, Cobb said that he had been misquoted completely. "They knew," said Ty, "that Mays and I never got along and had had a run-in a while before, but, on the occasion of poor Chapman's death, I had no comment whatever. When I was asked, I said I couldn't sit in judgment on something that happened a couple of hundred miles away."

But, of course, Ty was too proud to speak up at the time. If the New York public wanted to work him over, he could take it.

Two days later, the Tigers were in New York to play the Yankees in a Saturday game at the Polo Grounds. The park filled early with fans eager to cut loose with explosive verbal broadsides.

They sat puzzled through the Detroit batting practice, for Cobb did not appear. The Tigers went out for their fielding drill. Still no Cobb. Some felt cheated. Others exulted in the vain hope that fear of the inevitable demonstration had chased Cobb into hiding. They should have known better.

Finally, the game was about to begin. The door of the visiting team's clubhouse in center field opened and out stepped Cobb alone. The booing mounted as he descended the steps and roared to a crescendo as he walked down the middle of the field with quick light steps and his head held high.

He passed second base, the pitcher's box and home plate, then instead of turning toward the dugout stopped before the press box, then located on the ground level.

His smile was beatific as he removed his baseball cap. As he bowed to the reporters he executed a sweeping gesture with his cap to include them all. The reporters sat stunned but the hostile crowd was further infuriated by the proud arrogance of their appointed villain. The booing, if possible, increased in volume and was maintained throughout most of the ball game.

The Tigers won, 11 to 9, a disastrous defeat for the Yankees who were chasing Cleveland for the pennant. Cobb came to bat six times. Cobb got a double, a triple and three singles, stole two bases, scored two runs, and drove in two more before his howling critics.

Ty was a good outfielder, at home in all three picket positions. He played a great deal of center field in his younger days, later on was more likely to appear in right or left. He could cover ground, had good hands and threw well. There were other good outfielders, and a few were better.

The way he operated with his bat, of course, is the real reason why Cobb will be an immortal memory as long as the game is played.

He was a left-handed hitter who stood with his feet close together in the batter's box. He employed a shifting grip which started with his right hand about three inches from the knob of the bat and his left hand three inches above his right.

He was ready for anything at the plate. His reactions were so quick that he could slide his hands down to the end of the bat and pull a pitch with power into right field. Or he could maintain his hands-apart style and punch a hit into left field. He was a superb bunter with an exceptional percentage of beating out bunts for hits. A third baseman, expecting a bunt, was in danger of having his hair parted by a line drive if he charged in.

Cobb studied his pitchers and applied psychology as an instrument of success. For example, he hit the great, hard-throwing Walter Johnson uncommonly well because he was aware of Johnson's fear that he might accidentally maim a batter with his blazing fast ball.

So Ty would crowd the plate against Johnson, knowing that Walter would pitch him outside and Walter did. But more often than not, this would get Johnson behind on the ball-and-strike count. Then Cobb shifted back to his normal hitting position, knowing that Johnson must come in over the plate with a pitch or give Ty a base on balls.

Cobb's techniques were ideal for meeting the challenges of pitching in the old days of the dead ball. Nevertheless, there is no doubt whatever that Ty would have been great in any era of the game. The fact is that he proved it to the satisfaction of contemporary critics when he was 38 years old.

This was in 1925 and Babe Ruth was in his ascendancy as the all-time master of the home run.

Strictly speaking, Cobb never was much of a home run hitter although he did lead the American League in 1909, when nine home runs were enough to do it. In his 24-year career, he hit a total of 118 homers and his high water mark for single seasons was 12, in 1921 and again in 1925.

Anyway, the veteran, on this occasion, became irritated by one of the frequent stories that good as Cobb was with a bat, Ruth's power, figuratively speaking, put the Babe in another world.

He discussed the story with a group of sports writers in St. Louis and brashly announced that he intended to give a slugging demonstration in the next two games against the Browns.

The next day he hit three home runs against St. Louis pitching. The day after he hit two more homers and two balls bounced off the top of the outfield fence and back into the park for doubles.

"I did it without changing my style too," he proudly informed the astounded critics.

His point established, Cobb went right back to what he called "scientific" hitting. He and Ruth, after some early misunderstandings, ultimately became good friends and Cobb said that he never was jealous of the old Bam's slugging records.

It was inevitable that Cobb should become a manager. He succeeded Hughey Jennings at Detroit in 1921 and was playing-manager of the Tigers for the next six years, getting the team as high as second in 1923.

Like most of the really great ballplayers who try to manage, Cobb was considered a failure as a leader. The general theory is that men of great natural talent are too impatient with young players who are less gifted.

Cobb maintained until his death that his frustration as a manager was more due to Frank Navin, who controlled the purse-strings of the Detroit club and with whom Cobb rarely did see eye-to-eye.

Through at long last in Detroit, Cobb wound up his playing career with the Athletics for two seasons under Connie Mack, for whom he expressed boundless admiration and respect. He got into 134 games in 1927 and batted .357.

Mr. Mack urged Ty to return for one more year and Mr. Cobb finally promised. Ty was now 42. His legs, which he never spared from the day he started out so long before with Augusta of the Sally League, had begun to protest.

In later years, Ty said that, whenever possible that final season, he was in bed by eight in the evening, reading and resting until time to report to the ball park the next day. He played in 95 games, hit .323, and that was that.

TYRUS RAYMOND COBB

Born, December 18, 1886, Narrows, Georgia.
Died, July 17, 1961, Atlanta, Georgia.
Height 6'¾". Weight 175. Batted left- and threw right-handed.

Year	Club	League	Pos.	G	AB	R	H	2B	3B	HR	RBI	BA
1905	Detroit	Amer.	OF	41	150	19	36	6	0	1	...	.240
1906	Detroit	Amer.	OF	97	350	44	112	13	7	1	...	.320
1907	Detroit	Amer.	OF	150	605	97	212	29	15	5	116	.350
1908	Detroit	Amer.	OF	150	581	88	188	36	20	4	101	.324
1909	Detroit	Amer.	OF	156	573	116	216	33	10	9	115	.377
1910	Detroit	Amer.	OF	140	509	106	196	36	13	8	88	.385
1911	Detroit	Amer.	OF	146	591	147	248	47	24	8	144	.420
1912	Detroit	Amer.	OF	140	553	119	227	30	23	7	90	.410
1913	Detroit	Amer.	OF-2B	122	428	70	167	18	16	4	65	.390
1914	Detroit	Amer.	OF	97	345	69	127	22	11	2	57	.368
1915	Detroit	Amer.	OF	156	563	144	208	31	13	3	95	.369
1916	Detroit	Amer.	OF	145	542	113	201	31	10	5	67	.371
1917	Detroit	Amer.	OF-1B	152	588	107	225	44	23	7	108	.383
1918	Detroit	Amer.	OF-1B	111	421	83	161	19	14	3	64	.382
1919	Detroit	Amer.	OF	124	497	92	191	36	13	1	69	.384
1920	Detroit	Amer.	OF	112	428	86	143	28	8	2	63	.334
1921	Detroit	Amer.	OF	128	507	124	197	37	16	12	101	.389
1922	Detroit	Amer.	OF	137	526	99	211	42	16	4	99	.401
1923	Detroit	Amer.	OF	145	556	103	189	40	7	6	88	.340
1924	Detroit	Amer.	OF	155	625	115	211	38	10	4	74	.338
1925	Detroit	Amer.	OF-P	121	415	97	157	31	12	12	102	.378
1926	Detroit [1]	Amer.	OF	79	233	48	79	18	5	4	62	.339
1927	Philadelphia	Amer.	OF	134	490	104	175	32	7	5	93	.357
1928	Philadelphia	Amer.	OF	95	353	54	114	27	4	1	40	.323
Major League Totals				**3033**	**11429**	**2244**	**4191**	**724**	**297**	**118**	**1901**	**.367**

[1] Released, November 2, 1926. Signed by Philadelphia, February, 1927.

WORLD SERIES RECORD

Year	Club	League	Pos.	G	AB	R	H	2B	3B	HR	RBI	BA
1907	Detroit	Amer.	OF	5	20	1	4	0	1	0	0	.200
1908	Detroit	Amer.	OF	5	19	3	7	1	0	0	3	.368
1909	Detroit	Amer.	OF	7	26	3	6	3	0	0	5	.231
World Series Totals				**17**	**65**	**7**	**17**	**4**	**1**	**0**	**8**	**.262**

* key
Pos. = position
G = games
AB = at bat
R = runs
H = hits
2B = two-base hits or doubles
3B = three-base hits or triples
HR = home run
RBI = runs batted in
BA = batting average

24

THEODORE SAMUEL WILLIAMS

Hitting Unlimited

KIRBY HIGBE, the uninhibited knuckleballer, was seated in the club car, doing what comes naturally—talking—surrounded by four or five baseball writers who were on their way from Boston to Chicago after leaving behind them the wreck of the 1946 All-Star game in Fenway Park. The topic of conversation was Ted Williams, since the 1946 All-Star game was one it was impossible to discuss without Williams, who had made a one-man show of it.

Higbe had had quite a time of it in the All-Star game. He had pitched an inning and one-third, during which brief period the game had degenerated from a respectable 2–0 lead held by the Americans to a complete and uttter rout of the National League. A lesser man might have brooded but not ol' Hig.

"That Williams, tch!" spat Kirby. "Everybody thinks he's a great hitter. We got dozens better in our league."

When one of the audience suggested that Higbe name one, he changed the subject.

"That home run he hit against me today," continued the pitcher. "First, I thought I might catch it myself in the pitcher's box. Then I thought maybe Marty Marion might catch it at shortstop. Next I thought maybe Johnny Hopp might catch it in center. And what happened? It landed in the bleachers. Shucks, 'twarn't nothin' but a windblown pop fly!"

Again one of Higbe's auditors was unkind enough to point

out that the so-called "windblown pop fly" had landed eight rows deep in the bleachers in the farthermost reaches of Fenway's center field, a drive that carried 400 feet-plus on a rising trajectory, possibly as hard a blow as mortal man ever struck.

Williams was the first batter Higbe faced when he took over the National League pitching in the fourth and the count was two balls and one strike when Ted unloaded. Williams was the tenth and last batter Higbe faced in the fifth, when he lashed a terrific single to left to give Kirby the rest of the afternoon off. As a consequence, Higbe's belittling of the Red Sox slugger was rather difficult to fathom.

"I still say he ain't a great hitter," stoutly maintained Hig. "I just wish he wuz in our league. I'd like to pitch against him all year."

"I imagine Williams would like it, too," said one of the writers, ending the discussion.

As befits a hitter of his stature, Williams had many days of glory but it is improbable that Ted, or anybody else, ever gave a batting exhibition such as the one he presented before 34,906 fans on July 9, 1946, in Fenway Park. He hit two home runs, getting one off Rip Sewell in the eighth, which was one of the most remarkable of all time. He also drew a pass and hit two singles, having a perfect four-for-four day, scoring four runs for the American Leaguers and batting in five. His amazing performance glossed over the fact that the Nationals suffered a disgraceful 12–0 defeat.

Sewell developed what he called the "ephus" pitch, a delivery which was more spectacular than effective. It was an extraordinarily slow pitch which resembled a pitch shot in golf, since the apex of its arch toward the plate was a good 30 feet from the ground. You could have driven a load of hay under it.

There didn't seem to be much rhyme or reason to the pitch, there being some who were unkind enough to insinuate that Rip used it only to take the minds of the fans off his pitching. It was a diversion, no more, no less. He frequently got it over the plate for a called strike but rarely was anybody foolish enough to swing at it.

Williams, however, decided to have a swing at it. He timed it perfectly, ran up on it and smashed it into the right field bull-pen, where it was caught on the fly by one of the reservists after it had crossed the screen barrier for a home run. It was over 390 feet, a startling distance when you consider that on a slow-motion, looping pitch such as this, the batter has to supply all the power.

Let us leave Higbe and his conversation in the club car that July evening and advance some four months to an evening in October. The sixth game of the World Series has just been won by the Cardinals to pull them even with the Red Sox. Rogers Hornsby and a couple of writers are jolting through the streets of St. Louis from Sportsman's Park to press headquarters at the Hotel Jefferson.

"What ever has come over that Williams?" rasped Hornsby.

"He's not hitting," replied a writer, happy to have the correct answer. Ted's batting average of the moment being a neat, though not gaudy, .238. "That shift has got him all fouled up."

"It isn't just the shift," rasped Rog. "He just doesn't look like he's ever gonna hit. He's fiddlin' around up at the plate, jerkin' his bat one way and then the other as if he didn't know what town he was in. I never saw a good hitter look so bad in my life."

When the seventh game was played, Williams went four-for-oh, as the phrase has it, and wound up with five singles to show for 25 times at bat in the Series, an average of .200 and precisely one run batted in. It was one of the biggest flops of all time by a star player in World Series competition.

Somehow those two conversations, the one in the club car in July and the one in the cab in October, are illustrative of Williams. There was no middle ground for Ted. He was either a hero or a goat. Indisputably, the figures show Williams to be one of the greatest hitters of his time. Nobody can be part-hero and part-goat and maintain such an average, but with Ted the goat roles are remembered long after the hero roles are forgotten, maybe because there are so many of the latter.

Lou Boudreau, the quondam boy manager of Cleveland, probably did as much to cause Williams mental anguish and heartache as all the hooting of the fans and the barbs of the sportswriters put together. With Lou, however, it was not deliberate, but a matter of self-preservation. For it was Boudreau who decided that super-methods would have to be taken to check a super-hitter. And even Lou didn't realize the full effect his overshifted defense was going to have upon Williams.

It was in July of 1946, only five days after the All-Star game in which Williams clouted his two home runs. Ted was still riding on the momentum of those homers and in the first game of a Sunday double-header, he whacked three against an assortment of Cleveland pitchers. In the clubhouse between games, Boudreau devised the shift which was to cause Williams so much trouble.

Boudreau lined up the Indians on the right side of the diamond and dared Williams to pull the ball. The right fielder played on the foul line and so did the first baseman, who played deep. The second baseman was back on the grass and closer to first base than he was to second. The shortstop (Boudreau) was on the right side of second base, near the normal second baseman's position. The third baseman played directly behind second base. The center fielder moved over to right fielder's regular position, while the left fielder moved in to a position just behind shortstop.

This unorthodox alignment left only the pitcher or catcher to field bunts and nobody at all to field anything hit to left field, save the left fielder who was playing in a deep shortstop position. Ted, of course, didn't try to bunt nor did he try to hit

219

to left. He accepted Boudreau's challenge and that very afternoon whacked out two hits. In view of what has happened since, it might have been better if he had been horse-collared the first time he faced the shift.

Fenway Park has an unusual construction, with a short left field fence and a deep stretch in right. Boudreau first said that the purpose of the shift was to limit Williams to singles, but since has confessed in his biography that he regarded the efficacy of the shift as a psychological, rather than a tactical, victory. Ted, of course, could have defeated the purpose of the shift at any time by bunting or placing his hits to left. And since has, forcing teams who overshift against him to employ a much more modified version of the original Boudreau shift.

Eddie Dyer, who managed the Cardinals against Joe Cronin's Red Sox in the 1946 World Series, guessed that Williams would accept the challenge again, particularly since it was a World Series and the eyes of all baseball were upon him. Eddie guessed correctly. The Dyer shift was an offspring of the one devised by Boudreau, with the difference that the shortstop, Marty Marion, remained on the left side of second base, but close to the bag and Whitey Kurowski, the third baseman, played on the right side of second. The outfield swung around, but Eddie didn't bring his left fielder in as close as Boudreau had.

Williams succeeded in pulling a ball through this defense in the opener but was blanked in the second game. When the Series moved to Boston, Williams dropped a bunt down the third baseline and, thereafter, Dyer played Kurowski in the corner but some 20 feet off the base to protect against bunts. Ted never tried another bunt in the Series.

Considering all the trouble, mental and physical, which the Boudreau shift piled up for Williams in that year of 1946, there is an ironic twist to it. The Red Sox, who won 40 of their first 50 games that year and tow-roped the American League field, had difficulty in clinching the pennant, the first Red Sox flag in twenty-eight years. They finally made the grade in Cleveland on September 13, on a home run by Williams hit into left field over the head of Pat Seerey, the Cleveland left fielder, who was playing in close in accordance with his position in the Boudreau shift!

Because of Williams' well-known and oft-demonstrated eagerness to hit, many pitchers formed the hasty opinion that so impulsive a batter might be lured into hitting at bad pitches as Babe Ruth was. Nothing was farther from the case. Williams would not offer at a ball if it was a fraction of an inch out of the strike zone. Umpires had such respect for Ted's keen eye that he rarely was called out on strikes. As a result of pitchers trying to entice him into biting at bad pitches, pitching carefully to him because of the damage he could do and of giving him intentional passes, Williams drew more walks than any living player. He always got more than 100 bases on balls in a season and usually led the American League in that statistic.

Loose is the word for Williams at the plate. He looked like a marionette with the puppeteer's strings relaxed. Tall and gangly, he dipped his knees slightly, took a few nervous swishes with the bat, wrapped his fingers around the handle as though he were going to wring sawdust from it and then became immobile as the pitcher prepared to deliver. Ted stood fairly deep in the box, right foot somewhat closer to the plate than his left, which was about 15 inches behind the right. He used to bat with his feet somewhat closer together and take a longer stride but later he widened his stance somewhat and shortened his stride.

When Williams swung, it was a marvelously rhythmic and coordinated swing, with his strong wrists snapping into the swing at the moment of impact. Admitting that Ted had the fine sense of timing and the whiplash swing so vital to a good hitter, the two characteristics which made him a super-hitter were his exceptional eyesight and his great wrist action.

Considering how many raps Williams took for his fielding, it was ironical that it was a rap sustained *because* of his fielding that should give him the first major injury of his career. It happened in the 1950 All-Star game in Chicago's Comiskey Park when Ted gamely crashed into the left field scoreboard after catching a drive hit by Ralph Kiner.

Williams continued to play for a couple of innings after the collision but the pain became too severe and Casey Stengel, managing the All-Star for the first time, relieved him. It was only after the game that it was discovered that he had sustained a fracture in his left forearm.

The slugger was out for several weeks, but strangely enough the Red Sox made quite a run at the Yankees without him. By now Steve O'Neill had succeeded Joe McCarthy as the Bosox manager and he was criticized when he returned Williams to the lineup and the Red Sox tailed off.

"Good Lord," said Steve in quiet exasperation at his second guessers, "they didn't expect me to win the pennant *without* the best hitter in baseball, did they?"

Although he played in only 89 games that year, a couple of them as a pinch hitter, Williams managed to hit 28 home runs and knock in 97 runs. His average was only .317 and in 1951 Ted had what was for him an ordinary year. He played almost the entire season but he knocked in only 29 more runs than he had the year before and hit only two more homers.

It was in 1952 that Williams made his peace with the fans of Fenway—or vice versa. In April of that year he was summoned to appear before a Marine Corps agency in Jacksonville, Florida, to take his physical. Like Jerry Coleman of the Yankees, Ted had maintained a reserve commission after World War II, and the Marines, who were left desperately short of fliers after the emergence of the Army Air Forces as a separate fighting group, commenced the recalling of former pilots.

Williams passed and was given the customary 30 days to "get

his affairs in order" as the phrase so baldly puts it. He played only a half-dozen games, hitting one home run to raise his lifetime total to 324, but the Red Sox fans gave him a day before he reported back to service and showered him with gifts. And Ted responded by tipping his cap!

Williams himself had little hope of returning to baseball. It wasn't long before he was flying jets in Korea, and Ted was sure then that his baseball career was behind him, never more so than one day when he crash-landed in Korea with the tail of his plane afire.

Ted was away all that remained of 1952 and the most of 1953. He returned to the States in time to be present at the All-Star game in Cincinnati, where Commissioner Frick delegated to him the honor of throwing out the first ball.

When Ted finally returned to action he showed the amazing skills which were his. Playing the last 37 games, Williams batted .409. More remarkable was that he clouted 13 home runs in 91 official at bats. Since Ted goes to bat more than 500 times when he plays a full year, these 13 homers represented a full-season rate of 70!

Williams lent his name to a ghostwritten piece in the spring of 1954 which stirred up another great controversy in Boston. The Red Sox slugger announced that this was to be his last year. And before the first installment was on the stands, Ted fractured his collarbone in the first five minutes of the first day of spring training! He was hardly back in the lineup before he was down with an attack of pneumonia. The result was that, although he batted .345, he didn't play in enough games to accumulate the necessary 400 at bats to make himself eligible for the American League batting title.

The greatest of all Williams batting accomplishments, of course, is the .406 average he achieved in 1941. Bill Terry, who hit .401 in 1930, was the last major leaguer to hit .400 before Ted and nobody has hit that high since. Only eight men have broken .400 since the turn of the century, only two in the last quarter-century. It takes, as you will note, a bit of doing.

Williams was hitting over .400 when the schedule had a week to go and Manager Cronin told Ted he could take the rest of the season off and protect his average, if he wished. Ted refused on the grounds that if he was to be a .400 hitter, he'd be a legitimate one. The Yanks already had clinched the pennant and the remaining games were meaningless but Williams, to his everlasting credit, insisted on playing out the string.

On the final day of the season, with a Sunday doubleheader coming up in Philadelphia, it looked as though Williams had made a poor guess. His average had dipped to .399 and he would need at least four hits in the double-header to put him over the top. Ted did a little better than that—he belted four out of five in the opener, two out of three in the nightcap to wind up with a resplendent .406, highest American League average since George Sisler batted .420 in 1922. One of his hits was a home run and another would have been had it not hit the horn atop the scoreboard at Shibe Park and rebounded back to the playing field for a two-bagger.

Williams' batting average, particularly his home run production, was remarkable when you consider that he played 77 games each season in Fenway Park, the layout of which was diametrically and geometrically inimical to his hitting talent. Ted pulled to right field, the longest stretch in the Fenway, where the average home run to right field must travel 382 feet. Left field, which Ted avoided as though it were a leper colony, is a cozy 315 feet.

It is doubtful if Williams ever found a park more suited to his hitting talents than Nicollet Park in Minneapolis, where the Red Sox sent him in 1938. It was here for the first time that the long drink of water began to display the attributes which were to make him the scourge of rival pitchers. And traits which often drove his own manager to the aspirin bottle.

Billy Evans, general manager of the Red Sox, and vice-president Eddie Collins had plucked Williams from San Diego before he was ripe. And with good reason. Ted went right from Herbert Hoover High School in his native San Diego to the local club in the Pacific Coast League in midsummer of 1936. He finished out the season without doing anything spectacular, or even anything temperamental. The Red Sox had a working agreement with the Padres and the fine, level swing of the kid rookie was dutifully reported back to the home office. Williams didn't hit .300 in that first half-season with San Diego, nor did he hit it in his next year, either, but he already was showing signs of greatness. Before he took on too much glamour, the Red Sox closed the deal for him, getting him for something like $25,000 and five minor league players. And they got him just before some really big offers were in the making.

Williams aroused some little interest in Sarasota, mainly because he refused to wear a necktie and again because he missed a bus which was to take him for an exhibition game. Cronin decided that a year at Minneapolis would do Williams no harm and himself a lot of good.

Minneapolis then was owned by Mike Kelley, the last of the truly great "independent" owners, who stood off the chain-store system as long as he could. The manager of the Millers was Donie Bush, a mild-mannered little fellow who had played with Detroit's ferocious Tigers back in the century's first decade, a major and minor league manager of note with the reputation of being able to handle men.

That Donie could handle men there was no doubt. Apparently his special skills didn't extend to boys. Ted found American Association pitching inviting and the short fences of Nicollet Park even more so. He promptly proceeded to tear the league apart, eventually leading it in batting, in home runs, in runs batted in, in total bases, in runs scored and in bases on balls.

One morning Bush walked into President Kelley's office,

where Mike sat, guarded by his faithful and fierce Dalmatian, Jitterbug.

"Mike," said Donie, skillfully avoiding an attempted nip by Jitterbug, "either that kid takes off his uniform or I do."

"I've known you a long time now, Donie, haven't I?" began Kelley placatingly.

"Better than thirty years," moodily agreed Bush.

"How many years has it been," asked Mike, "since you saw a kid who could hit like that one? You certainly don't think that after all the years I've known you I'd ask you to turn in your uniform, do you? And, after all the years we've both known each other, you don't think I'm crazy enough to ask a hitter like that to take off his uniform, do you?"

Bush wasn't the first manager who felt that even Ted's great batting didn't compensate for other things, nor was he the last. Cronin on at least three occasions took Williams out of a ball game for loafing. Or, to put it more aptly, sulking.

When Joe McCarthy succeeded Cronin as manager of the Red Sox, the Hot Stove simmered and bubbled all winter with speculation as to how McCarthy, a strict disciplinarian, would handle Williams. Joe, for instance, had an aversion to sports shirts. He wanted his players to look and act like champions, in the dining room as well as on the ball field.

One fact nobody bothered to take into consideration was that McCarthy was a great handler of men only because he was a great handler of individuals. He solved the tieless problem, for instance, by wearing a sports shirt himself the first few days around the Sarasota training camp. The issue of neckties never came up because McCarthy buried it beforehand.

As to how McCarthy "handled" Williams, there is only this to report. Ted had two of the greatest seasons of his life under Joe and the Red Sox narrowly missed two straight pennants in the first two years of their association, losing one in a playoff and the other in the final game of the season.

Probably Williams irritated as many baseball fans as irritated

226

him, which is saying a great deal. Ted, even when he made a great play in the outfield, gave the impression that he was only half-trying. His nonchalance at the plate, so amazing when he hit safely, became annoying when he popped up.

A couple of Williams' mannerisms which irritated the fans were his refusal to tip his hat after hitting a home run. Another was the fact that when he was on base and Vernon (Junior) Stephens followed him with a home run, Ted never waited at home plate to shake Junior's hand. The rumor was printed that Ted was jealous of the newcomer to the Red Sox.

Ted never bothered to scotch such rumors, but on several occasions he tried to "water-down" the fans who were getting on him for it. In 1956, he was mockingly christened The Splendid Spitter when he was fined $5,000 by Boston owner Tom Yawkey for directing a few drops of saliva at several Red Sox spectators. Will Harridge, the American League president, added $250 to the league's coffers by fining Ted for spitting at the fans in Kansas City in 1958, the year he won his seventh and last league hitting crown.

There is much evidence at hand to indicate that Williams was not the self-centered athlete he so often was depicted as being. During the great batting streak of Joe DiMaggio in 1941, when Joe hit in 56 straight games, Ted, from his left field position in front of the scoreboard at Fenway Park, always had Bill Daley, the operator, let him know the progress of Joe's streak and he then shouted the information across to Dom DiMaggio in center. Hardly jealous that, considering that the rivalry between Williams and the older DiMaggio had practically split Boston and New York into armed camps.

Williams was close with Johnny Orlando, manager of the Red Sox clubhouse and considered the rotund Johnny one of his best friends. After the 1946 season, Ted gave Johnny a check which was bigger than the losers' share of the World Series' that fall. Certainly Johnny hardly would classify his favorite slugger as inconsiderate or self-centered.

Neither would the kids of Boston. For years, he has been the guiding light in the success of the Jimmy Fund, a local charity which treats children with cancer. Not only has he personally donated thousands of dollars and brought in hundreds of thousands more, but he has also unselfishly devoted himself to visiting them in hospitals. Ted demands only one favor for his efforts—no publicity. He may not try to be one of the guys on the field. But to them he's all man off it.

One of Williams' truly big days among his fellow American Leaguers was his performance in the All-Star game in Boston in 1946, related at the outset of this chapter. It is possible he enjoyed an even greater one in Detroit five years earlier when his ninth-inning home run smash against the roof of Briggs Stadium broke up the game.

The Americans went into the ninth trailing, 5–3. With one out and the bases filled, Claude Passeau was in a tough spot but he pitched craftily to Joe DiMaggio and the Yankee Clipper hit a perfect double-play ball to Eddie Miller at short. It should have ended the game but Billy Herman, taking the relay at second, pivoted and threw wide to first base. One run scored.

Herman, one of the best pivot men in the game, claimed he was confused by the collection of uniforms at first base, understandable enough since each player wears the uniform of his own team. Whatever the reason, the failure to make the double play was costly, since it brought Williams to bat.

Passeau had one strike and two balls on Ted when the kid's bat lashed out. The ball crashed against the façade atop the third tier of the stadium, fair by a comfortable margin. Joe Gordon and DiMaggio scored ahead of Williams, waited for him at home plate and smothered him with hugs. And so did as many of the other American League as could reach him. For one day at least, the lonesome Williams was one of the boys.

Casey Stengel, who forgets very little, certainly remembered that and has included Ted on every All-Star team until they both closed out their American League careers in 1960. But it is doubtful if even the ole Professor could have ignored a man with a .344 lifetime batting average, 521 home runs, and the title "Player of the Decade."

THEODORE SAMUEL WILLIAMS

Born, August 30, 1918, San Diego, California.
Height 6'4". Weight 200. Batted left- and threw right-handed.

Year	Club	League	Pos.	G	AB	R	H	2B	3B	HR	RBI	BA
1939	Boston	Amer.	OF	149	565	131	185	44	11	31	145	.327
1940	Boston	Amer.	OF	144	561	134	193	43	14	23	113	.344
1941	Boston	Amer.	OF	143	456	135	185	33	3	37	120	.406
1942	Boston	Amer.	OF	150	522	141	186	34	5	36	137	.356
1943–1944–1945	(In Military Service)											
1946	Boston	Amer.	OF	150	514	142	176	37	8	38	123	.342
1947	Boston	Amer.	OF	156	528	125	181	40	9	32	114	.343
1948	Boston	Amer.	OF	137	509	124	188	44	3	25	127	.369
1949	Boston	Amer.	OF	155	566	150	194	39	3	43	159	.343
1950	Boston	Amer.	OF	89	334	82	106	24	1	28	97	.317
1951	Boston	Amer.	OF	148	531	109	169	28	4	30	126	.318
1952	Boston [1]	Amer.	OF	6	10	2	4	0	1	1	3	.400
1953	Boston	Amer.	OF	37	91	17	37	6	0	13	34	.407
1954	Boston	Amer.	OF	117	386	93	133	23	1	29	89	.345
1955	Boston	Amer.	OF	98	320	77	114	21	3	28	83	.356
1956	Boston	Amer.	OF	136	400	71	138	28	2	24	82	.345
1957	Boston	Amer.	OF	132	420	96	163	28	1	38	87	.388
1958	Boston	Amer.	OF	129	411	81	135	23	2	26	85	.328
1959	Boston	Amer.	OF	103	272	32	69	15	0	10	43	.254
1960	Boston	Amer.	OF	113	310	56	98	15	0	29	72	.316
Major League Totals				**2292**	**7706**	**1798**	**2654**	**525**	**71**	**521**	**1839**	**.344**

[1] In Military Service most of 1952 and 1953 seasons.

WORLD SERIES RECORD

Year	Club	League	Pos.	G	AB	R	H	2B	3B	HR	RBI	BA
1946	Boston	Amer.	OF	7	25	2	5	0	0	0	1	.200

* key
Pos. = position
G = games
AB = at bat
R = runs
H = hits
2B = two-base hits or doubles
3B = three-base hits or triples
HR = home run
RBI = runs batted in
BA = batting average

25

WILLIE MAYS
The "Say-Hey" Kid

In 1954, his first full and uninterrupted season in the National League, the Giants' Willie Mays did everything except take tickets. He led the majors in batting with a .345 average, he led the majors in slugging with an awesome .667 percentage, his team won the National League pennant, swept Cleveland's Indians four straight in the World Series, and Mays was voted the Most Valuable Player in the National League.

There literally is no telling how far Mays can go in baseball, any more than there is any telling how far he can go for a baseball. As long ago as 1951, when Willie, a kid of nineteen, was called up by the Giants from Minneapolis, Manager Leo Durocher was raving about him. "I wouldn't trade Willie for any player in baseball—DiMaggio, Musial, Williams, or anybody," declared the Lip. At the time, while Mays' undeniable skills were appreciated, it was thought that Leo was overstating the case. It turns out he was right all along.

The writer who first tagged Willie "The Amazin' Mays" had something. The kid from Alabama is truly an amazing player. The catch he made on Vic Wertz of the Indians in the first game of the 1954 Series in all probability won, not just that game, but the Series for the Giants. In the annual poll conducted by baseball's bible, *The Sporting News*, the majority of sportswriters singled out this catch as the most exciting play of 1954 in any sport, not just baseball.

When Wertz came to bat, Cleveland had men on first and second and none out. It was the eighth inning and the score was tied, 2–2. The Indians hadn't scored against Sal Maglie since this same Wertz had tripled home two runs in the first inning, and the Giants hadn't scored against Bob Lemon since the third. The 52,751 fans at the Polo Grounds were silent in an agony of suspense, aware that the big moment was coming up.

Durocher, playing the percentages, lifted Maglie and brought in a young southpaw, Don Liddle, to pitch to the left-handed batting Wertz, who had made three straight hits. Liddle threw a ball, got over a called strike to even the count, and then Wertz fouled one off. Vic hit the next pitch about as far as a ball could be hit in the Polo Grounds and still stay in the ball park. It sailed dead to the bleachers just to the right of center.

Mays took one look, turned his back on home plate, and ran like a thief. He never looked again until he was within a couple of feet of the barrier, when he glanced backward and took the ball in his gloved hand over his left shoulder. He quickly whirled and fired the ball back to the infield, falling as he did so. That was all the pitching for Liddle that day, Marv Grissom taking over and holding the Indians at bay until Dusty Rhodes delivered a three-run pinch homer in the tenth.

I was sitting next to Joe DiMaggio in the press box when Mays made his catch. The Yankee Clipper agreed with the rest of us that it was one of the best catches he ever saw and then went on to point out why he considered it a great catch.

"As remarkable as the ground Willie had to cover to make the catch—and he just did get to the ball—was the judgment he showed in not letting the fence scare him," said DiMaggio. "There is no trick to catching a ball in the open field, no matter how far it is hit, as long as it stays in the air long enough. The test of an outfielder's skill comes when he has to go against the fence to make a catch."

Mays was a hit with the Giant fans from the day he joined

231

the club in 1951, even though he made only one hit in his first
21 times at bat in a Giant uniform. It was then he picked up
the "Say-Hey" nickname. Willie didn't know too many of the
other players on the club and, being unsure of name, he simply
yelled, "Say-Hey!" whenever he wanted somebody's attention.

Mays, on the bench or in the clubhouse, is the spirit of the
Giants. He talks a lot, laughs a lot. When he rode out on the
bus with the other National League players for the All-Star
game in Cleveland in 1954, Charley Grimm, the Milwaukee
manager and one of the National League coaches, declared,
"Mays is the only ballplayer I ever saw who could help a club
just by riding on the bus with it."

Willie, in demand for personal appearances these days, is
perhaps not as gay and as carefree as he was when he first came
up. It was then that Bill Roeder of the *World-Telegram & Sun*
said of him, "Willie answers all your questions breathlessly.
He sounds like a guy who has just been told that his house is
on fire."

Mays is a baseball genius but a kid in the ways of the world.
The only time he is sure of himself is when he is on the ball
field, whether it's Candlestick Park, a street in Harlem where
he used to play stickball with the neighborhood kids, or a ball
park in Puerto Rico where he played winter ball in the 1954–55
season.

When Willie learned he could play winter baseball, he was
like a kid who had been told there were two Christmases. Or
that Santa Claus was twins. Ripping out base hits and roaming
the outfield for Santurce in the Puerto Rican League, he was
completely happy, even though he didn't have a word of Spanish at his command. Willie can hit and field in any language,
including the Scandinavian.

It wasn't any happenstance that Mays spent the first winter
of his stardom in Puerto Rico. The Giant officials, confident that
they had as their property the greatest baseball player to come

along since Babe Ruth, pondered how to keep Willie happy between seasons. Winter baseball was the logical answer.

When Mays returned from the Army in 1954 to set the baseball world afire, he became a national figure. And Willie, at twenty-three, didn't know how to be a national figure. He only knew how to play ball.

Winter baseball in Puerto Rico was something Willie understood. There were familiar faces there: Herman Franks, the Giant third-base coach who managed Santurce, Reuben Gomez, Willie's teammate, and dozens of others, including some who had played with Mays when he was with the Birmingham Black Barons in the Negro League. It was all down Willie's alley.

Mays was a tremendous hit in Puerto Rico. He led the league, natch. The fans even learned to drop "Ole! Mira!"— the Spanish equivalent of "Say-Hey"—and to chant "Say-Hey" like a football cheer every time Mays came to bat. Willie's basket catches, his rifle throws, and his slashing base hits sent the Islanders into ecstasies. When he dashed around the bases or the field and his cap fell off, as it inevitably does anytime Willie gets up steam, he was applauded vigorously.

Frank Forbes, the Giant scout, a New York state boxing judge and an old Howard College athlete, accompanied Mays to Puerto Rico and revealed that Willie was a little unhappy in his first few days there. "He had a real nice apartment, three rooms, maybe nicer than he had had to himself before in his life," said Forbes, "but he just couldn't get over the fact that when he came home at night, there was nobody there to say 'Hello' to him."

Forbes explained that Mays grew up in Alabama as one of a large family of 10 half-brothers and half-sisters and that in Harlem, his landlady, Mrs. James Goosby, clucks over him like a mother hen. "He just couldn't get used to being alone when he first came to Puerto Rico," said Forbes. "Willie likes people." It might be added that people like Willie, too.

Mays went to Puerto Rico primarily to play ball and secondly to escape the confusion that enveloped him in New York. When fame descended on Willie like a hailstorm in the summer of 1954, he found himself being dragged from banquet table to television station like a guy running for office. There were fees, to be sure, and sizable ones at that, but Mays gladly would have passed them up for the sake of some peace.

Willie had hoped that the outside involvements would end with the World Series. Instead, they increased. He had all sorts of extracurricular offers, including a bizarre, and somewhat suspect, bid to take part in a floor show at a Las Vegas night club. This was prior to the days when Don Drysdale, Maury Wills, et al. made this desert town as much a part of the off-season as the Hot Stove League. The Giants, knowing that they have something special in Mays, keep him wrapped in jeweler's wool, insulated from the fast-buck chasers by club officials and by members of Art Flynn Associates, his agents.

Willie played the day after he landed in San Juan. He would have played the day he landed except that it rained. Franks, his manager, told him he only had to make a courtesy appearance, to pinch-hit or pinch-run. "I came down here to play, Herm," said Willie, and play he did. He made two hits in his first game and played center field at Parque Sixto Escobar as if he had been born and brought up there. It is, it may be parenthetically noted, probably the only ball field in the world named after a bantamweight champion.

If Mays has a fault, it is that his throwing is undisciplined. It was thought that perhaps Franks might have had some specific instructions from Durocher for handling Mays.

"Instructions?" repeated Franks. "What could you tell Willie? He doesn't smoke and he doesn't drink and he loves to sleep, so you don't have to worry about him being in shape. Maybe he shouldn't go after that first pitch so often, but that's the way he is. His throwing could be somewhat more restrained,

234

but his one idea is to get the ball and fire it home as quickly as possible. If Willie lets a fellow get an extra base once in a while because of his throws, it's nothing compared to the extra bases he takes away from 'em."

"When you've got a boy like Willie you don't burden him with instructions," interpolated Tom Sheehan, a Giant scout. "Would you try to teach Native Dancer how to run?"

Durocher has given Mays his head ever since the boy joined the club after the start of the 1951 season. When Willie got off a plane in the spring of 1954 and hit a ball over the center field fence at Phoenix in his first time at bat, Leo winked at the sportswriters and said, "Why tinker with a guy like that?"

The affinity between Durocher and Mays is out of this world. Willie takes every word of Leo's as gospel. If the Lip tells Willie to ask the umpire to inspect the ball, Mays won't step into the batter's box until the ball has been inspected.

Buster Clarkson, who had hit 42 home runs for Dallas in the Texas League, is a Negro infielder who was born about five years too early to take full advantage of Branch Rickey's emancipation proclamation. Before the erasure of the color line in baseball, Negroes had to take their play and their pay where they found it, which usually was south of the border. Buster was talking about playing baseball in Mexico under Adolpho Luque, the Cuban who once was one of the National League's craftiest right-handers.

"Smartest cookie I ever played for," said Buster appreciatively. "He had different signs for every player on the club and it seemed like he had a sign for every pitch. I don't see how he remembered them all. And, brother, you had to remember them or he'd fine you big if you missed one."

"I couldn't play for a man like that, I declare I couldn't," squeaked Willie in the high-pitched voice he lapses into when excited. "I just like to be let alone when I'm playing. That's why I like Leo. He never bothers me, just lets me go 'long

235

my own way. Oh, mebbe if we're a run or two behind in the late innings, I look over to him to see should I take or hit but mostly I'm free."

As a matter of fact, Durocher had Willie bunt only once during 1954. It resulted in a runner being thrown out at third. The Giants lost the game and Mays never was asked to bunt again.

The only advice given Mays since he first joined the club was a suggestion midway in the 1954 season that he modify his stance. Willie had been batting from a full spread and a semi-crouch. Durocher got him to bring his feet somewhat closer together and to stand more erectly. The results of the new stance were amazing, even for Mays.

Willie hit his 36th home run off Alpha Brazle of the Cardinals on July 28th in the 99th game on the Giants' schedule, a pace which was better than Babe Ruth's in 1927 when he smashed his record of 60 homers. Although he played in 55 more games, Mays hit only five more home runs, one of them inside the park. If this sounds as though the pitchers had solved Willie, don't kid yourself. He was batting .326 when he changed his stance and he batted .379 from that point on, to wind up leading the majors with an impressive .345 average.

The dip in home-run production and the boom in Mays' average were the result of the altered stance. Willie's power had been against high, inside pitches. Pitchers were keeping the ball away from his strength and were pitching low and outside. With the new stance, Mays was ripping this ball into right and right-center for base hits. Individual glory (homers) was sacrificed for the greater good of the team (base knocks).

Mays didn't stick to his new stance entirely during 1954. In the first two games of the World Series, he spread himself and tried for the fences but Bob Lemon and Early Wynn were able to get the ball past him and he didn't make a hit. Durocher talked with Willie on the plane to Cleveland and Mays modified his stance in the two games there, batting .444 and raising his Series average to .286.

In Puerto Rico, Mays used the modified stance for the first couple of weeks, batted up around .500, but hit no home runs. Then he went back to the spread and hit homers in four consecutive games. As the winter season progressed, Willie alternated the stances, allowing himself to be governed in many cases by the type of pitching he faced.

The one chink in Willie's armor is his impatience. He hates to let the first pitch go by if it is within range. In the 1954 Series, Willie chased the first pitch eight times and made only one hit, twice missing it for strikes and going out on it five times.

In these days, when players are switching to lighter and lighter bats, Mays is something of an oddity, swinging a 39 ounce club. Willie has amazingly powerful forearms and biceps, which account for him being able to whip the bat around so quickly and so strongly. Mays believed that his hitch in the Army developed his arms.

"I loved the calisthenics," explained Willie, "and they used to let me lead the new batches in the setting-up exercises. I think all those push-ups I did made my arms bigger."

The first time Durocher ever saw Mays was in 1951 at Melbourne, Florida, where the Giants had their minor league clubs training. That was the year that the Giants and Yankees swapped training bases for the spring, the Yankees going out to Phoenix and the Giants taking over St. Petersburg. Willie had been purchased from the Birmingham Black Barons the year before on the recommendation of Scout Eddie Montague. He had finished out 1950 with Trenton, New Jersey, in the Inter-State League, batted a cool .353, but with only four home runs, and was earmarked for advancement all the way up to Minneapolis in the American Association.

It was love at first sight. The pepper and hustle of Mays

made a great impression on Leo and he confided to Fred Weatherly, *Daily Mirror* cartoonist, that he was going to have Mays on the Giant squad as soon as he could. Weatherly probably was the first New York newspaperman to even hear of Mays.

Durocher was all for kidnaping Willie then and there and carting him right back to St. Pete with him. Rosie Ryan, general manager of Minneapolis, squealed in protest and held on to Mays but Ryan knew then that his number was up.

Mays was allowed to remain with the Millers through 35 ball games. All he did was to bat .477! When President Stoneham called him back to the Giants, the howls in Minneapolis could be heard as far away as Milwaukee. Stoneham took large ads in the Minneapolis papers to explain why he had called Willie up, but Willie's batting average explained that.

Although Mays didn't hit .300 in his first year with the Giants, evidence of his power was there in the 20 home runs he lashed. He made, as he still does, many spectacular fielding plays, including one in which he caught his cap with one hand and the ball with the other. Mays' cap was always falling off, as no Giant player's cap had since Frankie Frisch came from the Fordham campus in 1919.

Mays was an inspiration to the Giants in that first year but when he went away to the Army in May of 1952, the bottom dropped out of things. The Giants managed to stay close to the Brooks but never looked strong enough to make the Dodgers worry over a repetition of the miracle of the year before. It wasn't long after Willie had entered service that Charley Dressen, the Dodger manager and the victim of the '51 miracle, was able to publicly proclaim, "The Giants is dead!" Dressen was wrong grammatically but factually he was as right as rain.

From the very beginning in 1954, Mays was red-hot. He delighted 32,397 opening day fans at the Polo Grounds by belting a pitch from Brooklyn's Carl Erskine into the upper deck in left to break a 3–3 tie and give Sal Maglie another victory over the Dodgers.

As Mays' home runs increased, so did the outside pressure on him. It was the beginning of the log jam which caused him to seek sanctuary in Puerto Rico that winter. His aunt, who had been a foster mother to him after the death of his own mother, died in Alabama in July and Willie left the club to attend the funeral. He missed three games, the only games he has missed since joining the Giants.

Mays received $1000 a month and expenses for playing in Puerto Rico. He obviously could have made more than that by hanging around New York and making personal appearances but the Giant officials decided that Willie would be better off playing ball. He had an offer to go with a barnstorming team but Durocher nixed that, on the advice of Hank Thompson, Giant third baseman.

"Willie can't play ball unless it means something," said Thompson. "He'll be much better off playing in the winter league."

In addition to being named MVP in the National League, further honors were bestowed on Mays when the New York chapter of the Baseball Writers Association selected him as the player of the year at their annual dinner in January, 1955, and presented the Sid Mercer Memorial Award to him.

Willie became his own man after Leo was ousted from the Giant's managerial spot in 1955. He bought a sumptuous home in an exclusive San Francisco suburb, and hired an agent to attend to his major league high salary of $105,000 per year. It might also be added that he has collected 290 home runs in those eight years and averaged over 100 RBI's per season. In the Giant's pennant winning year in 1962, Willie hit .304, knocked in 141 runs, and hit a league-leading 49 homers.

Branch Rickey, Jr., head of the Pittsburgh farm system,

watched Mays play a couple of games in Puerto Rico and made an interesting observation:

"You can tell more about players in a couple of games down here than you can in a couple of weeks in the States," declared the Twig. "Down here you can tell who likes to play and who doesn't. In the States, there's always a manager putting pressure on the player, but down here the boys are on their own. The guy who puts out down here wants to play. And the fellow who likes to play will help your club."

Willie proves that theory—with and without a bat in his hands. In 1955, he became the first player to hit 50 or more home runs and steal 20 or more bases in a season, and in 1956 he set another adaptability record by hitting more than 30 HR's and stealing better than 30 bases. In the 1963 All-Star game in Cleveland, Wondrous Willie stood out again. He collected a hit, 2 RBI's, scored twice, walked, stole two bases and topped it off with the outstanding catch of the game.

That about sums up Willie. He likes to play. And he's pretty good at it, too—maybe the best there is today.

WILLIE HOWARD MAYS, JR.

Born, May 6, 1931, Westfield, Alabama.
Height 5'11". Weight 180. Bats and throws right-handed.

Year	Club	League	Pos.	G	AB	R	H	2B	3B	HR	RBI	BA
1951	New York	Nat.	OF	121	464	59	127	22	5	20	68	.274
1952	New York [1]	Nat.	OF	34	127	17	30	2	4	4	23	.236
1953	(In Military Service)											
1954	New York	Nat.	OF	151	565	119	195	33	13	41	110	.345
1955	New York	Nat.	OF	152	580	123	185	18	13	51	127	.319
1956	New York	Nat.	OF	152	578	101	171	27	8	36	84	.296
1957	New York	Nat.	OF	152	585	112	195	26	20	35	97	.333
1958	San Francisco	Nat.	OF	152	600	121	208	33	11	29	96	.347
1959	San Francisco	Nat.	OF	151	575	125	180	43	5	34	104	.313
1960	San Francisco	Nat.	OF	153	595	107	190	29	12	29	103	.319
1961	San Francisco	Nat.	OF	154	572	129	176	32	3	40	123	.308
1962	San Francisco	Nat.	OF	162	621	130	189	36	5	49	141	.304
1963	San Francisco	Nat.	OF	157	596	115	187	32	7	38	103	.314
Major League Totals				**1691**	**6458**	**1258**	**2033**	**333**	**106**	**406**	**1179**	**.315**

[1] In Military Service most of season.

WORLD SERIES RECORD

Year	Club	League	Pos.	G	AB	R	H	2B	3B	HR	RBI	BA
1951	New York	Nat.	OF	6	22	1	4	0	0	0	1	.182
1954	New York	Nat.	OF	4	14	4	4	1	0	0	3	.286
1962	San Francisco	Nat.	OF	7	28	3	7	2	0	0	1	.250
World Series Totals				**17**	**64**	**8**	**15**	**3**	**0**	**0**	**5**	**.234**

* key
Pos. = position
G = games
AB = at bat
R = runs
H = hits
2B = two-base hits or doubles
3B = three-base hits or triples
HR = home run
RBI = runs batted in
BA = batting average

26

STANLEY FRANK MUSIAL
The Man

MAN AND BOY, Tom Sheehan has been around baseball parks most of his life. He has been on the pitching mound and the batter's box, the coaching box and the dugout. He has been in the bullpen and in the bleachers, in the grandstand and the front row boxes. He was in one of the latter when the 1946 World Series opened at Sportsman's Park, St. Louis.

While others might loll in the luxury of their box seats, our hero leaned forward, almost bug-eyed in his intentness to catch every move on the field. Other people are fans and spectators but Tom is a student of baseball.

With particular interest, Sheehan watched the Red Sox pitcher Tex Hughson face Stan Musial, the Cardinal slugger who had led the National League that season with a .365 batting average. Tom had been away from the majors for some years, toiling in such places as Minneapolis and St. Cloud, Minnesota, and hadn't had much chance to study Musial.

He watched as Musial took his stand in the left-handed side of the batter's box, noted carefully that Stan gripped the bat down at the end, his right hand just above the knob. Tom noted with approval that Musial stood in the box with his feet close together, the stance of a batter who can hit to either field. Sheehan's eyes really popped, however, as Stan placed his right foot a little closer to the plate than his left, bent his knees slightly and turned his right shoulder toward the pitcher. He watched as Musial grounded crisply to Bobby Doerr at second base to end the inning.

"Well," said Tom as he turned to his new employer, Horace Stoneham, president of the Giants, "no wonder nobody can pitch to that guy. He hits at you from around the corner."

It was an apt description of Musial's stance. Stan almost has his back turned to the pitcher as the latter starts his delivery. The bent knees and the crouch give him the appearance of a coiled spring, although most pitchers think of him as a coiled rattlesnake. And when he unwinds and lashes into the ball, it spells trouble for somebody.

As is the case with an extraordinary hitter, Musial's timing is excellent, his vision perfect. With Stan, once more we encounter the feet-together theory, which says that only a batter who stands with his feet together and thus is able to hit to both fields ever can have a shot at a possible .400 average. The .376 average with which Musial led the league in 1948 was the highest compiled in the National League since Bill Terry hit .401 for the Giants in 1931, seventeen years earlier.

Musial's crouch and his habit of turning his right shoulder toward the pitcher created a great deal of comment in 1946. This set some inquisitive baseball writers to wondering and when baseball writers wonder they always ask questions. Terry Moore, the Cardinal team captain and one of the greatest ball hawks who ever played, supplied the answer.

"The crouch is something Stan picked up in the Navy," explained Moore. "He used to stand up straighter before he went into service. And now when he crouches, it exaggerates that shoulder he turns toward the pitcher. Although only the crouch is new, it makes him look entirely different."

Like Babe Ruth, George Sisler, Lefty O'Doul, Bill Terry, and many another great hitter, Stanley Frank Musial began his professional career as a southpaw pitcher. And, like another slugger, Lou Gehrig, the insistence of Musial's immigrant par-

243

ents upon the college education which they themselves never had almost kept him from professional baseball.

Musial was a fine athlete in high school at his native Donora, Pennsylvania, the same Donora High at which Arnold Galiffa was to star some years later before going to West Point to become one of the country's outstanding quarterbacks. Western Pennsylvania always has been fertile ground for high-school stars and Musial could have had his pick of several colleges with room, board, books, and tuition were it not that he had his heart set on baseball.

To Papa Lukasz Musial, America was the land of opportunity where every man had a right to an education. He wanted his oldest boy to have the best. And here was the boy with a choice of the very best turning it down to play some silly game which would pay him little money and that for only six months of the year. It was almost the same argument which Papa and Mom Gehrig used when Paul Krichell tried first to tell them of the gold and the glory that awaited their boy Louie as a Yankee.

Young Stan had been piling up the strikeouts as a skinny left-hander at Donora High. He had worked out with Monessen in the Penn State League and both the manager, Ollie Vanek, and the business manager, Andy French, thought the boy had possibilities. Pie Traynor, of the Pittsburgh Pirates, had one of his scouts, Johnny Gooch, chasing after the boy, too. Monessen was in the Cardinal chain and French had learned something of the spellbinders' art from Branch Rickey but he was getting nowhere fast with Papa Musial.

After French had spent several evenings in vain pleading with the elder Musial, young Stan saw it was a losing battle. Only seventeen at the time, he began to cry softly. Stanley's tears worked where all of French's oratory had failed. Reluctantly, Papa Lukasz allowed Mr. French to sign his boy to a Monessen contract.

244

As a left-handed kid starting out in organized ball, Musial was just about what you would expect, ordinary but promising. He had a fair curve and better control than could reasonably be expected from a southpaw of his inexperience. He finished the 1938 season with Williamson, West Virginia, in the Mountain State League and stayed there for all of 1939.

It was after that first full season when Musial married his school-days sweetheart, Lillian Labash, whose dad ran a grocery store in Donora, where Stan worked winters. The pair married on November 21, 1939, Stan's nineteenth birthday.

The married man of nineteen was moved up in the Cardinal organization in 1940, being sent to pitch for the Daytona Beach Islanders in the Florida State League. It was here he got the best and the worst breaks of his career. The best was when he met Dickie Kerr, one of the white White Sox of the 1919 World Series, the pitcher who won two games from Cincinnati while some of his teammates were trying to throw the Series. Kerr was an intelligent, understanding man and he polished Stan's pitching. Kerr also decided that the power of Musial could be utilized in the outfield and began playing Stan there on days when he wasn't pitching.

Musial was going well both as a pitcher and a batter when he ran into a bad break. By mid-August he had won 17 games for the Islanders and was hitting over .300. He essayed a diving catch of a sinking line drive in center and while he caught the ball, he injured his left shoulder so severely that he lost his pitching touch completely. More than that, he lost the ability to throw with any power at all. Stan still could hit but he was a dead-armed outfielder.

Still months short of his twentieth birthday, Musial was face to face with the harsh facts of life. His wife was going to have a baby, his salary was $100 a month, six months of the year, and his baseball future seemed washed up. It seemed as though he were headed for the very fate Papa Musial had sought to

245

avoid by having him enter college—a life in the steel mills of his native Donora.

J. Roy Stockton, the able St. Louis author and the first of Stan's many biographers, relates that Manager Kerr came to Musial's rescue in more ways than one. Dickie advised Stan not to quit baseball and told him he still had a chance to make the big wheel as an outfielder, that he was a natural hitter, and that hitting covered more sins than charity ever did. Besides, there was no reason to believe that the shoulder injury which impaired his throwing was going to be permanent.

Kerr did more than merely bolster Musial's morale. He gave him material aid as well. The Kerrs rented a larger house in Daytona Beach and moved Stan and his young bride in with them. This cut down Musial's expenses and enabled him to finish the season with the Islanders. He wound up with a batting average of .311—and a dead arm.

Horatio Alger wouldn't have dared to put down on paper the rags-to-riches story of our hero Stanley in 1941. It would have frightened even Burt L. Standish, the creator of the Merriwells. In March, there wasn't a manager in the far-flung baseball empire of the Cardinals who wanted him. By July, the New York Giants offered to buy him for $40,000 and by September, he was hitting better than .400 in the National League.

Branch Rickey, then the Cardinal brain, was the first to establish baseball camps, as distinguished from training camps. Some years before he had tried out the plan at St. Joseph, Missouri, and he felt it possessed distinct advantages. He since carried it to the point where it is virtually a baseball assembly line.

Briefly Rickey's plan was to establish a common pool of the Cardinals' minor league ballplayers under a faculty of minor league managers and coaches. Since the minor league seasons usually open much later than the major league, the camp usually was held at a site different from that used for training by the parent club.

Columbus, Georgia, was the spot Rickey selected for his 1940 proving grounds. Musial was one of more than two hundred young ballplayers. He soon showed that he had lost nothing of his batting skill. He had the same level, rhythmic swing, the same keen eye. And he was getting more distance to his drives than ever before. On the other hand, Stan couldn't throw for beans.

After the long afternoon workouts, the brain trusters would gather in solemn conclave in the evenings to compare notes. The opinion was unanimous that Musial could hit, but nobody was willing to say that he ever would be able to throw again. Or that his hitting skill would be sufficient to offset the liability of his lame arm.

Eventually Ollie Vanek, managing Springfield, Missouri, in the Class-C Western League, took the dead-armed Musial. Ollie had been managing Monessen when Stan worked out with that club before being signed to a Cardinal organization contract. Vanek knew the boy could hit but before he took him he exacted a promise from Rickey that Musial would be replaced with an able-bodied outfielder at the first opportunity.

Whether Rickey ever did dig up the able-bodied outfielder nobody knows, for Musial started hitting from the first day he put on a Springfield uniform and he didn't stop. At one stage, Stan was tearing the Western League apart with a batting average which at one time touched .440. Even when he tapered off, it was to a robust .379 before he was shifted to Rochester in the International League.

From Class-C to Class-AA, which was the alphabetical classification of the International League then, is a big jump but Musial took it in stride. The first time he went to bat for Manager Tony Kaufman he hit a home run and he was batting

.326 when he was called in to bolster the Cardinals in their ding-dong battle with the Dodgers for the pennant.

Nobody around the National League had heard about Musial and nobody knew how to pronounce his name when he joined the Cards on September 17, 1941. When he wound up the season with an average of .426 for a dozen games, everybody around the National League knew who he was and how his name was pronounced, everything about him, in fact, except how to pitch to him.

Musial won no batting crowns in 1941 for all of his great hitting simply because he played in no league long enough to be a contender for the title but his average in the Western Association, International League, and National League was higher than that of the leader in each of those circuits. Nor did he have the satisfaction of being with a pennant winner in any of the three leagues.

Although Musial won neither batting crowns nor pennants in his rags-to-riches year of 1941, he soon was to win more than his share of them. In each of his first three years as a regular with the Cardinals, the National League pennant went to St. Louis and by 1943 Stan was the batting leader of the league with a mark of .357. He was in the Navy in 1945 but when he returned in 1946, there was another batting championship for Musial, another pennant and another World Series triumph for the Cardinals.

The season of 1946 was one of the most sparkling in all the glamorous history of the Cardinals. For the first time there was a playoff for the National League pennant and the Cardinals beat the Dodgers twice to meet the Red Sox in the World Series and score a stunning upset victory by capturing both the sixth and seventh games. It was a great season for Musial, too, for he was switched to first base by his new manager, Eddie Dyer, and performed around the bag with the grace and skill of one to the manner born.

If 1946 ended in a blaze of glory for Musial, 1947 started in a most deplorable fashion for Stan and for his fellow Cardinals. The Cardinals won only two of their first thirteen games and Musial was hitting not only below .300, which was unprecedented for him, but actually below .200! By mid-May Musial was clocked at .140, a mark rarely achieved in the majors, even by third-string pitchers with defective vision.

Eventually Musial's trouble was traced to an unruly appendix. An immediate operation was advised while the club was in the East. Stan rebelled at being cut while the season was in progress and flew to St. Louis where he consulted with Dr. Robert F. Hyland, baseball's surgeon general. He asked Dr. Hyland if the appendix could be frozen for the duration, so to speak. Dr. Hyland said it could be done and, after a brief hospitalization, Musial returned to the wars.

The climb to the heights was slow for both Musial and the Cardinals. It wasn't until mid-July that the champions of the year before escaped from the dank precincts of the second division; even then Stan, although his average had climbed more than 100 points, still was hovering around the .250 mark. By now, however, he no longer was a slumping hitter. Like a horse which begins to roll in the stretch, Musial was now coming fastest of all, although there was plenty of distance separating him from the leaders. In the month of August, he batted well over .450 and by the time the season ended, his average was a respectable .312.

It was the fans of Brooklyn who gave Musial the only nickname he has had in baseball, save the semi-family one of "Stash," a diminutive of "Stashu," which his dad called him. With the simplicity which his greatness deserves the fans of Flatbush refer to Musial as "The Man."

Musial's hitting against the Dodgers, particularly at Ebbets Field, has been amazing. It is nothing for him to hit .400 there for a season, or even .500. National Leaguers consider Musial the best clutch hitter in baseball and it is principally because of his hitting against the Dodgers. Rarely is there a Dodger-St. Louis series which doesn't have a highly important bearing on the race and rarely is there a series between the two in which Stan the Man doesn't leave his imprint upon the Dodger pitching.

Bob Broeg, who covers the Cards for the St. Louis *Post-Dispatch*, tells of the time Musial came to Ebbets Field not feeling up to par—something any Dodger fan would find hard to believe. In the course of the game, in addition to getting his customary quota of hits, Musial had made some elegant catches in the outfield, one of them a bit of larceny which necessitated an acrobatic dive. Stan injured his shoulder on the play but said nothing about it until there were two out in Brooklyn's half of the ninth, with a man on second, the score tied and Pete Reiser at bat.

Musial called time and came into the Cardinal bench to speak to Manager Dyer. "Skip," said he, "I think you'd better take me out and put Chuck Diering in. My shoulder hurts and if Reiser should hit one to the outfield, I couldn't make the throw to the plate in time to keep the winning run from scoring."

For all of his great clutch hitting, which is attested to by his annual runs-batted-in totals, Musial has batted .300 only once in his four World Series. He never, however, has had a bad Series and in 1942 he made a spectacular catch against Joe Gordon in Yankee Stadium when he went into the boxes in left field to take a home run away from the Flash.

After the death of his father in late 1948, Musial entered into a partnership in a restaurant business in St. Louis, where he now has established a permanent home for himself and his family. When he came East for the first time with the Cardinals in 1949, he wasn't hitting well, which is to say he was hitting well enough for a mortal but not for a Musial. A story was printed that he was worried over his restaurant business, which was reported losing money, and that it was being reflected in his hitting.

Musial was genuinely perturbed over the story. When St. Louis came to Ebbets Field he asked me if I had seen the article and would I please inform the writer, and all the writers, that there wasn't any truth to it.

"I only wish I was going as well as the restaurant," said Stan honestly. "We're doing capacity every night at the dinner hour."

When the game started, Musial proceeded to do "capacity" himself, getting two home runs and a single against the Dodger pitching. Afterward, he was told that his batting display that afternoon should end the rumors about both his restaurant and his slump.

"Yes," he smiled modestly, "this always has been a lucky park for me."

Nobody will ever convince Brooklyn fans that Stan the Man is lucky. They happen to think he is simply great—and he proves it almost every chance he gets against their pitchers.

One of the big complaints against Musial is that he is "colorless." He doesn't stand on his head, unless in an effort to catch a fly ball, but he is neither a stoic nor a deadpan. There is always the trace of a smile, if not a full-blown one, playing about his face as he waits his turn to hit and he is one of the most easily approached ballplayers in the game, great or small.

Musial never has forgotten the kindness of Dickie Kerr at Daytona Beach in 1940 when he thought seriously about chucking it all and going into the steel mills of Western Pennsylvania. It was then Dickie, treated shabbily himself by baseball, convinced Musial that you don't just up and quit the game. And he convinced Stan, too, that he had a future as a hitter, if not as a southpaw pitcher. Musial named his first son, Dickie, after Kerr.

If Musial has not forgotten Kerr, neither did the game little

251

White Sox pitcher forget him. In 1947, when Musial was plagued by poisoned tonsils and a troublesome appendix and was hitting under .200, he received a letter from Kerr.

"You know you can hit," was the substance of what Kerr wrote to the ailing and slumping Musial. "Don't let anybody or anything get you down. You're a natural .300 hitter and you'll be one as long as you're young enough to play ball. All you have to do, is to keep trying."

Whether it bolstered his confidence or not, Musial went from that horrendous slump to finish up with a .312 average as already related. And he kept trying, for Stan doesn't know any other way to play ball.

Because he is a natural hustler, Musial sustained the injury which ruined him as a pitcher. He was trying to catch a ball which he could have played on one hop in safety. Yet the injury which ruined him as a pitcher, opened the gates to fame and fortune for him as an outfielder.

Stan rose above injury again in 1956 and copped his seventh and last batting title—despite a torn ligament that sidelined him for three weeks. Three years later, age began to take a heavier toll on Stan's marvelous talents. He sat out the second game of doubleheaders and spent frequent respites on the bench. His batting average plummeted to .255 and, for the first time, The Man was booed in St. Louis.

When the heat of summer cooled so did the fans' ire. That winter reality dawned on the Cardinal rooters and they publicly apologized to him with advertisements in the St. Louis papers.

With the fans back on his side—if, indeed, they have ever left it—Stan rolled on for four more years. And on May 19, 1962, he collected the greatest of his innumerable records when he smashed his 3,431st hit off his old cousins, the Dodgers, to set a National League record. He raised that total to 3,630 when he collected two hits in his final game on September 29, 1963, in St. Louis, Stan Musial Night.

Among the 51 records that Stan has set or tied include a career's highest total bases, 6,134; most games played in the National League, 3,026 (which includes a record streak of 895 in a row); and most consecutive years in the N.L. as a .300 hitter, 16.

"Musial is a free-swinger," explained an anonymous National League manager several years ago, "and while his eyes are as keen as ever, it takes longer for him to adjust his timing. Veterans just don't get enough batting practice in spring training any longer, what with the March 1 starting date, the early exhibitions, and the raft of youngsters in camp. You play the youngsters, because you have to see what they can do and you already know what the regulars can do. The result is that it takes a guy like Musial until June to get his swing going properly. And, as he gets older, it will take longer—maybe until July."

"And what will happen then?" the manager was asked.

"Why, Musial will probably hit only .320," sighed the manager.

Musial's philosophy of baseball and of life is simple, simple but effective.

"Unless you can give it all you've got," he says, "there isn't any sense in playing."

It never has been any effort for Stan to give it all he has. As the song so happily puts it, he's just doing what comes natural.

Now that he has assumed a vice-presidency in the Cardinals' front office, Stan intends to apply this philosophy off the field. You can bet he'll do it.

STANLEY FRANK MUSIAL

Born, November 21, 1920, Donora, Pennsylvania
Height 6'. Weight 180. Batted and threw left-handed.

Year	Club	League	Pos.	G	AB	R	H	2B	3B	HR	RBI	BA
1941	St. Louis	Nat.	OF	12	47	8	20	4	0	1	7	.426
1942	St. Louis	Nat.	OF	140	467	87	147	32	10	10	72	.315
1943	St. Louis	Nat.	OF	157	617	108	220	48	20	13	87	.357

STANLEY FRANK MUSIAL (*Continued*)

Year	Club	League	Pos.	G	AB	R	H	2B	3B	HR	RBI	BA
1944	St. Louis	Nat.	OF	146	568	112	197	51	14	12	94	.347
1945	(In Military Service)											
1946	St. Louis	Nat.	OF	156	624	124	228	50	20	16	103	.365
1947	St. Louis	Nat.	OF	149	587	113	183	30	13	19	95	.312
1948	St. Louis	Nat.	OF	155	611	135	230	46	18	39	131	.376
1949	St. Louis	Nat.	OF	157	612	128	207	41	13	36	123	.338
1950	St. Louis	Nat.	OF	146	555	105	192	41	7	28	109	.346
1951	St. Louis	Nat.	OF	152	578	124	205	30	12	32	108	.355
1952	St. Louis	Nat.	OF	154	578	105	194	42	6	21	91	.336
1953	St. Louis	Nat.	OF	157	593	127	200	53	9	30	113	.337
1954	St. Louis	Nat.	OF	153	591	120	195	41	9	35	126	.330
1955	St. Louis	Nat.	OF	154	562	97	179	30	5	33	108	.319
1956	St. Louis	Nat.	OF	156	594	87	184	33	6	27	109	.310
1957	St. Louis	Nat.	OF	134	502	82	176	38	3	29	102	.351
1958	St. Louis	Nat.	OF	135	472	64	159	35	2	17	62	.337
1959	St. Louis	Nat.	OF	115	341	37	87	13	2	14	44	.255
1960	St. Louis	Nat.	OF	116	331	49	91	17	1	17	63	.275
1961	St. Louis	Nat.	OF	123	372	46	107	22	4	15	70	.288
1962	St. Louis	Nat.	OF	135	433	57	143	18	1	19	82	.330
1963	St. Louis	Nat.	OF	124	337	34	86	10	2	12	58	.255
	Major League Totals			3026	10972	1949	3630	725	177	475	1951	.331

WORLD SERIES RECORD

Year	Club	League	Pos.	G	AB	R	H	2B	3B	HR	RBI	BA
1942	St. Louis	Nat.	OF	5	18	2	4	1	0	0	2	.222
1943	St. Louis	Nat.	OF	5	18	2	5	0	0	0	0	.278
1944	St. Louis	Nat.	OF	6	23	2	7	2	0	1	2	.304
1946	St. Louis	Nat.	OF	7	27	3	6	4	1	0	4	.222
	World Series Totals			23	86	9	22	7	1	1	8	.256

* key
Pos. = position
G   = games
AB = at bat
R   = runs
H   = hits
2B = two-base hits or doubles
3B = three-base hits or triples
HR = home run
RBI = runs batted in
BA = batting average

INDEX